Hands-On GPU Programming with Python and CUDA

Explore high-performance parallel computing with CUDA

Dr. Brian Tuomanen

BIRMINGHAM - MUMBAI

Hands-On GPU Programming with Python and CUDA

Commissioning Editor: Richa Tripathi
Acquisition Editor: Karan Sadawana
Content Development Editor: Akshada Iyer
Technical Editor: Mehul Singh
Copy Editor: Safis Editing
Project Coordinator: Prajakta Naik
Proofreader: Safis Editing
Indexer: Rekha Nair
Graphics: Jisha Chirayil
Production Coordinator: Jisha Chirayil

First published: November 2018

Production reference: 1231118

Published by Packt Publishing Ltd.
Livery Place
35 Livery Street
Birmingham
B3 2PB, UK.

ISBN 978-1-78899-391-3

www.packtpub.com

This one is for my mom.

`mapt.io`

Mapt is an online digital library that gives you full access to over 5,000 books and videos, as well as industry leading tools to help you plan your personal development and advance your career. For more information, please visit our website.

Why subscribe?

- Spend less time learning and more time coding with practical ebooks and videos from over 4,000 industry professionals

- Improve your learning with Skill Plans built especially for you

- Get a free eBook or video every month

- Mapt is fully searchable

- Copy and paste, print, and bookmark content

Packt.com

Did you know that Packt offers eBook versions of every book published, with PDF and ePub files available? You can upgrade to the eBook version at `www.packt.com` and as a print book customer, you are entitled to a discount on the eBook copy. Get in touch with us at `customercare@packtpub.com` for more details.

At `www.packt.com`, you can also read a collection of free technical articles, sign up for a range of free newsletters, and receive exclusive discounts and offers on Packt books and eBooks.

Contributors

About the author

Dr. Brian Tuomanen has been working with CUDA and general-purpose GPU programming since 2014. He received his bachelor of science in electrical engineering from the University of Washington in Seattle, and briefly worked as a software engineer before switching to mathematics for graduate school. He completed his PhD in mathematics at the University of Missouri in Columbia, where he first encountered GPU programming as a means for studying scientific problems. Dr. Tuomanen has spoken at the US Army Research Lab about general-purpose GPU programming and has recently led GPU integration and development at a Maryland-based start-up company. He currently works as a machine learning specialist (Azure CSI) for Microsoft in the Seattle area.

I would first like to thank Professor Michela Becchi of the NCSU ECE department and her student Andrew Todd for helping me get started in the world of GPU programming way back in 2014. I also thank my editor at Packt, Akshada Iyer, for her support in the process of writing this book. Finally, I thank Professor Andreas Kloeckner for writing his excellent PyCUDA library, which I have made heavy use of in the course of this text.

About the reviewer

Vandana Shah gained her bachelor's degree in electronics in 2001. She has also gained an MBA in human resource management and a master's in electronics engineering, specifically in the VLSI domain. She has also submitted her thesis for a PhD in electronics, specifically concerning the domain of image processing and deep learning for brain tumor detection, and is awaiting her award. Her area of interest is image processing with deep learning and embedded systems. She has more than 13 years of experience in research, as well as in teaching and guiding undergraduate and postgraduate students of electronics and communications. She has published many papers in renowned journals, such as IEEE, Springer, and Inderscience. She is also receiving a government grant for her upcoming research in the MRI image-processing domain. She has dedicated her life to mentoring students and researchers. She is also able to train students and faculty members in soft-skill development. Besides her prowess in technical fields, she also has a strong command of Kathak, an Indian dance.

I thank my family members for their full support.

Packt is searching for authors like you

If you're interested in becoming an author for Packt, please visit `authors.packtpub.com` and apply today. We have worked with thousands of developers and tech professionals, just like you, to help them share their insight with the global tech community. You can make a general application, apply for a specific hot topic that we are recruiting an author for, or submit your own idea.

Table of Contents

Preface

Greetings and salutations! This text is an introductory guide to GPU programming with Python and CUDA. **GPU** may stand for **Graphics Programming Unit**, but we should be clear that this book is *not* about graphics programming—it is essentially an introduction to **General-Purpose GPU Programming**, or **GPGPU Programming** for short. Over the last decade, it has become clear that GPUs are well suited for computations besides rendering graphics, particularly for parallel computations that require a great deal of computational throughput. To this end, NVIDIA released the CUDA Toolkit, which has made the world of GPGPU programming all the more accessible to just about anyone with some C programming knowledge.

The aim of *Hands-On GPU Programming with Python and CUDA* is to get you started in the world of GPGPU programming as quickly as possible. We have strived to come up with fun and interesting examples and exercises for each chapter; in particular, we encourage you to type in these examples and run them from your favorite Python environment as you go along (Spyder, Jupyter, and PyCharm are all suitable choices). This way, you will eventually learn all of the requisite functions and commands, as well as gain an intuition of how a GPGPU program should be written.

Initially, GPGPU parallel programming seems very complex and daunting, especially if you've only done CPU programming in the past. There are so many new concepts and conventions you have to learn that it may seem like you're starting all over again at zero. During these times, you'll have to have some faith that your efforts to learn this field are not for naught. With a little bit of initiative and discipline, this subject will seem like second nature to you by the time you reach the end of the text.

Happy programming!

Who this book is for

This book is aimed at one person in particular—that is, myself in the year 2014, when I was trying to develop a GPU-based simulation for my doctoral studies in math. I was poring over multiple books and manuals on GPU programming, trying to make the slightest sense of the field; most texts seemed happy to throw an endless parade of hardware schematics and buzzwords at the reader on every page, while the actual *programming* took a back seat.

This book is primarily aimed at those who want to actually *do GPU programming*, but without getting bogged down with gritty technical details and hardware schematics. We will program the GPU in proper C/C++ (CUDA C) in this text, but we will write it *inline* within Python code by way of the PyCUDA module. PyCUDA allows us to only write the necessary low-level GPU code that we need, while it automatically handles all of the redundancies of compiling, linking, and launching code onto a GPU for us.

What this book covers

Chapter 1, *Why GPU Programming?*, gives us some motivations as to why we should learn this field, and how to apply Amdahl's Law to estimate potential performance improvements from translating a serial program to making use of a GPU.

Chapter 2, *Setting Up Your GPU Programming Environment*, explains how to set up an appropriate Python and C++ development environment for CUDA under both Windows and Linux.

Chapter 3, *Getting Started with PyCUDA*, shows the most essential skills we will need for programming GPUs from Python. We will notably see how to transfer data to and from a GPU using PyCUDA's gpuarray class, and how to compile simple CUDA kernels with PyCUDA's ElementwiseKernel function.

Chapter 4, *Kernels, Threads, Blocks, and Grids*, teaches the fundamentals of writing effective CUDA kernels, which are parallel functions that are launched on the GPU. We will see how to write CUDA device functions ("serial" functions called directly by CUDA kernels), and learn about CUDA's abstract grid/block structure and the role it plays in launching kernels.

Chapter 5, *Streams, Events, Contexts, and Concurrency*, covers the notion of CUDA Streams, which is a feature that allows us to launch and synchronize many kernels onto a GPU concurrently. We will see how to use CUDA Events to time kernel launches, and how to create and use CUDA Contexts.

Chapter 6, *Debugging and Profiling Your CUDA Code*, fill in some of the gaps we have in terms of pure CUDA C programming, and shows us how to use the NVIDIA Nsight IDE for debugging and development, as well as how to use the NVIDIA profiling tools.

Chapter 7, *Using the CUDA Libraries with Scikit-CUDA*, gives us a brief tour of some of the important standard CUDA libraries by way of the Python Scikit-CUDA module, including cuBLAS, cuFFT, and cuSOLVER.

Chapter 8, *The CUDA Device Function Libraries and Thrust,* shows us how to use the cuRAND and CUDA Math API libraries in our code, as well as how to use CUDA Thrust C++ containers.

Chapter 9, *Implementation of a Deep Neural Network,* serves as a capstone in which we learn how to build an entire deep neural network from scratch, applying many of the ideas we have learned in the text.

Chapter 10, *Working with Compiled GPU Code,* shows us how to interface our Python code with pre-compiled GPU code, using both PyCUDA and Ctypes.

Chapter 11, *Performance Optimization in CUDA,* teaches some very low-level performance optimization tricks, especially in relation to CUDA, such as warp shuffling, vectorized memory access, using inline PTX assembly, and atomic operations.

Chapter 12, *Where to Go from Here,* is an overview of some of the educational and career paths you will have that will build upon your now-solid foundation in GPU programming.

To get the most out of this book

This is actually quite a technical subject. To this end, we will have to make a few assumptions regarding the reader's programming background. To this end, we will assume the following:

- You have an intermediate level of programming experience in Python.
- You are familiar with standard Python scientific packages, such as NumPy, SciPy, and Matplotlib.
- You have an intermediate ability in any C-based programming language (C, C++, Java, Rust, Go, and so on).
- You understand the concept of dynamic memory allocation in C (particularly how to use the C malloc and free functions.)

GPU programming is mostly applicable to fields that are very scientific or mathematical in nature, so many (if not most) of the examples will make use of some math. For this reason, we are assuming that the reader has some familiarity with first or second-year college mathematics, including:

- Trigonometry (the sinusoidal functions: sin, cos, tan …)
- Calculus (integrals, derivatives, gradients)
- Statistics (uniform and normal distributions)
- Linear Algebra (vectors, matrices, vector spaces, dimensionality).

Don't worry if you haven't learned some of these topics, or if it's been a while, as we will try to review some of the key programming and math concepts as we go along.

We will be making another assumption here. Remember that we will be working only with CUDA in this text, which is a proprietary programming language for NVIDIA hardware. We will, therefore, need to have some specific hardware in our possession before we get started. So, I will assume that the reader has access to the following:

- A 64-bit x86 Intel/AMD-based PC
- 4 Gigabytes (GB) of RAM or more
- An entry-level NVIDIA GTX 1050 GPU (Pascal Architecture) or better

The reader should know that most older GPUs will probably work fine with most, if not all, examples in this text, but the examples in this text have only been tested on a GTX 1050 under Windows 10 and a GTX 1070 under Linux. Specific instructions regarding setup and configuration are given in Chapter 2, *Setting Up Your GPU Programming Environment*.

Download the example code files

You can download the example code files for this book from your account at www.packt.com. If you purchased this book elsewhere, you can visit www.packt.com/support and register to have the files emailed directly to you.

You can download the code files by following these steps:

1. Log in or register at www.packt.com.
2. Select the **SUPPORT** tab.
3. Click on **Code Downloads & Errata**.
4. Enter the name of the book in the **Search** box and follow the onscreen instructions.

Once the file is downloaded, please make sure that you unzip or extract the folder using the latest version of:

- WinRAR/7-Zip for Windows
- Zipeg/iZip/UnRarX for Mac
- 7-Zip/PeaZip for Linux

The code bundle for the book is also hosted on GitHub at `https://github.com/PacktPublishing/Hands-On-GPU-Programming-with-Python-and-CUDA`. In case there's an update to the code, it will be updated on the existing GitHub repository.

We also have other code bundles from our rich catalog of books and videos available at `https://github.com/PacktPublishing/`. Check them out!

Download the color images

We also provide a PDF file that has color images of the screenshots/diagrams used in this book. You can download it here: `http://www.packtpub.com/sites/default/files/downloads/9781788993913_ColorImages.pdf`.

Conventions used

There are a number of text conventions used throughout this book.

`CodeInText`: Indicates code words in text, database table names, folder names, filenames, file extensions, pathnames, dummy URLs, user input, and Twitter handles. Here is an example: "We can now use the `cublasSaxpy` function."

A block of code is set as follows:

```
cublas.cublasDestroy(handle)
print 'cuBLAS returned the correct value: %s' % np.allclose(np.dot(A,x),
y_gpu.get())
```

When we wish to draw your attention to a particular part of a code block, the relevant lines or items are set in bold:

```
def compute_gflops(precision='S'):

if precision=='S':
    float_type = 'float32'
elif precision=='D':
    float_type = 'float64'
else:
    return -1
```

Any command-line input or output is written as follows:

```
$ run cublas_gemm_flops.py
```

Bold: Indicates a new term, an important word, or words that you see on screen. For example, words in menus or dialog boxes appear in the text like this.

 Warnings or important notes appear like this.

 Tips and tricks appear like this.

Get in touch

Feedback from our readers is always welcome.

General feedback: If you have questions about any aspect of this book, mention the book title in the subject of your message and email us at `customercare@packtpub.com`.

Errata: Although we have taken every care to ensure the accuracy of our content, mistakes do happen. If you have found a mistake in this book, we would be grateful if you would report this to us. Please visit `www.packt.com/submit-errata`, selecting your book, clicking on the Errata Submission Form link, and entering the details.

Piracy: If you come across any illegal copies of our works in any form on the internet, we would be grateful if you would provide us with the location address or website name. Please contact us at `copyright@packt.com` with a link to the material.

If you are interested in becoming an author: If there is a topic that you have expertise in, and you are interested in either writing or contributing to a book, please visit `authors.packtpub.com`.

Reviews

Please leave a review. Once you have read and used this book, why not leave a review on the site that you purchased it from? Potential readers can then see and use your unbiased opinion to make purchase decisions, we at Packt can understand what you think about our products, and our authors can see your feedback on their book. Thank you!

For more information about Packt, please visit `packt.com`.

Why GPU Programming? 1

It turns out that besides being able to render graphics for video games, **graphics processing units (GPUs)** also provide a readily accessible means for the general consumer to do *massively parallel computing*—an average person can now buy a $2,000 modern GPU card from a local electronics store, plug it into their PC at home, and then use it almost immediately for computational power that would only have been available in the supercomputing labs of top corporations and universities only 5 or 10 years ago. This open accessibility of GPUs has become apparent in many ways in recent years, which can be revealed by a brief observation of the news—cryptocurrency miners use GPUs to generate digital money such as Bitcoins, geneticists and biologists use GPUs for DNA analysis and research, physicists and mathematicians use GPUs for large-scale simulations, AI researchers can now program GPUs to write plays and compose music, while major internet companies, such as Google and Facebook, use *farms* of servers with GPUs for large-scale machine learning tasks… the list goes on and on.

This book is primarily aimed at bringing you up to speed with GPU programming, so that you too may begin using their power as soon as possible, no matter what your end goal is. We aim to cover the core essentials of how to program a GPU, rather than provide intricate technical details and schematics of how a GPU works. Toward the end of the book, we will provide further resources so that you may specialize further, and apply your new knowledge of GPUs. (Further details as to particular required technical knowledge and hardware follow this section.)

In this book, we will be working with **CUDA**, a framework for **general-purpose GPU (GPGPU)** programming from NVIDIA, which was first released back in 2007. While CUDA is proprietary for NVIDIA GPUs, it is a mature and stable platform that is relatively easy to use, provides an unmatched set of first-party accelerated mathematical and AI-related libraries, and comes with the minimal hassle when it comes to installation and integration. Moreover, there are readily available and standardized Python libraries, such as PyCUDA and Scikit-CUDA, which make GPGPU programming all the more readily accessible to aspiring GPU programmers. For these reasons, we are opting to go with CUDA for this book.

CUDA is *always* pronounced *coo-duh*, and <u>never</u> as the acronym *C-U-D-A*! CUDA originally stood for *Compute Unified Device Architecture*, but Nvidia has dropped the acronym and now uses CUDA as a proper name written in all-caps.

We will now start our journey into GPU programming with an overview of **Amdahl's Law**. Amdahl's Law is a simple but effective method to estimate potential speed gains we can get by offloading a program or algorithm onto a GPU; this will help us determine whether it's worth our effort to rewrite our code to make use of the GPU. We will then go over a brief review of how to profile our Python code with the *cProfile* module, to help us find the bottlenecks in our code.

The learning outcomes for this chapter are as follows:

- Understand Amdahl's Law
- Apply Amdahl's Law in the context of your code
- Using the *cProfile* module for basic profiling of Python code

Technical requirements

An installation of Anaconda Python 2.7 is suggested for this chapter:

`https://www.anaconda.com/download/`

This chapter's code is also available on GitHub:

`https://github.com/PacktPublishing/Hands-On-GPU-Programming-with-Python-and-CUDA`

 For more information about the pre-requisites, check the preface of this book; for the software and hardware requirements, check the README section in `https://github.com/PacktPublishing/Hands-On-GPU-Programming-with-Python-and-CUDA`.

Parallelization and Amdahl's Law

Before we can dive in and unlock the potential of GPUs, we first have to realize where their computational power lies in comparison to a modern Intel/AMD central processing unit (CPU)—the power does not lie in the fact that it has a higher clock speed than a CPU, nor in the complexity or particular design of the individual cores. An individual GPU core is actually quite simplistic, and at a disadvantage when compared to a modern individual CPU core, which use many fancy engineering tricks, such as branch prediction to reduce the **latency** of computations. **Latency** refers to the beginning-to-end duration of performing a single computation.

The power of the GPU derives from the fact that there are many, many more cores than in a CPU, which means a huge step forward in **throughput**. **Throughput** here refers to the number of computations that can be performed simultaneously. Let's use an analogy to get a better understanding of what this means. A GPU is like a very wide city road that is designed to handle many slower-moving cars at once (high throughput, high latency), whereas a CPU is like a narrow highway that can only admit a few cars at once, but can get each individual car to its destination much quicker (low throughput, low latency).

We can get an idea of the increase in throughput by seeing how many cores these new GPUs have. To give you an idea, the average Intel or AMD CPU has only two to eight cores—while an entry-level, consumer-grade NVIDIA GTX 1050 GPU has *640 cores*, and a new top-of-the-line NVIDIA RTX 2080 Ti has *4,352 cores*! We can exploit this massive throughput, provided we know how properly to **parallelize** any program or algorithm we wish to speed up. By **parallelize**, we mean to rewrite a program or algorithm so that we can split up our workload to run in parallel on multiple processors simultaneously. Let's think about an analogy from real-life.

Suppose that you are building a house and that you already have all of the designs and materials in place. You hire a single laborer, and you estimate it will take 100 hours to construct the house. Let's suppose that this particular house can be built in such a way that the work can be perfectly divided between every additional laborer you hire—that is to say, it will take 50 hours for two laborers, 25 hours for four laborers, and 10 hours for ten laborers to construct the house—the number of hours to construct your house will be 100 divided by the number of laborers you hire. This is an example of a **parallelizable task**.

We notice that this task is twice as fast to complete for two laborers, and ten times as fast for ten laborers to complete together (that is, in *parallel)* as opposed to one laborer building the house alone (that is, in *serial)*—that is, if N is the number of laborers, then it will be N times as fast. In this case, N is known as the **speedup** of parallelizing our task over the serial version of our task.

Before we begin to program a parallel version of a given algorithm, we often start by coming up with an estimate of the *potential speedup* that parallelization would bring to our task. This can help us determine whether it is worth expending resources and time writing a parallelization of our program or not. Because real life is more complicated than the example we gave here, it's pretty obvious that we won't be able to parallelize every program perfectly, all of the time—most of the time, only a part of our program will be nicely parallelizable, while the rest will have to run in serial.

Using Amdahl's Law

We will now derive **Amdahl's Law**, which is a simple arithmetic formula that is used to estimate potential speed gain that may arise from parallelizing some portion of code from a serial program onto multiple processors. We will do this by continuing with our prior analogy of building a house.

Last time, we only considered the actual physical construction of the house as the entire time duration, but now, we will also consider the time it takes to design the house into the time duration for building the house. Suppose that only one person in the world has the ability to design your house—you—and it takes you 100 hours to design the plans for your house. There is no possibility that any other person on the planet can compare to your architectural brilliance, so there is no possibility that this part of the task can be split up at all between other architects—that is, so it will take 100 hours to design your house, regardless of what resources you have or how many people you can hire. So, if you have only one laborer to build your house, the entire time it will take to build your home will be 200 hours—100 hours for you to design it, and 100 hours for a single laborer to build it. If we hire two laborers, this will take 150 hours—the time to design the house will remain at 100 hours, while the construction will take 50 hours. It's clear that the total number of hours to construct the house will be $100 + 100 / N$, where N is the number of laborers we hire.

Now, let's step back and think about how much time building the house takes if we hire one laborer—we ultimately use this to determine speedup as we hire additional laborers; that is, how many times faster the process becomes. If we hire a single laborer, we see that it takes the same amount of time to both design and construct the house—100 hours. So, we can say that that the portion of time spent on the design is .5 (50%), and the portion of the time it takes to construct the house is .5 (50%)—of course, both of these portions add up to 1, that is 100%. We want to make comparisons to this as we add laborers—if we have two laborers, the portion of time for the construction is halved, so in comparison to the original serial version of our task, this will take .5 + .5/2 = .75 (75%) of the time of the original task, and .75 x 200 hours is 150 hours, so we can see that this works. Moreover, we can see that if we have N laborers, we can calculate the percentage of time our *parallelized* construction with N laborers will take which the formula .5 + .5 / N.

Now, let's determine the *speedup* we are gaining by adding additional laborers. Since it takes 75% of the time to build a house if we have two laborers, we can take the reciprocal of .75 to determine the speedup of our parallelization—that is, the speedup will be 1 / .75, which is around 1.33 times faster than if we only have one laborer. In this case, we see that the speedup will be 1 / (.5 + .5 / N) if we have N laborers.

We know that .5 / N will shrink very close to 0 as we add more and more laborers, so we can see there is always an upper bound on the speedup you can get when you parallelize this task—that is, 1 / (.5 + 0) = 2. We can divide the original serial time with the estimated maximum speedup to determine an absolute minimum amount of time this task will take—200 / 2 = 100 hours.

The principle we have just applied to determine speedups in parallel programming is known as **Amdahl's Law**. It only requires knowledge of the parallelizable proportion of execution time for code in our original serial program, which is referred to as p, and the number of processor cores N that we have available.

The proportion of execution time for code that is not parallelizable in this case is always $1 - p$, so we only need to know p.

We can now calculate speedup with **Amdahl's Law** as follows:

$$Speedup = \frac{1}{(1 - p) + p/N}$$

To sum it up, Amdahl's Law is a simple formula that allows us to roughly (*very roughly*) estimate potential speedup for a program that can be at least partially parallelized. This can provide a general idea as to whether it will be worthwhile to write a parallel version of a particular serial program, provided we know what proportion of the code we can parallelize (p), and how many cores we can run our parallelized code on (N).

The Mandelbrot set

We are now prepared to see a very standard example for parallel computing that we will revisit later in this text—an algorithm to generate an image of the *Mandelbrot set*. Let's first define exactly what we mean.

For a given complex number, c, we define a recursive sequence for $n \geq 0$, with $z_0 = 0$ and $z_n = z_{n-1}^2 + c$ for $n \geq 1$. If $|z_n|$ remains bounded by 2 as n increases to infinity, then we will say that c is a member of the Mandelbrot set.

Recall that we can visualize the complex numbers as residing on a two-dimensional Cartesian plane, with the *x*-axis representing the real components and the y-axis representing the imaginary components. We can therefore easily visualize the Mandelbrot set with a very appealing (and well-known) graph. Here, we will represent members of the Mandelbrot set with a lighter shade, and nonmembers with a darker shade on the complex Cartesian plane as follows:

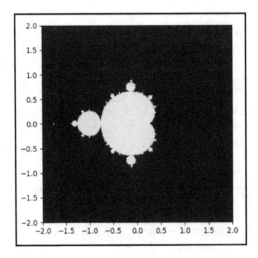

Now, let's think about how we would go about generating this set in Python. We have to consider a few things first—since we obviously can't check whether every single complex number is in the Mandelbrot set, we have to choose a certain range to check over; we have to determine how many points in each range we will consider (*width, height*); and the maximum value of *n* that we will check $|z_n|$ for (max_iters). We can now prepare to implement a function to generate a graph of the Mandelbrot set—here, we do this by iterating over every single point in the graph in *serial*.

We will start by importing the NumPy library, which is a numerical library that we will be making ample use of throughout this text. Our implementation here is in the simple_mandelbrot function. We start by using NumPy's linspace function to generate a lattice that will act as a discrete complex plane (the rest of the code that follows should be fairly straightforward):

```
import numpy as np

def simple_mandelbrot(width, height, real_low, real_high, imag_low,
imag_high, max_iters):
    real_vals = np.linspace(real_low, real_high, width)
    imag_vals = np.linspace(imag_low, imag_high, height)
    # we will represent members as 1, non-members as 0.
    mandelbrot_graph = np.ones((height,width), dtype=np.float32)
    for x in range(width):
        for y in range(height):
            c = np.complex64( real_vals[x] + imag_vals[y] * 1j  )
            z = np.complex64(0)
            for i in range(max_iters):
                z = z**2 + c
                if(np.abs(z) > 2):
                    mandelbrot_graph[y,x] = 0
                    break
    return mandelbrot_graph
```

Now, we want to add some code to dump the image of the Mandelbrot set to a PNG format file, so let's add the appropriate headers at the beginning:

```
from time import time
import matplotlib
# the following will prevent the figure from popping up
matplotlib.use('Agg')
from matplotlib import pyplot as plt
```

Now, let's add some code to generate the Mandelbrot set and dump it to a file, and use the time function to time both operations:

```
if __name__ == '__main__':
    t1 = time()
    mandel = simple_mandelbrot(512,512,-2,2,-2,2,256, 2)
    t2 = time()
    mandel_time = t2 - t1
    t1 = time()
    fig = plt.figure(1)
    plt.imshow(mandel, extent=(-2, 2, -2, 2))
    plt.savefig('mandelbrot.png', dpi=fig.dpi)
    t2 = time()
    dump_time = t2 - t1
    print 'It took {} seconds to calculate the Mandelbrot
graph.'.format(mandel_time)
    print 'It took {} seconds to dump the image.'.format(dump_time)
```

Now let's run this program (this is also available as the `mandelbrot0.py` file, in folder `1`, within the GitHub repository):

```
PS C:\Users\btuom\examples\1> python mandelbrot0.py
It took 14.617000103 seconds to calculate the Mandelbrot graph.
It took 0.110999822617 seconds to dump the image.
```

It took about 14.62 seconds to generate the Mandelbrot set, and about 0.11 seconds to dump the image. As we have seen, we generate the Mandelbrot set point by point; there is no interdependence between the values of different points, and it is, therefore, an intrinsically parallelizable function. In contrast, the code to dump the image cannot be parallelized.

Now, let's analyze this in terms of Amdahl's Law. What sort of speedups can we get if we parallelize our code here? In total, both pieces of the program took about 14.73 seconds to run; since we can parallelize the Mandelbrot set generation, we can say that the portion of execution time for parallelizable code is $p = 14.62 / 14.73 = .99$. This program is 99% parallelizable!

What sort of speedup can we potentially get? Well, I'm currently working on a laptop with an entry-level GTX 1050 GPU with 640 cores; our N will thus be 640 when we use the formula. We calculate the speedup as follows:

$$Speedup = \frac{1}{.01 + .99/640} \approx 86.6$$

That is definitely very good and would indicate to us that it is worth our effort to program our algorithm to use the GPU. Keep in mind that Amdahl's Law only gives a very rough estimate! There will be additional considerations that will come into play when we offload computations onto the GPU, such as the additional time it takes for the CPU to send and receive data to and from the GPU; or the fact that algorithms that are offloaded to the GPU are only partially parallelizable.

Profiling your code

We saw in the previous example that we can individually time different functions and components with the standard `time` function in Python. While this approach works fine for our small example program, this won't always be feasible for larger programs that call on many different functions, some of which may or may not be worth our effort to parallelize, or even optimize on the CPU. Our goal here is to find the bottlenecks and hotspots of a program—even if we were feeling energetic and used `time` around every function call we make, we might miss something, or there might be some system or library calls that we don't even consider that happen to be slowing things down. We should find candidate portions of the code to offload onto the GPU before we even think about rewriting the code to run on the GPU; we must always follow the wise words of the famous American computer scientist Donald Knuth: Premature optimization is the root of all evil.

We use what is known as a **profiler** to find these hot spots and bottlenecks in our code. A **profiler** will conveniently allow us to see where our program is taking the most time, and allow us to optimize accordingly.

Using the cProfile module

We will primarily be using the *cProfile* module to check our code. This module is a standard library function that is contained in every modern Python installation. We can run the profiler from the command line with `-m cProfile`, and specify that we want to organize the results by the cumulative time spent on each function with `-s cumtime`, and then redirect the output into a text file with the > operator.

This will work on both the Linux Bash or Windows PowerShell command line.

Let's try this now:

```
PS C:\Users\btuom\examples\1> python -m cProfile -s cumtime mandelbrot0.py > mandelbrot_profile.txt
PS C:\Users\btuom\examples\1>
```

We can now look at the contents of the text file with our favorite text editor. Let's keep in mind that the output of the program will be included at the beginning of the file:

```
It took 14.5690000057 seconds to calculate the Mandelbrot graph.
It took 0.136000156403 seconds to dump the image.
         564104 function calls (559254 primitive calls) in 14.965 seconds

   Ordered by: cumulative time

   ncalls  tottime  percall  cumtime  percall filename:lineno(function)
        1    0.002    0.002   14.966   14.966 mandelbrot0.py:1(<module>)
        1   14.363   14.363   14.572   14.572 mandelbrot0.py:10(simple_mandelbrot)
   263606    0.209    0.000    0.209    0.000 {range}
        1    0.007    0.007    0.134    0.134 __init__.py:101(<module>)
        1    0.003    0.003    0.123    0.123 pyplot.py:17(<module>)
       12    0.017    0.001    0.119    0.010 __init__.py:1(<module>)
        1    0.000    0.000    0.097    0.097 pyplot.py:694(savefig)
        2    0.000    0.000    0.082    0.041 backend_agg.py:418(draw)
      152/2    0.000    0.000    0.081    0.041 artist.py:47(draw_wrapper)
        2    0.000    0.000    0.081    0.041 figure.py:1264(draw)
      4/2    0.000    0.000    0.080    0.040 image.py:120(_draw_list_compositing_images)
```

Now, since we didn't remove the references to time in the original example, we see their output in the first two lines at the beginning. We can then see the total number of function calls made in this program, and the cumulative amount of time to run it.

Subsequently, we have a list of functions that are called in the program, ordered from the cumulatively most time-consuming functions to the least; the first line is the program itself, while the second line is, as expected, the simple_mandelbrot function from our program. (Notice that the time here aligns with what we measured with the time command). After this, we can see many libraries and system calls that relate to dumping the Mandelbrot graph to a file, all of which take comparatively less time. We use such output from *cProfile* to infer where our bottlenecks are within a given program.

Summary

The main advantage of using a GPU over a CPU is its increased throughput, which means that we can execute more *parallel* code simultaneously on GPU than on a CPU; a GPU cannot make recursive algorithms or nonparallelizable algorithms somewhat faster. We see that some tasks, such as the example of building a house, are only partially parallelizable—in this example, we couldn't speed up the process of *designing* the house (which is intrinsically *serial* in this case), but we could speed up the process of the *construction*, by hiring more laborers (which is parallelizable in this case).

We used this analogy to derive Amdahl's Law, which is a formula that can give us a rough estimate of potential speedup for a program if we know the percentage of execution time for code that is parallelizable, and how many processors we will have to run this code. We then applied Amdahl's Law to analyze a small program that generates the Mandelbrot set and dumps it to an image file, and we determined that this would be a good candidate for parallelization onto a GPU. Finally, we ended with a brief overview of profiling code with the *cPython* module; this allows us to see where the bottlenecks in a program are, without explicitly timing function calls.

Now that we have a few of the fundamental concepts in place, and have a motivator to learn GPU programming, we will spend the next chapter setting up a Linux- or Windows 10-based GPU programming environment. We will then immediately dive into the world of GPU programming in the following chapter, where we will actually write a GPU-based version of the Mandelbrot program that we saw in this chapter.

Questions

1. There are three `for` statements in this chapter's Mandelbrot example; however, we can only parallelize over the first two. Why can't we parallelize over all of the `for` loops here?

2. What is something that Amdahl's Law doesn't account for when we apply it to offloading a serial CPU algorithm to a GPU?

3. Suppose that you gain exclusive access to three new top-secret GPUs that are the same in all respects, except for core counts—the first has 131,072 cores, the second has 262,144 cores, and the third has 524,288 cores. If you parallelize and offload the Mandelbrot example onto these GPUs (which generates a 512 x 512 pixel image), will there be a difference in computation time between the first and second GPU? How about between the second and third GPU?

4. Can you think of any problems with designating certain algorithms or blocks of code as *parallelizable* in the context of Amdahl's Law?

5. Why should we use profilers instead of just using Python's `time` function?

2
Setting Up Your GPU Programming Environment

We will now see how to set up an appropriate environment for GPU programming under both Windows and Linux. In both cases, there are several steps we will have to take. We will proceed through these steps one-by-one, noting any differences between Linux and Windows as we proceed. You should, of course, feel free to skip or ignore any sections or comments that don't apply to your choice of operating system.

The reader should note that we will only cover two platforms for 64-bit Intel/AMD-based PCs in this chapter—Ubuntu LTS (long-term support) releases and Windows 10. Note that any Ubuntu LTS-based Linux operating systems (such as Xubuntu, Kubuntu, or Linux Mint) are also equally appropriate to the generic Unity/GNOME-based Ubuntu releases.

We suggest the use of Python 2.7 over Python 3.x. Python 2.7 has stable support across all libraries that we use in this text, and we have tested every example given in this book with Python 2.7 on both Windows and Linux platforms. Python 3.x users can make use of this book, but should be aware of the differences between Python 2.7 and Python 3.x. Some of the examples in this have been tested on using Python 3.7, but require standard changes, such as adding parentheses with the Python `print` function.

 Packt author Dr. Sebastian Raschka provides a list of key differences between Python 2.7 and 3.x at `https://sebastianraschka.com/Articles/2014_python_2_3_key_diff.html`.

We suggest the Anaconda Python 2.7 distribution in particular for both Windows and Linux users, since this can be installed on a user-by-user basis without `sudo` or `administrator` access, contains all necessary data science and visualization modules needed for this text, and uses fast pre-optimized NumPy/SciPy packages that make use of Intel's **Math Kernel Library** (**MKL**). (The default Linux `/usr/bin/python` installation should also be sufficient for this text, but you may have to install some packages manually, such as NumPy and Matplotlib.)

 Anaconda Python (both 2.7 and 3.x versions) can be downloaded for all platforms at `https://www.anaconda.com/download/`.

Users who are on other supported platforms (for example, macOS, Windows 7/8, Windows Server 2016, Red Hat/Fedora, OpenSUSE, and CENTOS) should consult the official NVIDIA CUDA documentation (`https://docs.nvidia.com/cuda/`) for further details. Furthermore, there are other possibilities for hardware: the reader interested in embedded systems or robotics with some experience in boards, such as the Raspberry Pi may wish to start with an ARM-based NVIDIA Jetson development board, while the reader interested in cloud computing or web programming may consider remotely using an appropriate Azure or AWS instance. In these cases, the reader is encouraged to read the official documentation to set up their drivers, compiler, and CUDA Toolkit. Some of the steps in this chapter may or may not apply.

The learning outcomes for this chapter are:

- Ensuring that we have the appropriate hardware
- Installing the NVIDIA GPU drivers
- Setting up an appropriate C/C++ programming environment
- Installing the NVIDIA CUDA Toolkit
- Setting up our Python environment for GPU programming

Technical requirements

An installation of Anaconda Python 2.7 is suggested for this chapter at `https://www.anaconda.com/download/`.

This chapter's code is also available on GitHub at `https://github.com/PacktPublishing/Hands-On-GPU-Programming-with-Python-and-CUDA`.

For more information about the pre-requisites, check the Preface of this book; and for the software and hardware requirements, check the README section in `https://github.com/PacktPublishing/Hands-On-GPU-Programming-with-Python-and-CUDA`.

Ensuring that we have the right hardware

For this book, we recommend that you have the following hardware as a minimum:

- 64-bit Intel/AMD-based PC
- 4 gigabytes (GB) of RAM
- NVIDIA GeForce GTX 1050 GPU (or higher)

This configuration will ensure that you can comfortably learn GPU programming, run all of the examples in this book, and also run some of the other newer and interesting GPU-based software, such as Google's TensorFlow (a machine learning framework) or the Vulkan SDK (a cutting-edge graphics API).

Note that you must have an NVIDIA brand GPU to make use of this book! The CUDA Toolkit is proprietary for NVIDIA cards, so it won't work for programming Intel HD or Radeon GPUs.

As stated, we will be assuming that you are using either the Windows 10 or Ubuntu LTS (long-term support) release.

Ubuntu LTS releases generally have version numbers of the form 14.04, 16.04, 18.04, and so on.

Ubuntu LTS, is by and large, the most mainstream version of Linux, which ensures maximum compatibility with new software and toolkits. Keep in mind there are many variations of Linux that are based on Ubuntu, such as Linux Mint or Xubuntu, and these generally work equally well. (I have personally found that Linux Mint works fairly well out of the box for GPU-equipped laptops.)

We should note that we are assuming that you have at least an entry-level GTX 1050 (Pascal) GPU, or the equivalent in any newer architecture. Note that many of the examples in this book will most likely work on most older GPUs, but they have only been tested on a GTX 1050 (under Windows 10) and GTX 1070 (under Linux) by the author. While the examples haven't been tested on older GPUs, a 2014-era entry level Maxwell architecture GPU, such as a GTX 750, should also be sufficient for the purposes of this text.

 If you are using a desktop PC, please ensure that you have physically installed your GPU by following all the included instructions before proceeding.

Checking your hardware (Linux)

We will now do a few basic checks in Linux to ensure that we have the right hardware. Let's first open up a Terminal and drop to the bash command line—you can do this quickly in Ubuntu by pressing the combination *Ctrl + Alt + T*.

Let's now check our processor by typing `lscpu` and pressing *Enter*. A lot of information will appear, but just look at the first line and make sure that the architecture is indeed x86_64:

```
Architecture:          x86_64
CPU op-mode(s):        32-bit, 64-bit
Byte Order:            Little Endian
CPU(s):                12
On-line CPU(s) list:   0-11
Thread(s) per core:    2
Core(s) per socket:    6
Socket(s):             1
NUMA node(s):          1
Vendor ID:             GenuineIntel
```

Next, we check our memory capacity by typing `free -g` at the bash prompt and then again press *Enter*. This will tell us the total number of proper memory that we have in gigabytes in the first entry of the first row, as well as the amount of memory in swap space in the following row:

```
           total     used     free     shared  buff/cache  available
Mem:          15        3        9          0           2         12
Swap:          5        0        5
```

This is certainly sufficient memory.

Finally, let's see whether we have an appropriate GPU. NVIDIA GPUs communicate with our PC via the PCI bus, so we can use the `lspci` command to list all PCI hardware. There is usually a lot of other hardware listed, so let's use the `grep` command to filter for just NVIDIA GPUs by entering `lspci | grep -e "NVIDIA"` at the bash prompt:

```
01:00.0 VGA compatible controller: NVIDIA Corporation GP104M [GeForce GTX 1070 Mobile] (rev a1)
```

This is a GTX 1070, which fortunately exceeds our need for at least a GTX 1050.

Checking your hardware (windows)

First, we must open the Windows panel. We do this by pressing *Windows + R* and then entering `Control Panel` at the prompt, as demonstrated in the following screenshot:

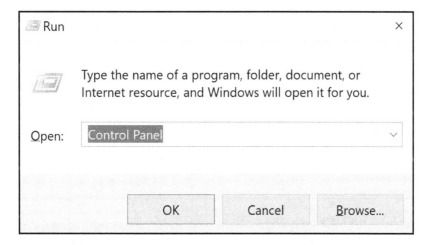

The Windows Control Panel will pop up. Now click on **System and Security**, and then choose **System** on the following screen. This will immediately tell us the amount of RAM that we have and whether we have a 64-bit processor:

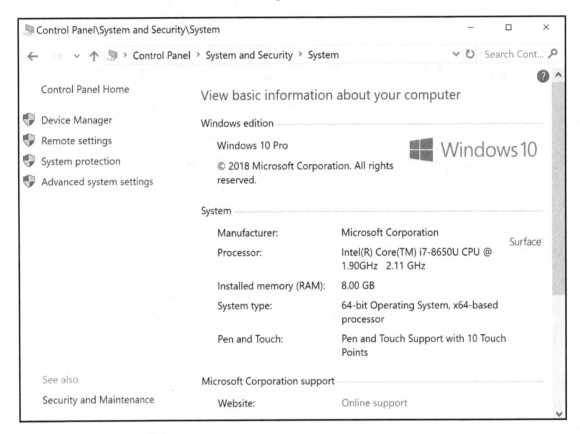

To check our GPU, click on **Device Manager** in the upper left-hand corner of this window. The Windows **Device Manager** will then pop up; you can then select the **Display adapters** drop-down box to check which GPUs are on your system:

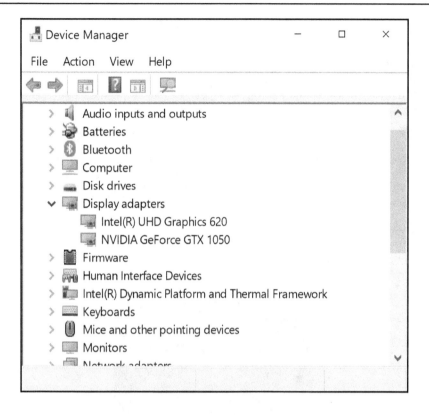

Installing the GPU drivers

If you already have drivers for your GPU installed, you may possibly skip this step; moreover, some versions of CUDA are pre-packaged with the latest drivers. Quite often, CUDA is very particular about which driver you have installed and may not even work with the CUDA Toolkit driver, so you may have to experiment with several different drivers before you find one that works.

Generally speaking, Windows has better CUDA driver compatibility and a more user-friendly installation than Linux. Windows users may consider skipping this step and just use the driver that is packaged with the CUDA Toolkit, which we will install a little later in this chapter. We would strongly suggest that Linux users (particularly Linux laptop users), however, closely follow all the steps in this section before proceeding.

Installing the GPU drivers (Linux)

In Ubuntu, the default driver for NVIDIA GPUs is an open-source driver called Nouveau; unfortunately, this does not work with CUDA at all, so we will have to install a proprietary driver. We will have to add the special `graphics-drivers` repository to our package manager to be able to download proprietary NVIDIA drivers to our Ubuntu system. We add the repository by typing the following line into the bash prompt:

```
sudo add-apt-repository ppa:graphics-drivers/ppa
```

Since this is a `sudo` superuser command, you will have to enter your password. We now synchronize our system with the new repository by typing the following line:

```
sudo apt-get update
```

We should now be ready to install our driver. From the Ubuntu desktop, press *Windows + R*, and then enter `software and drivers`:

The **Software & Drivers** setup menu should appear. From here, click on the tab marked **Additional Drivers**. You should see a selection of available stable proprietary drivers for your GPU; choose the newest one you see I(n my case, it is `nvidia-driver-396`, demonstrated as follows):

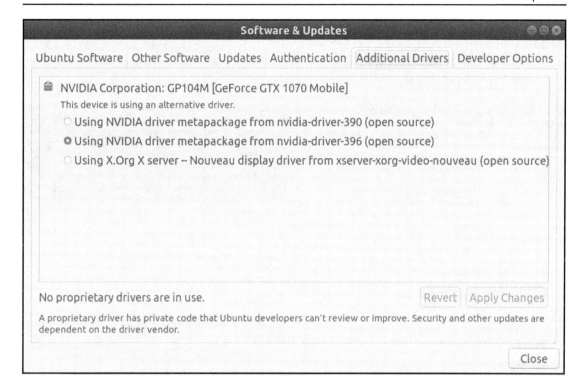

With the latest driver selected, click on **Apply Changes**. You will be prompted again for your sudo password, and then the driver will install; a progress bar should appear. Note that this process can take a long time and it may appear that your computer is *hanging*; this process can take well over an hour, so please be patient.

Finally, when the process is complete, reset your computer, and return to your Ubuntu desktop. Now type *Windows + A*, and then enter `nvidia-settings` (or alternatively, run this program from a bash prompt). The NVIDIA X Server Settings manager should appear, and indicate that you are using the appropriate driver version:

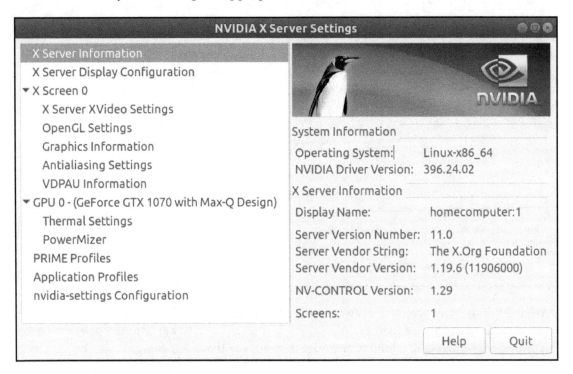

Installing the GPU drivers (Windows)

To reiterate—it is generally suggested that the reader initially skip this step, and then install the drivers that are included with the CUDA Toolkit.

The latest drivers for Windows are available directly from NVIDIA at `http://www.nvidia.com/Download/`. Simply choose the appropriate Windows 10 drivers for your GPU from the drop-down menu, which are executable (`.exe`) files. Simply install the driver by double-clicking on the file from the file manager.

Setting up a C++ programming environment

Now that we have our drivers installed, we have to set up our C/C++ programming environment; both Python and CUDA are particular about what compilers and IDEs they may integrate with, so you may have to be careful. In the case of Ubuntu Linux users, the standard repository compilers and IDEs generally work and integrate perfectly with the CUDA Toolkit, while Windows users might have to exercise a little more caution.

Setting up GCC, Eclipse IDE, and graphical dependencies (Linux)

Open up a Terminal from the Ubuntu desktop (*Ctrl* + *Alt* + *T*). We first update the apt repository as follows:

```
sudo apt-get update
```

Now we can install everything we need for CUDA with one additional line:

```
sudo apt-get install build-essential binutils gdb eclipse-cdt
```

Here, build-essential is the package with the gcc and g++ compilers, and other utilities such as make; binutils has some generally useful utilities, such as the LD linker, gdb is the debugger, and Eclipse is the IDE that we will be using.

Let's also install a few additional dependencies that will allow us to run some of the graphical (OpenGL) demos included with the CUDA Toolkit with this line:

```
sudo apt-get install freeglut3 freeglut3-dev libxi-dev libxmu-dev
```

Now you should be good to go to install the CUDA Toolkit.

Setting up Visual Studio (Windows)

At the time of writing, only one version of Visual Studio appears to ingrate perfectly with both Python and the latest CUDA Toolkits—Visual Studio 2015; that is, Visual Studio version 14.0.

While it may be possible to make a sub-installation of this under a later version of Visual Studio (for example, 2017), we would suggest to the reader that you directly install Visual Studio 2015 with C/C++ support onto your system.

Visual Studio Community 2015, the free version of this software, can be downloaded at `https://visualstudio.microsoft.com/vs/older-downloads/`.

Here, we will do a minimalist installation, with only the necessary components for CUDA. We run the installation software, and select the **Custom** installation:

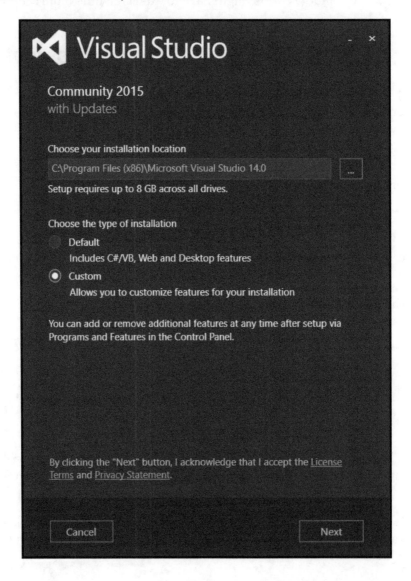

Click **Next**, then click the drop-down box for **Programming Languages**, and then choose **Visual C++** (feel free to select other packages or programming languages if you want or need them for other purposes, but Visual C++ is all we will need for GPU programming):

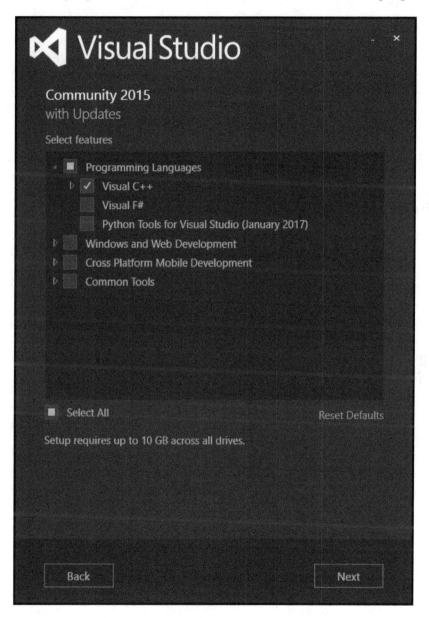

This should take some time to install. After this is complete, we will be ready to install the CUDA Toolkit.

Installing the CUDA Toolkit

Finally, we are beginning to get close to our goal! We now download our CUDA Toolkit by heading over to `https://developer.nvidia.com/cuda-downloads`. Select the appropriate operating system and you will see several options. In the case of both Windows and Linux, there are both network and local installations. I tend to use the local installation option under both Windows and Linux, because I prefer to download the entire package up-front; if there are any network problems, then you can be assured they won't occur while you are installing the CUDA Toolkit.

Installing the CUDA Toolkit (Linux)

In the case of Linux users, you will see that there are choices for using a `.deb` package and a `.run` file; for most users, I would suggest going with the `.deb` file, since this will install any missing packages that CUDA requires automatically. The `.run` file installs outside of your system's **Advanced Package Tool** (**APT**) system, which effectively just copies the appropriate files to the system's `/usr` binary and library directories. If you don't want to interfere with your system's APT system or repositories, and have a good understanding of Linux, the `.run` file may be more appropriate. In either case, carefully follow the instructions given on the site about installing the package, which can vary slightly from one version to the next.

After the package is finished installing, you may have to configure your `PATH` and `LD_SYSTEM_CONFIG` environment variables so that your system can find the appropriate binary executable and library files needed for CUDA. I would suggest doing this by appending the followiang lines to the end of your `.bashrc` file in your user directory. Open the `~/.bashrc` file with your favorite text editor, such as `gedit`, `nano`, `emacs`, or `vim`, and, at the very bottom of the file, add the following lines:

```
export PATH="/usr/local/cuda/bin:${PATH}
export LD_LIBRARY_PATH="/usr/local/cuda/lib64:${LD_LIBRARY_PATH}"
```

Save the file and then exit the Terminal. You can now ensure that you've correctly installed the toolkit by opening a new Terminal and typing `nvcc --version` and then pressing *Enter*, which will give you the version information of the compiler for your toolkit. (`nvcc` is the command-line CUDA C compiler, which is analogous to the `gcc` compiler.)

Installing the CUDA Toolkit (Windows)

In the case of Windows users, you can install the package by double-clicking on the `.exe` file and following all the on-screen prompts.

Once the installation is complete, reset your system. We will now ensure that CUDA was installed correctly by checking the `nvcc` compiler. Under the **Start** menu, click on the `Visual Studio 2015` folder, and then click **VS2015 x64 Native Tools Command Prompt**. A Terminal window will pop up; now type `nvcc --version` and press *Enter*, which should give you the version information of the NVIDIA compiler.

Setting up our Python environment for GPU programming

With our compilers, IDEs, and the CUDA Toolkit properly installed on our system, we now can set up an appropriate Python environment for GPU programming. There are many options here, but we explicitly recommend that you work with the Anaconda Python Distribution. Anaconda Python is a self-contained and user-friendly distribution that can be installed directly in your user directory, and which does not require any administrator or `sudo` level system access to install, use, or update.

Keep in mind that Anaconda Python comes in two flavors—Python 2.7, and Python 3. Since Python 3 is currently not as well-supported for some of the libraries we will be using, we will be using Python 2.7 in this book, which still has a broad mainstream usage.

You can install Anaconda Python by going to `https://www.anaconda.com/download`, choosing your operating system, and then by choosing to download the Python 2.7 version of the distribution. Follow the instructions given on the Anaconda site to install the distribution, which is relatively straightforward. We can now set up our local Python installation for GPU programming.

We will now set up what is arguably the most important Python package for this book: Andreas Kloeckner's PyCUDA package.

Installing PyCUDA (Linux)

Open up a command line in Linux. Ensure that your `PATH` variable is set up correctly to use the local Anaconda installation of Python (rather than the system-wide installation) by typing `which python` at the bash prompt and pressing *Enter* (Anaconda should have automatically configured your `.bashrc` during installation); this should tell you that the Python binary is in your local `~/anaconda2/bin` directory, rather than in the `/usr/bin` directory. If this isn't the case, open a text editor and put the line `export PATH="/home/${USER}/anaconda2/bin:${PATH}"` at the end of your `~/.bashrc` file, save this, open a new Terminal, and then check again.

There are several options for installation of PyCUDA. The easiest option is to install the latest stable version from the PyPI repository by typing `pip install pycuda`. You can also install the latest version of PyCUDA by following the instructions at the PyCUDA official website at `https://mathema.tician.de/software/pycuda/`. Please note that if you wish to re-install PyCUDA from a different source, be sure to uninstall it first with `pip uninstall pycuda`.

Creating an environment launch script (Windows)

Windows users will need to be particularly careful that both their Visual Studio and Anaconda Python environment variables are set up correctly in order to use PyCUDA; otherwise, Python will not be able to find NVIDIA's `nvcc` CUDA compiler or Microsoft's `cl.exe` C++ compiler. Fortunately, batch scripts are included that will set up these environments for us automatically, but we will have to be careful that these are executed each and every time we want to do GPU programming.

We will, therefore, create a batch script that will launch an appropriate IDE or command-line environment by calling these other two scripts in succession. (This script is also available at `https://github.com/PacktPublishing/Hands-On-GPU-Programming-with-Python-and-CUDA/blob/master/2/launch-python-cuda-environment.bat`.)

Be sure to first open up Windows Notepad, and follow along:

First, find where your `vcvars.bat` file for Visual Studio is; in the case of Visual Studio 2015, it is at `C:\Program Files (x86)\Microsoft Visual Studio 14.0\VC\vcvarsall.bat`.

Type the following line into your text editor, and then press *Enter*:

```
call "C:\Program Files (x86)\Microsoft Visual Studio 14.0\VC\vcvarsall.bat" amd64
```

We now need to call the Anaconda's `activate.bat` script to set up the Anaconda Python environment variables; the standard path is `Anaconda2\Scripts\activate.bat`. We have to further indicate where the Anaconda libraries are with an argument to this script. In my case, the second line in my launch script would be `call "C:\Users\%username%\Anaconda2\Scripts\activate.bat" C:\Users\%username%\Anaconda2`.

Finally, the last line of our batch script will launch whatever environment—IDE or command-line prompt—you prefer to program in, which will inherit all of the necessary environment and system variables the prior two scripts will set up. If you prefer the old standard DOS-style Command Prompt, this line should just be `cmd`. If you like to work from PowerShell, change this to `powershell`. It will be necessary to use the command line in some cases, particularly for accessing the command line `pip` and `conda` for updating your Python library.

Finally, save this file to your desktop with the filename `launch-python-cuda-environment.bat`. You can now launch our Python GPU programming environment by double-clicking this file.

(Keep in mind that if you wish to use the Jupyter Notebook or Spyder Python IDEs, you can simply launch these from the command line with `jupyter-notebook` or `spyder`, or alternatively, you can make a batch script that just replaces `cmd` with the appropriate IDE launch command.)

Installing PyCUDA (Windows)

Due to the fact that most Python libraries are primarily written by and for Linux users, it is suggested that you install a pre-built PyCUDA wheel binary from Christoph Gohlke's site at the following address: `https://www.lfd.uci.edu/~gohlke/pythonlibs/#pycuda`. Download a file of the from `pycuda-2017.1.1+cuda(VERSION)-cp27-cp27m-win_amd64.whl` where version is your CUDA version number. You can now install PyCUDA by typing the following on the command line, and replacing `pycuda.whl` with the full path and filename of your PyCUDA wheel:

```
pip install pycuda.whl
```

(Alternatively, you can try installing PyCUDA from the PyPI repository with `pip install pycuda`, or by following the instructions on the PyCUDA website.)

Testing PyCUDA

Finally, we're at the point where we can see whether our GPU programming environment actually works. We will run a small program from the next chapter that will query our GPU and yield some relevant information about the model number, memory, number of cores, architecture, and so forth. Get the Python file (`deviceQuery.py`) from directory 3 in the repository, which is also available at `https://github.com/PacktPublishing/Hands-On-GPU-Programming-with-Python-and-CUDA/blob/master/3/deviceQuery.py`.

If you are using Windows, be sure to launch the GPU programming environment by launching the `.bat` file on our desktop we made in the last section. Otherwise, if you are using Linux, open a bash Terminal. Now type the following line and press *Enter*—`python deviceQuery.py`.

This will output many lines of data, but the first few lines should indicate that your GPU has been detected by PyCUDA, and you should see the model number in the following line:

```
PS C:\Users\btuom\examples\3> python .\deviceQuery.py
CUDA device query (PyCUDA version)

Detected 1 CUDA Capable device(s)

Device 0: GeForce GTX 1050
```

Congratulations, you are now ready to embark upon the world of GPU programming!

Summary

Setting up your Python environment for GPU programming can be a very delicate process. The Anaconda Python 2.7 distribution is suggested for both Windows and Linux users for the purposes of this text. First, we should ensure that we have the correct hardware for GPU programming; generally speaking, a 64-bit Windows or Linux PC with 4 gigabytes of RAM and any entry-level NVIDIA GPU from 2016 or later will be sufficient for our ends. Windows users should be careful in using a version of Visual Studio that works well with both the CUDA Toolkit and Anaconda (such as VS 2015), while Linux users should be particularly careful in the installation of their GPU drivers, and set up the appropriate environment variables in their .bashrc file. Furthermore, Windows users should create an appropriate launch script that will set up their environment for GPU programming and should use a pre-compiled wheel file for the installation of the PyCUDA library.

Now, with our programming environment set up and in place, we will spend the next chapter learning the very basics of GPU programming. We will see how to write and read data to and from the GPU's memory, and how to write some very simple *elementwise* GPU functions in CUDA C. (If you have seen the classic 1980's film *The Karate Kid*, then you might think of the following chapter as the "wax on, wax off" of GPU programming.)

Questions

1. Can we run CUDA on our main processor's built-in Intel HD GPU? What about on a discrete AMD Radeon GPU?
2. Does this book use Python 2.7 or Python 3.7 for examples?
3. What program do we use in Windows to see what GPU hardware we have installed?
4. What command-line program do we use in Linux to see what GPU hardware we have installed?
5. What is the command we use in Linux to determine how much memory our system has?
6. If we don't want to alter our Linux system's APT repository, should we use the run or deb installer for CUDA?

3
Getting Started with PyCUDA

In the last chapter, we set up our programming environment. Now, with our drivers and compilers firmly in place, we will begin the actual GPU programming! We will start by learning how to use PyCUDA for some basic and fundamental operations. We will first see how to query our GPU—that is, we will start by writing a small Python program that will tell us what the characteristics of our GPU are, such as the core count, architecture, and memory. We will then spend some time getting acquainted with how to transfer memory between Python and the GPU with PyCUDA's gpuarray class and how to use this class for basic computations. The remainder of this chapter will be spent showing how to write some basic functions (which we will refer to as **CUDA Kernels**) that we can directly launch onto the GPU.

The learning outcomes for this chapter are as follows:

- Determining GPU characteristics, such as memory capacity or core count, using PyCUDA
- Understanding the difference between host (CPU) and device (GPU) memory and how to use PyCUDA's gpuarray class to transfer data between the host and device
- How to do basic calculations using only gpuarray objects
- How to perform basic element-wise operations on the GPU with the PyCUDA ElementwiseKernel function
- Understanding the functional programming concept of reduce/scan operations and how to make a basic reduction or scan CUDA kernel

Technical requirements

A Linux or Windows 10 PC with a modern NVIDIA GPU (2016 onward) is required for this chapter, with all necessary GPU drivers and the CUDA Toolkit (9.0 onward) installed. A suitable Python 2.7 installation (such as Anaconda Python 2.7) with the PyCUDA module is also required.

This chapter's code is also available on GitHub at `https://github.com/PacktPublishing/ Hands-On-GPU-Programming-with-Python-and-CUDA`.

 For more information about the prerequisites, check the *Preface* of this book; for the software and hardware requirements, check the README section in `https://github.com/PacktPublishing/Hands-On-GPU- Programming-with-Python-and-CUDA`.

Querying your GPU

Before we begin to program our GPU, we should really know something about its technical capacities and limits. We can determine this by doing what is known as a **GPU query**. A GPU query is a very basic operation that will tell us the specific technical details of our GPU, such as available GPU memory and core count. NVIDIA includes a command-line example written in pure CUDA-C called `deviceQuery` in the `samples` directory (for both Windows and Linux) that we can run to perform this operation. Let's take a look at the output that is produced on the author's Windows 10 laptop (which is a Microsoft Surface Book 2 with a GTX 1050 GPU):

```
PS C:\ProgramData\NVIDIA Corporation\CUDA Samples\v9.1\bin\win64\Debug> .\deviceQuery.exe
C:\ProgramData\NVIDIA Corporation\CUDA Samples\v9.1\bin\win64\Debug\deviceQuery.exe Starting...

 CUDA Device Query (Runtime API) version (CUDART static linking)

Detected 1 CUDA Capable device(s)

Device 0: "GeForce GTX 1050"
  CUDA Driver Version / Runtime Version          9.1 / 9.1
  CUDA Capability Major/Minor version number:    6.1
  Total amount of global memory:                 2048 MBytes (2147483648 bytes)
  ( 5) Multiprocessors, (128) CUDA Cores/MP:     640 CUDA Cores
  GPU Max Clock rate:                            1493 MHz (1.49 GHz)
  Memory Clock rate:                             3504 Mhz
  Memory Bus Width:                              128-bit
  L2 Cache Size:                                 524288 bytes
  Maximum Texture Dimension Size (x,y,z)         1D=(131072), 2D=(131072, 65536), 3D=(16384, 16384, 16384)
  Maximum Layered 1D Texture Size, (num) layers  1D=(32768), 2048 layers
  Maximum Layered 2D Texture Size, (num) layers  2D=(32768, 32768), 2048 layers
  Total amount of constant memory:               65536 bytes
  Total amount of shared memory per block:       49152 bytes
  Total number of registers available per block: 65536
  Warp size:                                     32
  Maximum number of threads per multiprocessor:  2048
  Maximum number of threads per block:           1024
  Max dimension size of a thread block (x,y,z): (1024, 1024, 64)
  Max dimension size of a grid size    (x,y,z): (2147483647, 65535, 65535)
  Maximum memory pitch:                          2147483647 bytes
  Texture alignment:                             512 bytes
  Concurrent copy and kernel execution:          Yes with 2 copy engine(s)
  Run time limit on kernels:                     No
  Integrated GPU sharing Host Memory:            No
  Support host page-locked memory mapping:       Yes
  Alignment requirement for Surfaces:            Yes
  Device has ECC support:                        Disabled
  CUDA Device Driver Mode (TCC or WDDM):         WDDM (Windows Display Driver Model)
  Device supports Unified Addressing (UVA):      Yes
  Supports Cooperative Kernel Launch:            No
  Supports MultiDevice Co-op Kernel Launch:      No
  Device PCI Domain ID / Bus ID / location ID:   0 / 2 / 0
  Compute Mode:
     < Default (multiple host threads can use ::cudaSetDevice() with device simultaneously) >

deviceQuery, CUDA Driver = CUDART, CUDA Driver Version = 9.1, CUDA Runtime Version = 9.1, NumDevs = 1
Result = PASS
```

Let's look at some of the essentials of all of the technical information displayed here. First, we see that there is only one GPU installed, Device 0—it is possible that a host computer has multiple GPUs and makes use of them, so CUDA will designate each *GPU device* an individual number. There are some cases where we may have to be specific about the device number, so it is always good to know. We can also see the specific type of device that we have (here, GTX 1050), and which CUDA version we are using. There are two more things we will take note of for now: the total number of cores (here, 640), and the total amount of global memory on the device (in this case, 2,048 megabytes, that is, 2 gigabytes).

While you can see many other technical details from `deviceQuery`, the core count and amount of memory are usually the first two things your eyes should zero in on the first time you run this on a new GPU, since they can give you the most immediate idea of the capacity of your new device.

Querying your GPU with PyCUDA

Now, finally, we will begin our foray into the world of GPU programming by writing our own version of `deviceQuery` in Python. Here, we will primarily concern ourselves with only the amount of available memory on the device, the compute capability, the number of multiprocessors, and the total number of CUDA cores.

We will begin by initializing CUDA as follows:

```
import pycuda.driver as drv
drv.init()
```

Note that we will always have to initialize PyCUDA with `pycuda.driver.init()` or by importing the PyCUDA `autoinit` submodule with `import pycuda.autoinit`!

We can now immediately check how many GPU devices we have on our host computer with this line:

```
print 'Detected {} CUDA Capable device(s)'.format(drv.Device.count())
```

Let's type this into IPython and see what happens:

```
In [8]: import pycuda.driver as drv

In [9]: drv.init()

In [10]: print 'Detected {} CUDA Capable device(s)'.format(drv.Device.count())
Detected 1 CUDA Capable device(s)
```

Great! So far, I have verified that my laptop does indeed have one GPU in it. Now, let's extract some more interesting information about this GPU (and any other GPU on the system) by adding a few more lines of code to iterate over each device that can be individually accessed with `pycuda.driver.Device` (indexed by number). The name of the device (for example, GeForce GTX 1050) is given by the `name` function. We then get the **compute capability** of the device with the `compute_capability` function and total amount of device memory with the `total_memory` function.

 Compute capability can be thought of as a *version number* for each NVIDIA GPU architecture; this will give us some important information about the device that we can't otherwise query, as we will see in a minute.

Here's how we will write it:

```
for i in range(drv.Device.count()):
    gpu_device = drv.Device(i)
    print 'Device {}: {}'.format( i, gpu_device.name() )
    compute_capability = float( '%d.%d' % gpu_device.compute_capability() )
    print '\t Compute Capability: {}'.format(compute_capability)
    print '\t Total Memory: {} megabytes'.format(gpu_device.total_memory()//(1024**2))
```

Now, we are ready to look at some of the remaining attributes of our GPU, which PyCUDA yields to us in the form of a Python dictionary type. We will use the following lines to convert this into a dictionary that is indexed by strings indicating attributes:

```
device_attributes_tuples = gpu_device.get_attributes().iteritems()
device_attributes = {}
for k, v in device_attributes_tuples:
    device_attributes[str(k)] = v
```

We can now determine the number of *multiprocessors* on our device with the following:

```
num_mp = device_attributes['MULTIPROCESSOR_COUNT']
```

A GPU divides its individual cores up into larger units known as **Streaming Multiprocessors (SMs)**; a GPU device will have several SMs, which will each individually have a particular number of CUDA cores, depending on the compute capability of the device. To be clear: the number of cores per multiprocessor is not indicated directly by the GPU—this is given to us implicitly by the compute capability. We will have to look up some technical documents from NVIDIA to determine the number of cores per multiprocessor (see `http://docs.nvidia.com/cuda/cuda-c-programming-guide/index.html#compute-capabilities`), and then create a lookup table to give us the number of cores per multiprocessor. We do so as such, using the `compute_capability` variable to look up the number of cores:

```
cuda_cores_per_mp = { 5.0 : 128, 5.1 : 128, 5.2 : 128, 6.0 : 64, 6.1 : 128, 6.2 : 128}[compute_capability]
```

We can now finally determine the total number of cores on our device by multiplying these two numbers:

```
print '\t ({}) Multiprocessors, ({}) CUDA Cores / Multiprocessor: {} CUDA Cores'.format(num_mp, cuda_cores_per_mp, num_mp*cuda_cores_per_mp)
```

We now can finish up our program by iterating over the remaining keys in our dictionary and printing the corresponding values:

```
device_attributes.pop('MULTIPROCESSOR_COUNT')
for k in device_attributes.keys():
    print '\t {}: {}'.format(k, device_attributes[k])
```

So, now we finally completed our first true GPU program of the text! (Also available at `https://github.com/PacktPublishing/Hands-On-GPU-Programming-with-Python-and-CUDA/blob/master/3/deviceQuery.py`). Now, we can run it as follows:

```
PS C:\Users\btuom\examples\3> python deviceQuery.py
CUDA device query (PyCUDA version)

Detected 1 CUDA Capable device(s)

Device 0: GeForce GTX 1050
        Compute Capability: 6.1
        Total Memory: 2048 megabytes
        (5) Multiprocessors, (128) CUDA Cores / Multiprocessor: 640 CUDA Cores
        MAXIMUM_TEXTURE2D_LINEAR_PITCH: 2097120
        MAXIMUM_TEXTURE2D_GATHER_WIDTH: 32768
        MAXIMUM_TEXTURE2D_GATHER_HEIGHT: 32768
        PCI_DEVICE_ID: 0
        MAXIMUM_TEXTURE3D_WIDTH: 16384
        MAXIMUM_SURFACE2D_WIDTH: 131072
        MAXIMUM_TEXTURE1D_MIPMAPPED_WIDTH: 16384
        GLOBAL_MEMORY_BUS_WIDTH: 128
        LOCAL_L1_CACHE_SUPPORTED: 1
        MAXIMUM_SURFACE3D_DEPTH: 16384
        MAXIMUM_TEXTURE3D_HEIGHT: 16384
        PCI_DOMAIN_ID: 0
        COMPUTE_CAPABILITY_MINOR: 1
        MULTI_GPU_BOARD_GROUP_ID: 0
        MAX_REGISTERS_PER_BLOCK: 65536
        MAXIMUM_TEXTURE2D_ARRAY_WIDTH: 32768
        COMPUTE_CAPABILITY_MAJOR: 6
        MAXIMUM_SURFACE2D_LAYERED_HEIGHT: 32768
        MAXIMUM_TEXTURE1D_LAYERED_LAYERS: 2048
        UNIFIED_ADDRESSING: 1
```

We can now have a little pride that we can indeed write a program to query our GPU!
Now, let's actually begin to learn to *use* our GPU, rather than just observe it.

Using PyCUDA's gpuarray class

Much like how NumPy's `array` class is the cornerstone of numerical programming within
the NumPy environment, PyCUDA's `gpuarray` class plays an analogously prominent role
within GPU programming in Python. This has all of the features you know and love from
NumPy—multidimensional vector/matrix/tensor shape structuring, array-slicing, array
unraveling, and overloaded operators for point-wise computations (for example, +, −, *, /,
and **).

`gpuarray` is really an indispensable tool for any budding GPU programmer. We will spend this section going over this particular data structure and gaining a strong grasp of it before we move on.

Transferring data to and from the GPU with gpuarray

As we note from writing our prior `deviceQuery` program in Python, a GPU has its own memory apart from the host computer's memory, which is known as **device memory**. (Sometimes this is known more specifically as **global device memory**, to differentiate this from the additional cache memory, shared memory, and register memory that is also on the GPU.) For the most part, we treat (global) device memory on the GPU as we do dynamically allocated heap memory in C (with the `malloc` and `free` functions) or C++ (as with the `new` and `delete` operators); in CUDA C, this is complicated further with the additional task of transferring data back and forth between the CPU to the GPU (with commands such as `cudaMemcpyHostToDevice` and `cudaMemcpyDeviceToHost`), all while keeping track of multiple pointers in both the CPU and GPU space and performing proper memory allocations (`cudaMalloc`) and deallocations (`cudaFree`).

Fortunately, PyCUDA covers all of the overhead of memory allocation, deallocation, and data transfers with the `gpuarray` class. As stated, this class acts similarly to NumPy arrays, using vector/ matrix/tensor shape structure information for the data. `gpuarray` objects even perform automatic cleanup based on the lifetime, so we do not have to worry about *freeing* any GPU memory stored in a `gpuarray` object when we are done with it.

How exactly do we use this to transfer data from the host to the GPU? First, we must contain our host data in some form of NumPy array (let's call it `host_data`), and then use the `gpuarray.to_gpu(host_data)` command to transfer this over to the GPU and create a new GPU array.

Let's now perform a simple computation within the GPU (pointwise multiplication by a constant on the GPU), and then retrieve the GPU data into a new with the `gpuarray.get` function. Let's load up IPython and see how this works (note that here we will initialize PyCUDA with `import pycuda.autoinit`):

```
In [24]: import numpy as np

In [25]: import pycuda.autoinit

In [26]: from pycuda import gpuarray

In [27]: host_data = np.array([1,2,3,4,5],dtype=np.float32)

In [28]: device_data = gpuarray.to_gpu(host_data)

In [29]: device_data_x2 = 2 * device_data

In [30]: host_data_x2 = device_data_x2.get()

In [31]: print host_data_x2
[  2.   4.   6.   8.  10.]

In [32]:
```

One thing to note is that we specifically denoted that the array on the host had its type specifically set to a NumPy `float32` type with the `dtype` option when we set up our NumPy array; this corresponds directly with the float type in C/C++. Generally speaking, it's a good idea to specifically set data types with NumPy when we are sending data to the GPU. The reason for this is twofold: first, since we are using a GPU for increasing the performance of our application, we don't want any unnecessary overhead of using an unnecessary type that will possibly take up more computational time or memory, and second, since we will soon be writing portions of code in inline CUDA C, we will have to be very specific with types or our code won't work correctly, keeping in mind that C is a statically-typed language.

Remember to specifically set data types for NumPy arrays that will be transferred to the GPU. This can be done with the dtype option in the constructor of the numpy.array class.

Basic pointwise arithmetic operations with gpuarray

In the last example, we saw that we can use the (overloaded) Python multiplication operator (*) to multiply each element in a gpuarray object by a scalar value (here it was 2); note that a pointwise operation is intrinsically parallelizable, and so when we use this operation on a gpuarray object PyCUDA is able to offload each multiplication operation onto a single thread, rather than computing each multiplication in serial, one after the other (in fairness, some versions of NumPy can use the advanced SSE instructions found in modern x86 chips for these computations, so in some cases the performance will be comparable to a GPU). To be clear: these pointwise operations performed on the GPU are in parallel since the computation of one element is not dependent on the computation of any other element.

To get a feel for how the operators work, I would suggest that the reader load up IPython and create a few gpuarray objects on the GPU, and then play around with these operations for a few minutes to see that these operators do work similarly to arrays in NumPy. Here is some inspiration:

```
In [14]: x_host = np.array([1,2,3], dtype=np.float32)

In [15]: y_host = np.array([1,1,1], dtype=np.float32)

In [16]: z_host = np.array([2,2,2], dtype=np.float32)

In [17]: x_device = gpuarray.to_gpu(x_host)

In [18]: y_device = gpuarray.to_gpu(y_host)

In [19]: z_device = gpuarray.to_gpu(z_host)

In [20]: x_host + y_host
Out[20]: array([ 2.,   3.,   4.], dtype=float32)

In [21]: (x_device + y_device).get()
Out[21]: array([ 2.,   3.,   4.], dtype=float32)

In [22]: x_host ** z_host
Out[22]: array([ 1.,   4.,   9.], dtype=float32)

In [23]: (x_device ** z_device).get()
Out[23]: array([ 1.,   4.,   9.], dtype=float32)

In [24]: x_host / x_host
Out[24]: array([ 1.,   1.,   1.], dtype=float32)

In [25]: (x_device / x_device).get()
Out[25]: array([ 1.,   1.,   1.], dtype=float32)

In [26]: z_host - x_host
Out[26]: array([ 1.,   0.,  -1.], dtype=float32)

In [27]: (z_device - x_device).get()
Out[27]: array([ 1.,   0.,  -1.], dtype=float32)

In [28]: z_host / 2
Out[28]: array([ 1.,   1.,   1.], dtype=float32)

In [29]: (z_device / 2).get()
Out[29]: array([ 1.,   1.,   1.], dtype=float32)

In [30]: x_host - 1
Out[30]: array([ 0.,   1.,   2.], dtype=float32)

In [31]: (x_device - 1).get()
Out[31]: array([ 0.,   1.,   2.], dtype=float32)
```

Now, we can see that `gpuarray` objects act predictably and are in accordance with how NumPy arrays act. (Notice that we will have to pull the output off the GPU with the `get` function!) Let's now do some comparison between CPU and GPU computation time to see if and when there is any advantage to doing these operations on the GPU.

A speed test

Let's write up a little program (`time_calc0.py`) that will do a speed comparison test between a scalar multiplication on the CPU and then the same operation on the GPU. We will then use NumPy's `allclose` function to compare the two output values. We will generate an array of 50 million random 32-bit floating point values (this will amount to roughly 48 megabytes of data, so this should be entirely feasible with several gigabytes of memory on any somewhat modern host and GPU device), and then we will time how long it takes to scalar multiply the array by two on both devices. Finally, we will compare the output values to ensure that they are equal. Here's how it's done:

```
import numpy as np
import pycuda.autoinit
from pycuda import gpuarray
from time import time
host_data = np.float32( np.random.random(50000000) )

t1 = time()
host_data_2x =  host_data * np.float32(2)
t2 = time()

print 'total time to compute on CPU: %f' % (t2 - t1)
device_data = gpuarray.to_gpu(host_data)

t1 = time()
device_data_2x =  device_data * np.float32( 2 )
t2 = time()

from_device = device_data_2x.get()
print 'total time to compute on GPU: %f' % (t2 - t1)

print 'Is the host computation the same as the GPU computation? :
{}'.format(np.allclose(from_device, host_data_2x) )
```

(You can find the `time_calc0.py` file on the repository provided to you earlier.)

Now, let's load up IPython and run this a few times to get an idea of the general speed of these, and see if there is any variance. (Here, this is being run on a 2017-era Microsoft Surface Book 2 with a Kaby Lake i7 processor and a GTX 1050 GPU.):

```
In [1]: run time_calc0.py
total time to compute on CPU: 0.078000
total time to compute on GPU: 1.094000
Is the host computation the same as the GPU computation? : True

In [2]: run time_calc0.py
total time to compute on CPU: 0.079000
total time to compute on GPU: 0.008000
Is the host computation the same as the GPU computation? : True

In [3]: run time_calc0.py
total time to compute on CPU: 0.080000
total time to compute on GPU: 0.007000
Is the host computation the same as the GPU computation? : True

In [4]: run time_calc0.py
total time to compute on CPU: 0.078000
total time to compute on GPU: 0.009000
Is the host computation the same as the GPU computation? : True

In [5]: run time_calc0.py
total time to compute on CPU: 0.079000
total time to compute on GPU: 0.009000
Is the host computation the same as the GPU computation? : True
```

We first notice that the CPU computation time is about the same for each computation (roughly 0.08 seconds). Yet, we notice that the GPU computation time is far slower than the CPU computation the first time we run this (1.09 seconds), and it becomes much faster in the subsequent run, which remains roughly constant in every following run (in the range of 7 or 9 milliseconds). If you exit IPython, and then run the program again, the same thing will occur. What is the reason for this phenomenon? Well, let's do some investigative work using IPython's built-in prun profiler. (This works similarly to the cProfiler module that was featured in Chapter 1, *Why GPU Programming?*.)

First, let's load our program as text within IPython with the following lines, which we can then run with our profiler via Python's `exec` command:

```
with open('time_calc0.py','r') as f:
    time_calc_code = f.read()
```

We now type `%prun -s cumulative exec(time_calc_code)` into our IPython console (with the leading `%`) and see what operations are taking the most time:

```
In [2]: %prun -s cumulative exec(time_calc_code)
total time to compute on CPU: 0.078000
total time to compute on GPU: 1.100000
Is the host computation the same as the GPU computation? : True
         17353 function calls (17146 primitive calls) in 3.175 seconds

   Ordered by: cumulative time

   ncalls  tottime  percall  cumtime  percall filename:lineno(function)
        1    0.000    0.000    1.101    1.101 gpuarray.py:452(__mul__)
        1    0.000    0.000    1.092    1.092 gpuarray.py:317(_axpbz)
        1    0.000    0.000    1.091    1.091 <decorator-gen-122>:1(get_axpbz_kernel)
        1    0.000    0.000    1.091    1.091 tools.py:414(context_dependent_memoize)
        1    0.000    0.000    1.091    1.091 elementwise.py:413(get_axpbz_kernel)
        1    0.000    0.000    1.091    1.091 elementwise.py:155(get_elwise_kernel)
        1    0.000    0.000    1.091    1.091 elementwise.py:126(get_elwise_kernel_and_types)
        1    0.000    0.000    1.091    1.091 elementwise.py:41(get_elwise_module)
        1    0.001    0.001    1.089    1.089 compiler.py:285(__init__)
        1    0.001    0.001    1.089    1.089 compiler.py:190(compile)
        1    0.001    0.001    1.070    1.070 compiler.py:69(compile_plain)
        2    0.000    0.000    1.061    0.531 prefork.py:222(call_capture_output)
        2    0.000    0.000    1.061    0.531 prefork.py:43(call_capture_output)
        1    0.000    0.000    0.950    0.950 compiler.py:36(preprocess_source)
        2    0.000    0.000    0.837    0.419 subprocess.py:448(communicate)
        2    0.000    0.000    0.837    0.419 subprocess.py:698(_communicate)
        6    0.000    0.000    0.836    0.139 threading.py:309(wait)
```

Now, there are a number of suspicious calls to a Python module file, `compiler.py`; these take roughly one second total, a little less than the time it takes to do the GPU computation here. Now let's run this again and see if there are any differences:

```
In [3]: %prun -s cumulative exec(time_calc_code)
total time to compute on CPU: 0.101000
total time to compute on GPU: 0.015000
Is the host computation the same as the GPU computation? : True
        342 function calls (336 primitive calls) in 1.315 seconds

   Ordered by: cumulative time

   ncalls  tottime  percall  cumtime  percall filename:lineno(function)
        1    0.000    0.000    1.606    1.606 <string>:1(<module>)
        1    0.016    0.016    0.650    0.650 numeric.py:2397(allclose)
        1    0.069    0.069    0.630    0.630 numeric.py:2463(isclose)
        1    0.400    0.400    0.554    0.554 numeric.py:2522(within_tol)
        1    0.452    0.452    0.452    0.452 {method 'random_sample' of 'mtrand.Rand
omState' objects}
        2    0.191    0.096    0.191    0.096 gpuarray.py:1174(_memcpy_discontig)
        2    0.154    0.077    0.154    0.077 {abs}
        1    0.000    0.000    0.107    0.107 gpuarray.py:248(get)
        1    0.000    0.000    0.094    0.094 gpuarray.py:990(to_gpu)
        1    0.000    0.000    0.085    0.085 gpuarray.py:230(set)
        2    0.018    0.009    0.018    0.009 gpuarray.py:162(__init__)
        3    0.000    0.000    0.012    0.004 fromnumeric.py:1973(all)
```

Notice that this time, there are no calls to `compiler.py`. Why is this? By the nature of the PyCUDA library, GPU code is often compiled and linked with NVIDIA's `nvcc` compiler the first time it is run in a given Python session; it is then cached and, if the code is called again, then it doesn't have to be recompiled. This may include even *simple* operations such as this scalar multiply! (We will see eventually see that this can be ameliorated by using the pre-compiled code in, `Chapter 10`, *Working with Compiled GPU Code*, or by using NVIDIA's own linear algebra libraries with the Scikit-CUDA module, which we will see in `Chapter 7`, *Using the CUDA Libraries with Scikit-CUDA*).

> In PyCUDA, GPU code is often compiled at runtime with the NVIDIA `nvcc` compiler and then subsequently called from PyCUDA. This can lead to an unexpected slowdown, usually the first time a program or GPU operation is run in a given Python session.

Using PyCUDA's ElementWiseKernel for performing pointwise computations

We will now see how to program our own point-wise (or equivalently, *element-wise*) operations directly onto our GPU with the help of PyCUDA's `ElementWiseKernel` function. This is where our prior knowledge of C/C++ programming will become useful—we'll have to write a little bit of *inline code* in CUDA C, which is compiled externally by NVIDIA's `nvcc` compiler and then launched at runtime by our code via PyCUDA.

We use the term **kernel** quite a bit in this text; by *kernel*, we always mean a function that is launched directly onto the GPU by CUDA. We will use several functions from PyCUDA that generate templates and design patterns for different types of kernels, easing our transition into GPU programming.

Let's dive right in; we're going to start by explicitly rewriting the code to multiply each element of a `gpuarray` object by 2 in CUDA-C; we will use the `ElementwiseKernel` function from PyCUDA to generate our code. You should try typing the following code directly into an IPython console. (The less adventurous can just download this from this text's Git repository, which has the filename `simple_element_kernel_example0.py`):

```
import numpy as np
import pycuda.autoinit
from pycuda import gpuarray
from time import time
from pycuda.elementwise import ElementwiseKernel
host_data = np.float32( np.random.random(50000000) )
gpu_2x_ker = ElementwiseKernel(
"float *in, float *out",
"out[i] = 2*in[i];",
"gpu_2x_ker")
```

Let's take a look at how this is set up; this is, of course, several lines of inline C. We first set the input and output variables in the first line (`"float *in, float *out"`), which will generally be in the form of C pointers to allocated memory on the GPU. In the second line, we define our element-wise operation with `"out[i] = 2*in[i];"`, which will multiply each point in `in` by two and place this in the corresponding index of `out`.

Note that PyCUDA automatically sets up the integer index i for us. When we use i as our index, ElementwiseKernel will automatically parallelize our calculation over i among the many cores in our GPU. Finally, we give our piece of code its internal CUDA C kernel name ("gpu_2x_ker"). Since this refers to CUDA C's namespace and not Python's, it's fine (and also convenient) to give this the same name as in Python.

Now, let's do a speed comparison:

```
def speedcomparison():
    t1 = time()
    host_data_2x =  host_data * np.float32(2)
    t2 = time()
    print 'total time to compute on CPU: %f' % (t2 - t1)
    device_data = gpuarray.to_gpu(host_data)
    # allocate memory for output
    device_data_2x = gpuarray.empty_like(device_data)
    t1 = time()
    gpu_2x_ker(device_data, device_data_2x)
    t2 = time()
    from_device = device_data_2x.get()
    print 'total time to compute on GPU: %f' % (t2 - t1)
    print 'Is the host computation the same as the GPU computation? :
{}'.format(np.allclose(from_device, host_data_2x) )

if __name__ == '__main__':
    speedcomparison()
```

Now, let's run this program:

```
PS C:\Users\btuom\examples\3> python simple_element_kernel_example0.py
total time to compute on CPU: 0.092000
total time to compute on GPU: 1.494000
Is the host computation the same as the GPU computation? : True
PS C:\Users\btuom\examples\3>
```

Whoa! That doesn't look good. Let's run the `speedcomparison()` function a few times from IPython:

```
In [1]: run simple_element_kernel_example0.py
total time to compute on CPU: 0.080000
total time to compute on GPU: 0.989000
Is the host computation the same as the GPU computation? : True

In [2]: speedcomparison()
total time to compute on CPU: 0.081000
total time to compute on GPU: 0.000000
Is the host computation the same as the GPU computation? : True

In [3]: speedcomparison()
total time to compute on CPU: 0.096000
total time to compute on GPU: 0.000000
Is the host computation the same as the GPU computation? : True

In [4]: speedcomparison()
total time to compute on CPU: 0.085000
total time to compute on GPU: 0.000000
Is the host computation the same as the GPU computation? : True

In [5]: speedcomparison()
total time to compute on CPU: 0.085000
total time to compute on GPU: 0.000000
Is the host computation the same as the GPU computation? : True

In [6]:
```

As we can see, the speed increases dramatically after the first time we use a given GPU function. Again, as with the prior example, this is because PyCUDA compiles our inline CUDA C code the first time a given GPU kernel function is called using the `nvcc` compiler. After the code is compiled, then it is cached and re-used for the remainder of a given Python session.

Now, let's cover something else important before we move on, which is very subtle. The little kernel function we defined operates on C float pointers; this means that we will have to allocate some empty memory on the GPU that is pointed to by the `out` variable. Take a look at this portion of code again from the `speedcomparison()` function:

```
device_data = gpuarray.to_gpu(host_data)
# allocate memory for output
device_data_2x = gpuarray.empty_like(device_data)
```

As we did before, we send a NumPy array over to the GPU (host_data) via the gpuarray.to_gpu function, which automatically allocates data onto the GPU and copies it over from the CPU space. We will plug this into the in part of our kernel function. In the next line, we allocate empty memory on the GPU with the gpuarray.empty_like function. This acts as a plain malloc in C, allocating an array of the same size and data type as device_data, but without copying anything. We can now use this for the out part of our kernel function. We now look at the next line in speedcomparison() to see how to launch our kernel function onto the GPU (ignoring the lines we use for timing):

```
gpu_2x_ker(device_data, device_data_2x)
```

Again, the variables we set correspond directly to the first line we defined with ElementwiseKernel (here being, "float *in, float *out").

Mandelbrot revisited

Let's again look at the problem of generating the Mandelbrot set from Chapter 1, *Why GPU Programming?*. The original code is available under the 1 folder in the repository, with the filename mandelbrot0.py, which you should take another look at before we continue. We saw that there were two main components of this program: the first being the generation of the Mandelbrot set, and the second concerning dumping the Mandelbrot set into a PNG file. In the first chapter, we realized that we could parallelize only the generation of the Mandelbrot set, and considering that this takes the bulk of the time for the program to do, this would be a good candidate for an algorithm to offload this onto a GPU. Let's figure out how to do this. (We will refrain from re-iterating over the definition of the Mandelbrot set, so if you need a deeper review, please re-read the *Mandelbrot revisited* section of Chapter 1, *Why GPU Programming?*)

First, let's make a new Python function based on simple_mandelbrot from the original program. We'll call it gpu_mandelbrot, and this will take in the same exact input as before:

```
def gpu_mandelbrot(width, height, real_low, real_high, imag_low, imag_high,
    max_iters, upper_bound):
```

We will proceed a little differently from here. We will start by building a complex lattice that consists of each point in the complex plane that we will analyze.

Here, we'll use some tricks with the NumPy matrix type to easily generate the lattice, and then typecast the result from a NumPy `matrix` type to a two-dimensional NumPy `array` (since PyCUDA can only handle NumPy `array` types, not `matrix` types). Notice how we are very carefully setting our NumPy types:

```
    real_vals = np.matrix(np.linspace(real_low, real_high, width),
dtype=np.complex64)
    imag_vals = np.matrix(np.linspace( imag_high, imag_low, height),
dtype=np.complex64) * 1j
    mandelbrot_lattice = np.array(real_vals + imag_vals.transpose(),
dtype=np.complex64)
```

So, we now have a two-dimensional complex array that represents the lattice from which we will generate our Mandelbrot set; as we will see, we can operate on this very easily within the GPU. Let's now transfer our lattice to the GPU and allocate an array that we will use to represent our Mandelbrot set:

```
    # copy complex lattice to the GPU
    mandelbrot_lattice_gpu = gpuarray.to_gpu(mandelbrot_lattice)
    # allocate an empty array on the GPU
    mandelbrot_graph_gpu = gpuarray.empty(shape=mandelbrot_lattice.shape,
dtype=np.float32)
```

To reiterate—the `gpuarray.to_array` function only can operate on NumPy `array` types, so we were sure to have type-cast this beforehand before we sent it to the GPU. Next, we have to allocate some memory on the GPU with the `gpuarray.empty` function, specifying the size/shape of the array and the type. Again, you can think of this as acting similarly to `malloc` in C; remember that we won't have to deallocate or `free` this memory later, due to the `gpuarray` object destructor taking care of memory clean-up automatically when the end of the scope is reached.

 When you allocate memory on the GPU with the PyCUDA functions `gpuarray.empty` or `gpuarray.empty_like`, you do not have to deallocate this memory later due to the destructor of the `gpuarray` object managing all memory clean up.

We're now ready to launch the kernel; the only change we have to make is to change the

We haven't written our kernel function yet to generate the Mandelbrot set, but let's just write how we want the rest of this function to go:

```
mandel_ker( mandelbrot_lattice_gpu, mandelbrot_graph_gpu,
np.int32(max_iters), np.float32(upper_bound))
    mandelbrot_graph = mandelbrot_graph_gpu.get()
    return mandelbrot_graph
```

So this is how we want our new kernel to act—the first input will be the complex lattice of points (NumPy `complex64` type) we generated, the second will be a pointer to a two-dimensional floating point array (NumPy `float32` type) that will indicate which elements are members of the Mandelbrot set, the third will be an integer indicating the maximum number of iterations for each point, and the final input will be the upper bound for each point used for determining membership in the Mandelbrot class. Notice that we are *very* careful in typecasting everything that goes into the GPU!

The next line retrieves the Mandelbrot set we generated from the GPU back into CPU space, and the end value is returned. (Notice that the input and output of `gpu_mandelbrot` is exactly the same as that of `simple_mandelbrot`).

Let's now look at how to properly define our GPU kernel. First, let's add the appropriate `include` statements to the header:

```
import pycuda.autoinit
from pycuda import gpuarray
from pycuda.elementwise import ElementwiseKernel
```

We are now ready to write our GPU kernel! We'll show it here and then go over this line-by-line:

```
mandel_ker = ElementwiseKernel(
"pycuda::complex<float> *lattice, float *mandelbrot_graph, int max_iters,
float upper_bound",
"""
mandelbrot_graph[i] = 1;
pycuda::complex<float> c = lattice[i];
pycuda::complex<float> z(0,0);
for (int j = 0; j < max_iters; j++)
    {
     z = z*z + c;
     if(abs(z) > upper_bound)
         {
          mandelbrot_graph[i] = 0;
          break;
         }
    }
```

```
""",
"mandel_ker")
```

First, we set our input with the first string passed to `ElementwiseKernel`. We have to realize that when we are working in CUDA-C, particular C datatypes will correspond directly to particular Python NumPy datatypes. Again, note that when arrays are passed into a CUDA kernel, they are seen as C pointers by CUDA. Here, a CUDA C `int` type corresponds exactly to a NumPy `int32` type, while a CUDA C `float` type corresponds to a NumPy `float32` type. An internal PyCUDA class template is then used for complex types—here PyCUDA `::complex<float>` corresponds to Numpy `complex64`.

Let's look at the content of the second string, which is deliminated with three quotes (`"""`). This allows us to use multiple lines within the string; we will use this when we write larger inline CUDA kernels in Python.

While the arrays we have passed in are two-dimensional arrays in Python, CUDA will only see these as being one-dimensional and indexed by i. Again, `ElementwiseKernel` indexes i across multiple cores and threads for us automatically. We initialize each point in the output to one with `mandelbrot_graph[i] = 1;`, as i will be indexed over every single element of our Mandelbrot set; we're going to assume that every point will be a member unless proven otherwise. (Again, the Mandelbrot set is over two dimensions, real and complex, but `ElementwiseKernel` will automatically translate everything into a one-dimensional set. When we interact with the data again in Python, the two-dimensional structure of the Mandelbrot set will be preserved.)

We set up our c value as in Python to the appropriate lattice point with `pycuda::complex<float> c = lattice[i];` and initialize our z value to 0 with `pycuda::complex<float> z(0,0);` (the first zero corresponds to the real part, while the second corresponds to the imaginary part). We then perform a loop over a new iterator, j, with `for(int j = 0; j < max_iters; j++)`. (Note that this algorithm will not be parallelized over j or any other index—only i! This `for` loop will run serially over j—but the entire piece of code will be parallelized across i.)

We then set the new value of z with `z = z*z + c;` as per the Mandelbrot algorithm. If the absolute value of this element exceeds the upper bound (`if(abs(z) > upper_bound)`), we set this point to 0 (`mandelbrot_graph[i] = 0;`) and break out of the loop with the `break` keyword.

In the final string passed into `ElementwiseKernel` we give the kernel its internal CUDA C name, here `"mandel_ker"`.

We're now ready to launch the kernel; the only change we have to make is to change the reference from `simple_mandelbrot` in the main function to `gpu_mandelbrot`, and we're ready to go. Let's launch this from IPython:

```
In [1]: run gpu_mandelbrot0.py
It took 0.894000053406 seconds to calculate the Mandelbrot graph.
It took 0.102999925613 seconds to dump the image.
```

Let's check the dumped image to make sure this is correct:

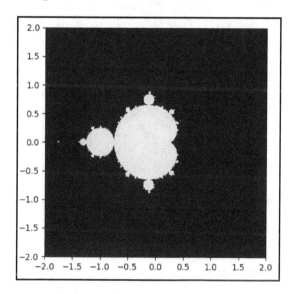

This is certainly the same Mandelbrot image that is produced in the first chapter, so we have successfully implemented this onto a GPU! Let's now look at the speed increase we're getting: in the first chapter, it took us 14.61 seconds to produce this graph; here, it only took 0.894 seconds. Keep in mind that PyCUDA also has to compile and link our CUDA C code at runtime, and the time it takes to make the memory transfers to and from the GPU. Still, even with all of that extra overhead, it is a very worthwhile speed increase! (You can view the code for our GPU Mandelbrot with the file named `gpu_mandelbrot0.py` in the Git repository.)

A brief foray into functional programming

Before we continue, let's briefly do a review of two functions available in Python for **functional programming**—map and reduce. These are both considered to be *functional* because they both act on *functions* for their operation. We find these interesting because these both correspond to common design patterns in programming, so we can swap out different functions in the input to get a multitude of different (and useful) operations.

Let's first recall the lambda keyword in Python. This allows us to define an **anonymous function**—in most cases, these can be thought of as a throwaway function that we may only wish to use once, or functions that are able to be defined on a single line. Let's open up IPython right now and define a little function that squares a number as such—pow2 = lambda x : x**2. Let's test it out on a few numbers:

```
In [2]: pow2 = lambda x : x**2

In [3]: pow2(2)
Out[3]: 4

In [4]: pow2(3)
Out[4]: 9

In [5]: pow2(4)
Out[5]: 16
```

Let's recall that map acts on two input values: a function and a list of objects that the given function can act on. map outputs a list of the function's output for each element in the original list. Let's now define our squaring operation as an anonymous function which we input into map, and a list of the last few numbers we checked with the following—map(lambda x : x**2, [2,3,4]):

```
In [6]: map(lambda x : x**2, [2,3,4])
Out[6]: [4, 9, 16]
```

We see that `map` acts as `ElementwiseKernel`! This is actually a standard design pattern in functional programming. Now, let's look at `reduce`; rather than taking in a list and outputting a directly corresponding list, reduce takes in a list, performs a recursive binary operation on it, and outputs a singleton. Let's get a notion of this design pattern by typing `reduce(lambda x, y : x + y, [1,2,3,4])`. When we type this in IPython, we will see that this will output a single number, 10, which is indeed the sum of *1+2+3+4*. You can try replacing the summation above with multiplication, and seeing that this indeed works for recursively multiplying a long list of numbers together. Generally speaking, we use reduce operations with *associative binary operations*; this means that, no matter the order we perform our operation between sequential elements of the list, will always invariably give the same result, provided that the list is kept in order. (This is not to be confused with the *commutative property*.)

We will now see how PyCUDA handles programming patterns akin to `reduce`—with **parallel scan** and **reduction kernels**.

Parallel scan and reduction kernel basics

Let's look at a basic function in PyCUDA that reproduces the functionality of reduce—`InclusiveScanKernel`. (You can find the code under the `simple_scankernel0.py` filename.) Let's execute a basic example that sums a small list of numbers on the GPU:

```
import numpy as np
import pycuda.autoinit
from pycuda import gpuarray
from pycuda.scan import InclusiveScanKernel
seq = np.array([1,2,3,4],dtype=np.int32)
seq_gpu = gpuarray.to_gpu(seq)
sum_gpu = InclusiveScanKernel(np.int32, "a+b")
print sum_gpu(seq_gpu).get()
print np.cumsum(seq)
```

We construct our kernel by first specifying the input/output type (here, NumPy `int32`) and in the string, `"a+b"`. Here, `InclusiveScanKernel` sets up elements named a and b in the GPU space automatically, so you can think of this string input as being analogous to `lambda a,b: a + b` in Python. We can really put any (associative) binary operation here, provided we remember to write it in C.

When we run `sum_gpu`, we see that we will get an array of the same size as the input array. Each element in the array represents the value for each step in the calculation (the NumPy `cumsum` function gives the same output, as we can see). The last element will be the final output that we are seeking, which corresponds to the output of reduce:

```
In [1]: run simple_scankernel0.py
[ 1   3   6 10]
[ 1   3   6 10]
```

Let's try something a little more challenging; let's find the maximum value in a `float32` array:

```python
import numpy as np
import pycuda.autoinit
from pycuda import gpuarray
from pycuda.scan import InclusiveScanKernel
seq = np.array([1,100,-3,-10000, 4, 10000, 66, 14, 21],dtype=np.int32)
seq_gpu = gpuarray.to_gpu(seq)
max_gpu = InclusiveScanKernel(np.int32, "a > b ? a : b")
print max_gpu(seq_gpu).get()[-1]
print np.max(seq)
```

(You can find the complete code in the file named `simple_scankernal1.py`.)

Here, the main change we made is to replace the `a + b` string with `a > b ? a : b`. (In Python, this would be rendered within a `reduce` statement as `lambda a, b: max(a,b)`). Here, we are using a trick to give the max among a and b with the C language's `?` operator. We finally display the last value of the resulting element in the output array, which will be exactly the last element (which we can always retrieve with the `[-1]` index in Python).

Now, let's finally look one more PyCUDA function for generating GPU kernels—`ReductionKernel`. Effectively, `ReductionKernel` acts like a `ElementwiseKernel` function followed by a parallel scan kernel. What algorithm is a good candidate for implementing with a `ReductionKernel`? The first that tends to come to mind is the dot product from linear algebra. Let's remember computing the dot product of two vectors has two steps:

1. Multiply the vectors pointwise
2. Sum the resulting pointwise multiples

These two steps are also called *multiply and accumulate*. Let's set up a kernel to do this computation now:

```
dot_prod = ReductionKernel(np.float32, neutral="0", reduce_expr="a+b",
map_expr="vec1[i]*vec2[i]", arguments="float *vec1, float *vec2")
```

First, note the datatype we use for our kernel (a `float32`). We then set up the input arguments to our CUDA C kernel with `arguments`, (here two float arrays representing each vector designated with `float *`) and set the pointwise calculation with `map_expr`, here it is pointwise multiplication. As with `ElementwiseKernel`, this is indexed over `i`. We set up `reduce_expr` the same as with `InclusiveScanKernel`. This will take the resulting output from the element-wise operation and perform a reduce-type operation on the array. Finally, we set the *neutral element* with neutral. This is an element that will act as an identity for `reduce_expr`; here, we set `neutral=0`, because 0 is always the identity under addition (under multiplication, one is the identity). We'll see why exactly we have to set this up when we cover parallel prefix in greater depth later in this book.

Summary

We first saw how to query our GPU from PyCUDA, and with this re-create the CUDA `deviceQuery` program in Python. We then learned how to transfer NumPy arrays to and from the GPU's memory with the PyCUDA `gpuarray` class and its `to_gpu` and `get` functions. We got a feel for using `gpuarray` objects by observing how to use them to do basic calculations on the GPU, and we learned to do a little investigative work using IPython's `prun` profiler. We saw there is sometimes some arbitrary slowdown when running GPU functions from PyCUDA for the first time in a session, due to PyCUDA launching NVIDIA's `nvcc` compiler to compile inline CUDA C code. We then saw how to use the `ElementwiseKernel` function to compile and launch element-wise operations, which are automatically parallelized onto the GPU from Python. We did a brief review of functional programming in Python (in particular the `map` and `reduce` functions), and finally, we covered how to do some basic reduce/scan-type computations on the GPU using the `InclusiveScanKernel` and `ReductionKernel` functions.

Now that we have the absolute basics down about writing and launching kernel functions, we should realize that PyCUDA has covered the vast amount of the overhead in writing a kernel for us with its templates. We will spend the next chapter learning about the principles of CUDA kernel execution, and how CUDA arranges concurrent threads in a kernel into abstract **grids** and **blocks**.

Questions

1. In `simple_element_kernel_example0.py`, we don't consider the memory transfers to and from the GPU in measuring the time for the GPU computation. Try measuring the time that the `gpuarray` functions, `to_gpu` and `get`, take with the Python time command. Would you say it's worth offloading this particular function onto the GPU, with the memory transfer times in consideration?

2. In `Chapter 1`, *Why GPU Programming?*, we had a discussion of Amdahl's Law, which gives us some idea of the gains we can potentially get by offloading portions of a program onto a GPU. Name two issues that we have seen in this chapter that Amdahl's law does not take into consideration.

3. Modify `gpu_mandel0.py` to use smaller and smaller lattices of complex numbers, and compare this to the same lattices CPU version of the program. Can we choose a small enough lattice such that the CPU version is actually faster than the GPU version?

4. Create a kernel with `ReductionKernel` that takes two `complex64` arrays on the GPU of the same length and returns the absolute largest element among both arrays.

5. What happens if a `gpuarray` object reaches end-of-scope in Python?

6. Why do you think we need to define `neutral` when we use `ReductionKernel`?

7. If in `ReductionKernel` we set `reduce_expr ="a > b ? a : b"`, and we are operating on int32 types, then what should we set "`neutral`" to?

Kernels, Threads, Blocks, and Grids

4

In this chapter, we'll see how to write effective **CUDA kernels**. In GPU programming, a **kernel** (which we interchangeably use with terms such as *CUDA kernel* or *kernel function*) is a parallel function that can be launched directly from the **host** (the CPU) onto the **device** (the GPU), while a **device function** is a function that can only be called from a kernel function or another device function. (Generally speaking, device functions look and act like normal serial C/C++ functions, only they are running on the GPU and are called in parallel from kernels.)

We'll then get an understanding of how CUDA uses the notion of **threads**, **blocks**, and **grids** to abstract away some of the underlying technical details of the GPU (such as cores, warps, and streaming multiprocessors, which we'll cover later in this book), and how we can use these notions to ease the cognitive overhead in parallel programming. We'll learn about thread synchronization (both block-level and grid-level), and intra-thread communication in CUDA using both **global** and **shared memory**. Finally, we'll delve into the technical details of how to implement our own parallel prefix type algorithms on the GPU (that is, the scan/reduce type functions we covered in the last chapter), which allow us to put all of the principles we'll learn in this chapter into practice.

The learning outcomes for this chapter are as follows:

- Understanding the difference between a kernel and a device function
- How to compile and launch a kernel in PyCUDA and use a device function within a kernel
- Effectively using threads, blocks, and grids in the context of launching a kernel and how to use `threadIdx` and `blockIdx` within a kernel
- How and why to synchronize threads within a kernel, using both `__syncthreads()` for synchronizing all threads among a single block and the host to synchronize all threads among an entire grid of blocks

- How to use device global and shared memory for intra-thread communication
- How to use all of our newly acquired knowledge about kernels to properly implement a GPU version of the parallel prefix sum

Technical requirements

A Linux or Windows 10 PC with a modern NVIDIA GPU (2016 onward) is required for this chapter, with all necessary GPU drivers and the CUDA Toolkit (9.0 onward) installed. A suitable Python 2.7 installation (such as Anaconda Python 2.7) with the PyCUDA module is also required.

This chapter's code is also available on GitHub at:

`https://github.com/PacktPublishing/Hands-On-GPU-Programming-with-Python-and-CUDA`

 For more information about the prerequisites, check the *Preface* of this book; for the software and hardware requirements, check the `README` section in `https://github.com/PacktPublishing/Hands-On-GPU-Programming-with-Python-and-CUDA`.

Kernels

As in the last chapter, we'll be learning how to write CUDA kernel functions as inline CUDA C in our Python code and launch them onto our GPU using PyCUDA. In the last chapter, we used templates provided by PyCUDA to write kernels that fall into particular design patterns; in contrast, we'll now see how to write our own kernels from the ground up, so that we can write a versatile variety of kernels that may not fall into any particular design pattern covered by PyCUDA, and so that we may get a more fine-tuned control over our kernels. Of course, these gains will come at the expense of greater complexity in programming; we'll especially have to get an understanding of **threads**, **blocks**, and **grids** and their role in kernels, as well as how to **synchronize** the threads in which our kernel is executing, as well as understand how to exchange data among threads.

Let's start simple and try to re-create some of the element-wise operations we saw in the last chapter, but this time without using the `ElementwiseKernel` function; we'll now be using the `SourceModule` function. This is a very powerful function in PyCUDA that allows us to build a kernel from scratch, so as usual it's best to start simple.

The PyCUDA SourceModule function

We'll use the `SourceModule` function from PyCUDA to compile raw inline CUDA C code into usable kernels that we can launch from Python. We should note that `SourceModule` actually compiles code into a **CUDA module**, this is like a Python module or Windows DLL, only it contains a collection of compiled CUDA code. This means we'll have to "pull out" a reference to the kernel we want to use with PyCUDA's `get_function`, before we can actually launch it. Let's start with a basic example of how to use a CUDA kernel with `SourceModule`.

As before, we'll start with making one of the most simple kernel functions possible—one that multiplies a vector by a scalar. We'll start with the imports:

```
import pycuda.autoinit
import pycuda.driver as drv
import numpy as np
from pycuda import gpuarray
from pycuda.compiler import SourceModule
```

Now we can immediately dive into writing our kernel:

```
ker = SourceModule("""
__global__ void scalar_multiply_kernel(float *outvec, float scalar, float
*vec)
{
 int i = threadIdx.x;
 outvec[i] = scalar*vec[i];
}
""")
```

So, let's stop and contrast this with how it was done in `ElementwiseKernel`. First, when we declare a kernel function in CUDA C proper, we precede it with the `__global__` keyword. This will distinguish the function as a kernel to the compiler. We'll always just declare this as a `void` function, because we'll always get our output values by passing a pointer to some empty chunk of memory that we pass in as a parameter. We can declare the parameters as we would with any standard C function: first we have `outvec`, which will be our output scaled vector, which is of course a floating-point array pointer. Next, we have `scalar`, which is represented with a mere `float`; notice that this is not a pointer! If we wish to pass simple singleton input values to our kernel, we can always do so without using pointers. Finally, we have our input vector, `vec`, which is of course another floating-point array pointer.

Singleton input parameters to a kernel function can be passed in directly from the host without using pointers or allocated device memory.

Let's peer into the kernel before we continue with testing it. We recall that `ElementwiseKernel` automatically parallelized over multiple GPU threads by a value, `i`, which was set for us by PyCUDA; the identification of each individual thread is given by the `threadIdx` value, which we retrieve as follows: `int i = threadIdx.x;`.

 `threadIdx` is used to tell each individual thread its identity. This is usually used to determine an index for what values should be processed on the input and output data arrays. (This can also be used for assigning particular threads different tasks than others with standard C control flow statements such as `if` or `switch`.)

Now, we are ready to perform our scalar multiplication in parallel as before: `outvec[i] = scalar*vec[i];`.

Now, let's test this code: we first must *pull out* a reference to our compiled kernel function from the CUDA module we just compiled with `SourceModule`. We can get this kernel reference with Python's `get_function` as follows:

```
scalar_multiply_gpu = ker.get_function("scalar_multiply_kernel")
```

Now, we have to put some data on the GPU to actually test our kernel. Let's set up a floating-point array of 512 random values, and then copy these into an array in the GPU's global memory using the `gpuarray.to_gpu` function. (We're going to multiply this random vector by a scalar both on the GPU and CPU, and see if the output matches.) We'll also allocate a chunk of empty memory to the GPU's global memory using the `gpuarray.empty_like` function:

```
testvec = np.random.randn(512).astype(np.float32)
testvec_gpu = gpuarray.to_gpu(testvec)
outvec_gpu = gpuarray.empty_like(testvec_gpu)
```

We are now prepared to launch our kernel. We'll set the scalar value as 2. (Again, since the scalar is a singleton, we don't have to copy this value to the GPU—we should be careful that we typecast it properly, however.) Here we'll have to specifically set the number of threads to 512 with the `block` and `grid` parameters. We are now ready to launch:

```
scalar_multiply_gpu( outvec_gpu, np.float32(2), testvec_gpu,
block=(512,1,1), grid=(1,1,1))
```

We can now check whether the output matches with the expected output by using the `get` function in our `gpuarray` output object and comparing this to the correct output with NumPy's `allclose` function:

```
print "Does our kernel work correctly? :
{}".format(np.allclose(outvec_gpu.get() , 2*testvec) )
```

(The code to this example is available as the `simple_scalar_multiply_kernel.py` file, under 4 in the repository.)

Now we are starting to remove the training wheels of the PyCUDA kernel templates we learned in the previous chapter—we can now directly write a kernel in pure CUDA C and launch it to use a specific number of threads on our GPU. However, we'll have to learn a bit more about how CUDA structures threads into collections of abstract units known as **blocks** and **grids** before we can continue with kernels.

Threads, blocks, and grids

So far in this book, we have been taking the term **thread** for granted. Let's step back for a moment and see exactly what this means—a thread is a sequence of instructions that is executed on a single core of the GPU—*cores* and *threads* should not be thought of as synonymous! In fact, it is possible to launch kernels that use many more threads than there are cores on the GPU. This is because, similar to how an Intel chip may only have four cores and yet be running hundreds of processes and thousands of threads within Linux or Windows, the operating system's scheduler can switch between these tasks rapidly, giving the appearance that they are running simultaneously. The GPU handles threads in a similar way, allowing for seamless computation over tens of thousands of threads.

Multiple threads are executed on the GPU in abstract units known as **blocks**. You should recall how we got the thread ID from `threadIdx.x` in our scalar multiplication kernel; there is an x at the end because there is also `threadIdx.y` and `threadIdx.z`. This is because you can index blocks over three dimensions, rather than just one dimension. Why do we do this? Let's recall the example regarding the computation of the Mandelbrot set from Chapter 1, *Why GPU Programming?* and Chapter 3, *Getting Started with PyCUDA*. This is calculated point-by-point over a two-dimensional plane. It may therefore make more sense for us to index the threads over two dimensions for algorithms like this. Similarly, it may make sense to use three dimensions in some cases—in a physics simulation, we may have to calculate the positions of moving particles within a 3D grid.

Blocks are further executed in abstract batches known as **grids**, which are best thought of as *blocks of blocks*. As with threads in a block, we can index each block in the grid in up to three dimensions with the constant values that are given by blockIdx.x, blockIdx.y, and blockIdx.z. Let's look at an example to help us make sense of these concepts; we'll only use two dimensions here for simplicity.

Conway's game of life

The Game of Life (often called *LIFE* for short) is a cellular automata simulation that was invented by the British mathematician John Conway back in 1970. This sounds complex, but it's really quite simple—LIFE is a zero-player *game* that consists of a two-dimensional binary lattice of *cells* that are either considered *live* or *dead*. The lattice is iteratively updated by the following set of rules:

- Any live cell with fewer than two live neighbors dies
- Any live cell with two or three neighbors lives
- Any live cell with more than three neighbors dies
- Any dead cell with exactly three neighbors comes to life

These four simple rules give rise to a complex simulation with interesting mathematical properties that is also aesthetically quite pleasing to watch when animated. However, with a large number of cells in the lattice, it can run quite slowly, and usually results in *choppy* animation when programmed in pure serial Python. However, this is parallelizable, as it is clear that each cell in the lattice can be managed by a single CUDA thread.

We'll now implement LIFE as a CUDA kernel and animate it as using the matplotlib.animation module. This will be interesting to us right now because namely we'll be able to apply our new knowledge of blocks and grids here.

We'll start by including the appropriate modules as follows:

```
import pycuda.autoinit
import pycuda.driver as drv
from pycuda import gpuarray
from pycuda.compiler import SourceModule
import numpy as np
import matplotlib.pyplot as plt
import matplotlib.animation as animation
```

Now, let's dive into writing our kernel via `SourceModule` . We're going to start by using the C language's `#define` directive to set up some constants and macros that we'll use throughout our kernel. Let's look at the first two we'll set up, _X and _Y:

```
ker = SourceModule("""
#define _X  ( threadIdx.x + blockIdx.x * blockDim.x )
#define _Y  ( threadIdx.y + blockIdx.y * blockDim.y )
```

Let's first remember how `#define` works here—it will literally replace any text of _X or _Y with the defined values (in the parentheses here) at compilation time—that is, it creates macros for us. (As a matter of personal style, I usually precede all of my C macros with an underscore.)

 In C and C++, `#define` is used for creating **macros**. This means that `#define` doesn't create any function or set up a proper constant variables—it just allows us to write things shorthand in our code by swapping text out right before compilation time.

Now, let's talk about what _X and _Y mean specifically—these will be the Cartesian *x* and *y* values of a single CUDA thread's cell on the two-dimensional lattice we are using for LIFE. We'll launch the kernel over a two-dimensional grid consisting of two-dimensional blocks that will correspond to the entire cell lattice. We'll have to use both thread and block constants to find the Cartesian point on the lattice. Let's look at some diagrams to make the point. A thread residing in a two-dimensional CUDA block can be visualized as follows:

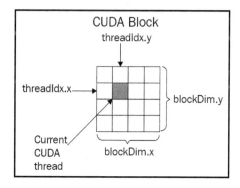

At this point, you may be wondering why we don't launch our kernel over a single block, so we can just set _X as `threadIdx.x` and _Y as `threadIdx.y` and be done with it. This is due to a limitation on block size imposed on us by CUDA—currently, only blocks consisting of at most 1,024 threads are supported. This means that we can only make our cell lattice of dimensions 32 x 32 at most, which would make for a rather boring simulation that might be better done on a CPU, so we'll have to launch multiple blocks over a grid. (The dimensions of our current block will be given by `blockDim.x` and `blockDim.y`, which will help us determine the objective *x* and *y* coordinates, as we'll see.)

Similarly, as before, we can determine which block we are in within a two-dimensional grid with `blockIdx.x` and `blockIdx.y`:

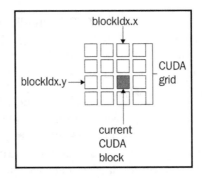

After we think of the math a little bit, it should be clear that _X should be defined as (`threadIdx.x` + `blockIdx.x` * `blockDim.x`) and _Y should be defined as (`threadIdx.y` + `blockIdx.y` * `blockDim.y`). (The parentheses are added so as not to interfere with the order of operations when the macros are inserted in the code.) Now, let's continue defining the remaining macros:

```
#define _WIDTH  ( blockDim.x * gridDim.x )
#define _HEIGHT ( blockDim.y * gridDim.y )

#define _XM(x)  ( (x + _WIDTH) % _WIDTH )
#define _YM(y)  ( (y + _HEIGHT) % _HEIGHT )
```

The _WIDTH and _HEIGHT macros will give us the width and height of our cell lattice, respectively, which should be clear from the diagrams. Let's discuss the _XM and _YM macros. In our implementation of LIFE, we'll have the endpoints "wrap around" to the other side of the lattice—for example, we'll consider the *x*-value of –1 to be _WIDTH - 1, and a *y*-value of –1 to be _HEIGHT - 1, and we'll likewise consider an *x*-value of _WIDTH to be 0 and a *y*-value of _HEIGHT to be 0. Why do we need this? When we calculate the number of living neighbors of a given cell, we might be at some edge and the neighbors might be external points—defining these macros to modulate our points will cover this for us automatically. Notice that we have to add the width or height before we use C's modulus operator—this is because, unlike Python, the modulus operator in C can return negative values for integers.

We now have one final macro to define. We recall that PyCUDA passes two-dimensional arrays into CUDA C as one-dimensional pointers; two-dimensional arrays are passed in **row-wise** from Python into one dimensional C pointers. This means that we'll have to translate a given Cartesian (*x*,*y*) point for a given cell on the lattice into a one dimensional point within the pointer corresponding to the lattice. Here, we can do so as follows:

```
#define _INDEX(x,y)  ( _XM(x)  + _YM(y) * _WIDTH )
```

Since our cell lattice is stored row-wise, we have to multiply the *y*-value by the width to offset to the point corresponding to the appropriate row. We can now finally begin with our implementation of LIFE. Let's start with the most important part of LIFE—counting the number of living neighbors a given cell has. We'll implement this using a CUDA **device function**, as follows:

```
__device__ int nbrs(int x, int y, int * in)
{
     return ( in[ _INDEX(x -1, y+1) ] + in[ _INDEX(x-1, y) ] + in[
_INDEX(x-1, y-1) ] \
                   + in[ _INDEX(x, y+1)] + in[_INDEX(x, y - 1)] \
                   + in[ _INDEX(x+1, y+1) ] + in[ _INDEX(x+1, y) ] + in[
_INDEX(x+1, y-1) ] );
}
```

A device function is a C function written in serial, which is called by an individual CUDA thread in kernel. That is to say, this little function will be called in parallel by multiple threads from our kernel. We'll represent our cell lattice as a collection of 32-bit integers (1 will represent a living cell and 0 will represent a dead one), so this will work for our purposes; we just have to add the values of the neighbors around our current cell.

A CUDA **device function** is a serial C function that is called by an individual CUDA thread from within a kernel. While these functions are serial in themselves, they can be run in parallel by multiple GPU threads. Device functions cannot by themselves by launched by a host computer onto a GPU, only kernels.

We are now prepared to write our kernel implementation of LIFE. Actually, we've done most of the hard work already—we check the number of neighbors of the current thread's cell, check whether the current cell is living or dead, and then use the appropriate switch-case statements to determine its status for the next iteration according to the rules of LIFE. We'll use two integer pointer arrays for this kernel—one will be in reference to the last iteration as input (`lattice`) and the other in reference to the iteration that we'll calculate as output (`lattice_out`):

```
__global__ void conway_ker(int * lattice_out, int * lattice  )
{
    // x, y are the appropriate values for the cell covered by this thread
    int x = _X, y = _Y;
    // count the number of neighbors around the current cell
    int n = nbrs(x, y, lattice);
     // if the current cell is alive, then determine if it lives or dies for
the next generation.
    if ( lattice[_INDEX(x,y)] == 1)
       switch(n)
       {
          // if the cell is alive: it remains alive only if it has 2 or 3
neighbors.
          case 2:
          case 3: lattice_out[_INDEX(x,y)] = 1;
                  break;
          default: lattice_out[_INDEX(x,y)] = 0;
       }
    else if( lattice[_INDEX(x,y)] == 0 )
         switch(n)
         {
            // a dead cell comes to life only if it has 3 neighbors that
are alive.
            case 3: lattice_out[_INDEX(x,y)] = 1;
                    break;
            default: lattice_out[_INDEX(x,y)] = 0;
         }
}
""")


conway_ker = ker.get_function("conway_ker")
```

We remember to close off the inline CUDA C segment with the triple-parentheses, and then get a reference to our CUDA C kernel with `get_function`. Since the kernel will only update the lattice once, we'll set up a short function in Python that will cover for all of the overhead of updating the lattice for the animation:

```
def update_gpu(frameNum, img, newLattice_gpu, lattice_gpu, N):
```

The `frameNum` parameter is just a value that is required by Matplotlib's animation module for update functions that we can ignore, while `img` will be the representative image of our cell lattice that is required by the module that will be iteratively displayed.

Let's focus on the other three remaining parameters—`newLattice_gpu` and `lattice_gpu` will be PyCUDA arrays that we'll keep persistent, as we want to avoid re-allocating chunks of memory on the GPU when we can. `lattice_gpu` will be the current generation of the cell array that will correspond to the `lattice` parameter in the kernel, while `newLattice_gpu` will be the next generation of the lattice. `N` will indicate the the height and width of the lattice (in other words, we'll be working with an *N x N* lattice).

We launch the kernel with the appropriate parameters and set the block and grid sizes as follows:

```
    conway_ker(newLattice_gpu, lattice_gpu, grid=(N/32,N/32,1),
  block=(32,32,1)  )
```

We'll set the block sizes as 32 x 32 with `(32, 32, 1)`; since we are only using two dimensions for our cell lattice, we can just set the *z*-dimension as one. Remember that blocks are limited to 1,024 threads—*32 x 32 = 1024*, so this will work. (Keep in mind that there is nothing special here about 32 x 32; we could use values such as 16 x 64 or 10 x 10 if we wanted to, as long as the total number of threads does not exceed 1,024.)

 The number of threads in a CUDA block is limited to a maximum of 1,024.

We now look at grid value—here, since we are working with dimensions of 32, it should be clear that *N* (in this case) should be divisible by 32. That means that in this case, we are limited to lattices such as 64 x 64, 96 x 96, 128 x 128, and 1024 x 1024. Again, if we want to use lattices of a different size, then we'll have to alter the dimensions of the blocks. (If this doesn't make sense, then please look at the previous diagrams and review how we defined the width and height macros in our kernel.)

We can now set up the image data for our animation after grabbing the latest generated lattice from the GPU's memory with the `get()` function. We finally copy the new lattice data into the current data using the PyCUDA slice operator, `[:]`, which will copy over the previously allocated memory on the GPU so that we don't have to re-allocate:

```
img.set_data(newLattice_gpu.get() )
lattice_gpu[:] = newLattice_gpu[:]
return img
```

Let's set up a lattice of size 256 x 256. We now will set up an initial state for our lattice using the choice function from the `numpy.random` module. We'll populate a *N* x *N* graph of integers randomly with ones and zeros; generally, if around 25% of the points are ones and the rest zeros, we can generate some interesting lattice animations, so we'll go with that:

```
if __name__ == '__main__':
    # set lattice size
    N = 256
    lattice = np.int32( np.random.choice([1,0], N*N, p=[0.25,
0.75]).reshape(N, N) )
    lattice_gpu = gpuarray.to_gpu(lattice)
```

Finally, we can set up the lattices on the GPU with the appropriate `gpuarray` functions and set up the Matplotlib animation accordingly, as follows:

```
lattice_gpu = gpuarray.to_gpu(lattice)
    lattice_gpu = gpuarray.to_gpu(lattice)
    newLattice_gpu = gpuarray.empty_like(lattice_gpu)

    fig, ax = plt.subplots()
    img = ax.imshow(lattice_gpu.get(), interpolation='nearest')
    ani = animation.FuncAnimation(fig, update_gpu, fargs=(img,
newLattice_gpu, lattice_gpu, N, ) , interval=0, frames=1000,
save_count=1000)
    plt.show()
```

We can now run our program and enjoy the show (the code is also available as the `conway_gpu.py` file under the 4 directory in the GitHub repository):

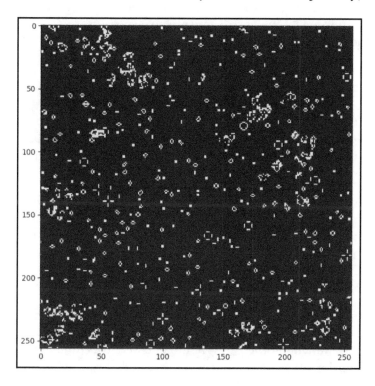

Thread synchronization and intercommunication

We'll now discuss two important concepts in GPU programming—**thread synchronization** and **thread intercommunication**. Sometimes, we need to ensure that every single thread has reached the same exact line in the code before we continue with any further computation; we call this thread synchronization. Synchronization works hand-in-hand with thread intercommunication, that is, different threads passing and reading input from each other; in this case, we'll usually want to make sure that all of the threads are aligned at the same step in computation before any data is passed around. We'll start here by learning about the CUDA __syncthreads device function, which is used for synchronizing a single block in a kernel.

Using the __syncthreads() device function

In our prior example of Conway's *Game of Life*, our kernel only updated the lattice once for every time it was launched by the host. There are no issues with synchronizing all of the threads among the launched kernel in this case, since we only had to work with the lattice's previous iteration that was readily available.

Now let's suppose that we want to do something slightly different—we want to re-write our kernel so that it performs a certain number of iterations on a given cell lattice without being re-launched over and over by the host. This may initially seem trivial—a naive solution would be to just put an integer parameter to indicate the number of iterations and a `for` loop in the inline `conway_ker` kernel, make some additional trivial changes, and be done with it.

However, this raises the issue of **race conditions**; this is the issue of multiple threads reading and writing to the same memory address and the problems that may arise from that. Our old `conway_ker` kernel avoids this issue by using two arrays of memory, one that is strictly read from, and one that is strictly written to for each iteration. Furthermore, since the kernel only performs a single iteration, we are effectively using the host for the synchronization of the threads.

We want to do multiple iterations of LIFE on the GPU that are fully synchronized; we also will want to use a single array of memory for the lattice. We can avoid race conditions by using a CUDA device function called `__syncthreads()`. This function is a **block level synchronization barrier**—this means that every thread that is executing within a block will stop when it reaches a `__syncthreads()` instance and wait until each and every other thread within the same block reaches that same invocation of `__syncthreads()` before the the threads continue to execute the subsequent lines of code.

`__syncthreads()` can only synchronize threads within a single CUDA block, not all threads within a CUDA grid!

Let's now create our new kernel; this will be a modification of the prior LIFE kernel that will perform a certain number of iterations and then stop. This means we'll not represent this as an animation, just as a static image, so we'll load the appropriate Python modules in the beginning. (This code is also available in the `conway_gpu_syncthreads.py` file, in the GitHub repository):

```
import pycuda.autoinit
import pycuda.driver as drv
from pycuda import gpuarray
from pycuda.compiler import SourceModule
import numpy as np
import matplotlib.pyplot as plt
```

Now, let's again set up our kernel that will compute LIFE:

```
ker = SourceModule("""
```

Of course, our CUDA C code will go here, which will be largely the same as before. We'll have to only make some changes to our kernel. Of course, we can preserve the device function, `nbrs`. In our declaration, we'll use only one array to represent the cell lattice. We can do this since we'll be using proper thread synchronization. We'll also have to indicate the number of iterations with an integer. We set the parameters as follows:

```
__global__ void conway_ker(int * lattice, int iters)
{
```

We'll continue similarly as before, only iterating with a `for` loop:

```
int x = _X, y = _Y;
for (int i = 0; i < iters; i++)
{
    int n = nbrs(x, y, lattice);
    int cell_value;
```

Let's recall that previously, we directly set the new cell lattice value directly within the array. Here, we'll hold the value in the `cell_value` variable until all of the threads in the block are synchronized. We proceed similarly as before, blocking execution with `__syncthreads` until all of the new cell values are determined for the current iteration, and only then setting the values within the lattice array:

```
if ( lattice[_INDEX(x,y)] == 1)
switch(n)
{
// if the cell is alive: it remains alive only if it has 2 or 3 neighbors.
case 2:
case 3: cell_value = 1;
break;
default: cell_value = 0;
}
else if( lattice[_INDEX(x,y)] == 0 )
switch(n)
{
// a dead cell comes to life only if it has 3 neighbors that are alive.
case 3: cell_value = 1;
break;
default: cell_value = 0;
}
__syncthreads();
lattice[_INDEX(x,y)] = cell_value;
__syncthreads();
}
}
""")
```

We'll now launch the kernel as before and display the output, iterating over the lattice 1,000,000 times. Note that we are using only a single block in our grid, which is of a size of 32 x 32, due to the limit of 1,024 threads per block. (Again, it should be emphasized that `__syncthreads` only works over all threads in a block, rather than over all threads in a grid, which is why we are limiting ourselves to a single block here):

```
conway_ker = ker.get_function("conway_ker")
if __name__ == '__main__':
 # set lattice size
 N = 32
 lattice = np.int32( np.random.choice([1,0], N*N, p=[0.25,
0.75]).reshape(N, N) )
 lattice_gpu = gpuarray.to_gpu(lattice)
 conway_ker(lattice_gpu, np.int32(1000000), grid=(1,1,1), block=(32,32,1))
 fig = plt.figure(1)
 plt.imshow(lattice_gpu.get())
```

When we run the program, we'll get the desired output as follows (this is what a random LIFE lattice will converge to after one million iterations!):

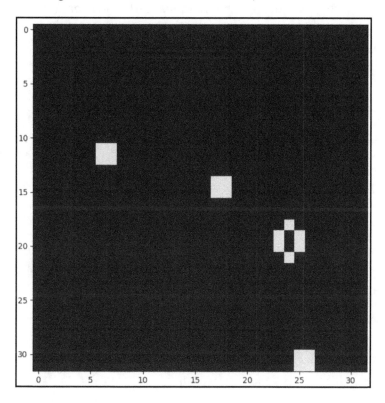

Using shared memory

We can see from the prior example that the threads in the kernel can intercommunicate using arrays within the GPU's global memory; while it is possible to use global memory for most operations, we can speed things up by using **shared memory**. This is a type of memory meant specifically for intercommunication of threads within a single CUDA block; the advantage of using this over global memory is that it is much faster for pure inter-thread communication. In contrast to global memory, though, memory stored in shared memory cannot directly be accessed by the host—shared memory must be copied back into global memory by the kernel itself first.

Let's first step back for a moment before we continue and think about what we mean. Let's look at some of the variables that are declared in our iterative LIFE kernel that we just saw. Let's first look at x and y, two integers that hold the Cartesian coordinates of a particular thread's cell. Remember that we are setting their values with the _X and _Y macros. (Compiler optimizations notwithstanding, we want to store these values in variables to reduce computation because directly using _X and _Y will recompute the x and y values every time these macros are referenced in our code):

```
int x = _X, y = _Y;
```

We note that, for every single thread, there will be a unique Cartesian point in the lattice that will correspond to x and y. Similarly, we use a variable, n, which is declared with `int n = nbrs(x, y, lattice);`, to indicate the number of living neighbors around a particular cell. This is because, when we normally declare variables in CUDA, they are by default local to each individual thread. Note that, even if we declare an array within a thread such as `int a[10];`, there will be an array of size 10 that is local to each thread.

 Local thread arrays (for example, a declaration of `int a[10];` within the kernel) and pointers to global GPU memory (for example, a value passed as a kernel parameter of the form `int * b`) may look and act similarly, but are very different. For every thread in the kernel, there will be a separate a array that the other threads cannot read, yet there is a single b that will hold the same values and be equally accessible for all of the threads.

We are prepared to use shared memory. This allows us to declare variables and arrays that are shared among the threads within a single CUDA block. This memory is much faster than using global memory pointers (as we have been using till now), as well as reduces the overhead of allocating memory in the case of pointers.

Let's say we want a shared integer array of size 10. We declare it as follows—`__shared__ int a[10]`. Note that we don't have to limit ourselves to arrays; we can make shared singleton variables as follows: `__shared__ int x`.

Let's rewrite a few lines of iterative version of LIFE that we saw in the last sub-section to make use of shared memory. First, let's just rename the input pointer to p_lattice, so we can instead use this variable name on our shared array, and lazily preserve all of the references to " lattice" in our code. Since we'll be sticking with a 32 x 32 cell lattice here, we set up the new shared lattice array as follows:

```
__global__ void conway_ker_shared(int * p_lattice, int iters)
{
 int x = _X, y = _Y;
 __shared__ int lattice[32*32];
```

We'll now have to copy all values from the global memory p_lattice array into lattice. We'll index our shared array exactly in the same way, so we can just use our old _INDEX macro here. Note that we make sure to put __syncthreads() after we copy, to ensure that all of the memory accesses to lattice are entirely completed before we proceed with the LIFE algorithm:

```
lattice[_INDEX(x,y)] = p_lattice[_INDEX(x,y)];
__syncthreads();
```

The rest of the kernel is exactly as before, only we have to copy from the shared lattice back into the GPU array. We do so as follows and then close off the inline code:

```
__syncthreads();
p_lattice[_INDEX(x,y)] = lattice[_INDEX(x,y)];
__syncthreads();
} """)
```

We can now run this as before, with the same exact test code. (This example can be seen in conway_gpu_syncthreads_shared.py in the GitHub repository.)

The parallel prefix algorithm

We'll now be using our new knowledge of CUDA kernels to implement the **parallel prefix algorithm**, also known as the **scan design pattern**. We have already seen simple examples of this in the form of PyCUDA's InclusiveScanKernel and ReductionKernel functions in the previous chapter. We'll now look into this idea in a little more detail.

The central motivation of this design pattern is that we have a binary operator $\oplus$, that is to say a function that acts on two input values and gives one output value (such as—+, ×, ∨ (maximum), ∧ (minimum)), and collection of elements, $x_0, x_1, x_2, \ldots, x_{n-1}$, and from these we wish to compute $x_0 \oplus x_1 \oplus x_2 \oplus \cdots \oplus x_{n-1}$ efficiently. Furthermore, we make the assumption that our binary operator $\oplus$ is **associative**—this means that, for any three elements, x, y, and z, we always have: $x \oplus (y \oplus z) = (x \oplus y) \oplus z$.

We wish to retain the partial results, that is the *n - 1* sub-computations— $x_0, x_0 \oplus x_1, x_0 \oplus x_1 \oplus x_2, \ldots, x_0 \oplus \cdots \oplus x_{n-2}$. The aim of the parallel prefix algorithm is to produce this collection of *n* sums efficiently. It normally takes *O(n)* time to produce these *n* sums in a serial operation, and we wish to reduce the time complexity.

 When the terms "parallel prefix" or "scan" are used, it usually means an algorithm that produces all of these *n* results, while "reduce"/"reduction" usually means an algorithm that only yields the single final result, $x_0 \oplus x_1 \oplus \cdots \oplus x_{n-1}$. (This is the case with PyCUDA.)

There are actually several variations of the parallel prefix algorithm, and we'll first start with the simplest (and oldest) version first, which is called the naive parallel prefix algorithm.

The naive parallel prefix algorithm

The **naive parallel prefix algorithm** is the original version of this algorithm; this algorithm is "naive" because it makes an assumption that given *n* input elements, $x_0, \ldots, x_{n-1}$, with the further assumption that *n* is *dyadic* (that is, $n = 2^k$ for some positive integer, *k*), and we can run the algorithm in parallel over *n* processors (or *n* threads). Obviously, this will impose strong limits on the cardinality *n* of sets that we may process. However, given these conditions are satisfied, we have a nice result in that its computational time complexity is only *O(log n)*. We can see this from the pseudocode of the algorithm. Here, we'll indicate the input values with $x_0, \ldots, x_{n-1}$ and the output values as $y_0, \ldots, y_{n-1}$:

```
input: x₀, ..., xₙ₋₁
initialize:
for k=0 to n-1:
    yₖ := xₖ
begin:
parfor i=0 to n-1 :
    for j=0 to log₂(n):
        if i >= 2ʲ :
            yᵢ := yᵢ ⊕ yᵢ ₋ ₂ʲ
    else:
```

```
            continue
        end if
    end for
end parfor
end
output: y₀, ..., yₙ₋₁
```

Now, we can clearly see that this will take *O(log n)* asymptotic time, as the outer loop is parallelized over the `parfor` and the inner loop takes $log_2(n)$. It should be easy to see after a few minutes of thought that the y_i values will yield our desired output.

Now let's begin our implementation; here, our binary operator will simply be addition. Since this example is illustrative, this kernel will be strictly over 1,024 threads.

Let's just set up the header and dive right into writing our kernel:

```python
import pycuda.autoinit
import pycuda.driver as drv
import numpy as np
from pycuda import gpuarray
from pycuda.compiler import SourceModule
from time import time

naive_ker = SourceModule("""
__global__ void naive_prefix(double *vec, double *out)
{
     __shared__ double sum_buf[1024];
     int tid = threadIdx.x;
     sum_buf[tid] = vec[tid];
```

So, let's look at what we have: we represent our input elements as a GPU array of doubles, that is `double *vec`, and represent the output values with `double *out`. We declare a shared memory `sum_buf` array that we'll use for the calculation of our output. Now, let's look at the implementation of the algorithm itself:

```c
int iter = 1;
for (int i=0; i < 10; i++)
{
     __syncthreads();
     if (tid >= iter )
     {
          sum_buf[tid] = sum_buf[tid] + sum_buf[tid - iter];
     }
     iter *= 2;
}
__syncthreads();
```

Of course, there is no `parfor`, which is implicit over the `tid` variable, which indicates the thread number. We are also able to omit the use of log_2 and 2^i by starting with a variable that is initialized to 1, and then iteratively multiplying by 2 every iteration of i. (Note that if we want to be even more technical, we can do this with the bitwise shift operators .) We bound the iterations of i by 10, since $2^{10} = 1024$. Now we'll close off our new kernel as follows:

```
__syncthreads();
out[tid] = sum_buf[tid];
__syncthreads();


}
""")
naive_gpu = naive_ker.get_function("naive_prefix")
```

Let's now look at the test code following the kernel:

```
if __name__ == '__main__':
 testvec = np.random.randn(1024).astype(np.float64)
 testvec_gpu = gpuarray.to_gpu(testvec)

 outvec_gpu = gpuarray.empty_like(testvec_gpu)
 naive_gpu( testvec_gpu , outvec_gpu, block=(1024,1,1), grid=(1,1,1))

 total_sum = sum( testvec)
 total_sum_gpu = outvec_gpu[-1].get()

 print "Does our kernel work correctly? :
 {}".format(np.allclose(total_sum_gpu , total_sum) )
```

We're only going to concern ourselves with the final sum in the output, which we retrieve with `outvec_gpu[-1].get()`, recalling that the "-1" index gives the last member of an array in Python. This will be the sum of every element in `vec`; the partial sums are in the prior values of `outvec_gpu`. (This example can be seen in the `naive_prefix.py` file in the GitHub repository.)

By its nature, the parallel prefix algorithm has to run over n threads, corresponding to a size-n array, where n is dyadic (again, this means that n is some power of 2). However, we can extend this algorithm to an arbitrary non-dyadic size assuming that our operator has a **identity element** (or equivalently, **neutral element**)—that is to say, that there is some value e so that for any x value, we have—$x = e \oplus x = x \oplus e$. In the case that our operator is + , the identity element is 0; in the case that it is ×, it is 1; all we do then is just pad the elements $x_0, \cdots, x_{n-1}$ with a series of e values so that we have the a dyadic cardinality of the new set $x_0 \oplus \cdots \oplus x_{n-1} \oplus e \oplus \cdots \oplus e$.

Inclusive versus exclusive prefix

Let's stop for a moment and make a very subtle, but very important distinction. So far, we have been concerned with taking inputs of the form $x_0, \cdots, x_{n-1}$, and as output producing an array of sums of the form $x_0, x_0 \oplus x_1, \ldots, x_0 \oplus \cdots \oplus x_{n-1}$. Prefix algorithms that produce output as such are called **inclusive**; in the case of an **inclusive prefix algorithm**, the corresponding element at each index is included in the summation in the same index of the output array. This is in contrast to prefix algorithms that are **exclusive**. An **exclusive prefix algorithm** differs in that it similarly takes n input values of the form $x_0, \cdots, x_{n-1}$ and produces the length-n output array $e, x_0, x_0 \oplus x_1, \ldots, x_0 \oplus \cdots \oplus x_{n-2}$.

This is important because some efficient variations of the prefix algorithm are exclusive by their nature. We'll see an example of one in the next sub-section.

 Note that the exclusive algorithm yields nearly the same output as the inclusive algorithm, only it is right-shifted and omits the final value. We can therefore trivially obtain the equivalent output from either algorithm, provided we keep a copy of $x_0, \cdots, x_{n-1}$.

A work-efficient parallel prefix algorithm

Before we continue with our new algorithm, we'll look at the naive algorithm from two perspectives. In an ideal case, the computational time complexity is *O(log n)*, but this is only when we have a sufficient number of processors for our data set; when the cardinality (number of elements) of our dataset, n, is much larger than the number of processors, we have that this becomes an *O(n log n)* time algorithm.

Let's define a new concept with relation to our binary operator ⊕—the **work** performed by a parallel algorithm here is the number of invocations of this operator across all threads for the duration of the execution. Similarly, the **span** is the number of invocations a thread makes in the duration of execution of the kernel; while the **span** of the whole algorithm is the same as the longest span among each individual thread, which will tell us the total execution time.

We seek to specifically reduce the amount of work performed by the algorithm across all threads, rather than focus merely span. In the case of the naive prefix, the additional work that is required costs a more time when the number of available processors falls short; this extra work will just spill over into the limited number of processors available.

We'll present a new algorithm that is **work efficient**, and hence more suitable for a limited number of processors. This consists of two separate two distinct parts—the **up-sweep (or reduce) phase** and the **down-sweep phase**. We should also note the algorithm we'll see is an exclusive prefix algorithm.

The **up-sweep phase** is similar to a single reduce operation to produce the value that is given by the reduce algorithm, that is $x_0 \oplus \cdots \oplus x_{n-1}$; in this case we retain the partial sums ($x_0 \oplus x_1, x_2 \oplus x_3, x_4 \oplus x_5, \ldots$) that are required the achieve the end result. The down-sweep phase will then operate on these partial sums and give us the final result. Let's look at some pseudocode, starting with the up-sweep phase. (The next subsection will then dive into the implementation from the pseudocode immediately.)

Work-efficient parallel prefix (up-sweep phase)

This is the pseudocode for the up-sweep. (Notice the `parfor` over the j variable, which means that this block of code can be parallelized over threads indexed by j):

```
input: x₀, ..., xₙ₋₁
initialize:
    for i = 0 to n - 1:
        yᵢ := xᵢ
begin:
for k=0 to log₂(n) - 1:
    parfor j=0 to n - 1:
        if j is divisible by 2^(k+1):
            y_(j+2^(k+1)-1) = y_(j+2^k-1) ⊕ y_(j+2^(k+1)-1)
    else:
            continue
end
output: y₀, ..., yₙ₋₁
```

Work-efficient parallel prefix (down-sweep phase)

Now let's continue with the down-sweep, which will operate on the output of the up-sweep:

```
input: x₀, ..., xₙ₋₁
initialize:
    for i = 0 to n - 2:
        yᵢ := xᵢ
    yₙ₋₁ := 0
begin:
for k = log₂(n) - 1 to 0:
    parfor j = 0 to n - 1:
        if j is divisible by 2ᵏ⁺¹:
            temp := y_{j+2ᵏ-1}
            y_{j+2ᵏ-1} := y_{j+2ᵏ⁺¹-1}
            y_{j+2ᵏ⁺¹-1} := y_{j+2ᵏ⁺¹-1} ⊕ temp
        else:
            continue
end
output: y₀ , y₁ , ..., yₙ₋₁
```

Work-efficient parallel prefix — implementation

As a capstone for this chapter, we'll write an implementation of this algorithm that can operate on arrays of arbitrarily large size over 1,024. This will mean that this will operate over grids as well as blocks; that being such, we'll have to use the host for synchronization; furthermore, this will require that we implement two separate kernels for up-sweep and down-sweep phases that will act as the parfor loops in both phases, as well as Python functions that will act as the outer for loop for the up- and down-sweeps.

Let's begin with an up-sweep kernel. Since we'll be iteratively re-launching this kernel from the host, we'll also need a parameter that indicates current iteration (k). We'll use two arrays for the computation to avoid race conditions—x (for the current iteration) and x_old (for the prior iteration). We declare the kernel as follows:

```
up_ker = SourceModule("""
__global__ void up_ker(double *x, double *x_old, int k)
{
```

Now let's set the `tid` variable, which will be the current thread's identification among *all* threads in *all blocks* in the grid. We use the same trick as in our original grid-level implementation of Conway's *Game of Life* that we saw earlier:

```
int tid =  blockIdx.x*blockDim.x + threadIdx.x;
```

We'll now use C bit-wise shift operators to generate 2^k and 2^{k+1} directly from k. We now set j to be `tid` times _2k1—this will enable us to remove the "if j is divisible by 2^{k+1}", as in the pseudocode, enabling us to only launch as many threads as we'll need:

```
int _2k = 1 << k;
int _2k1 = 1 << (k+1);

int j = tid* _2k1;
```

 We can easily generate dyadic (power-of-2) integers in CUDA C with the left bit-wise shift operator (<<). Recall that the integer 1 (that is 2^0) is represented as 0001, 2 (2^1) is represented as 0010, 4 (2^2) is represented as 0100, and so on. We can therefore compute 2^k with the 1 << k operation.

We can now run the up-sweep phase with a single line, noting that j is indeed divisible by 2^{k+1} by its construction:

```
 x[j + _2k1 - 1] = x_old[j + _2k -1 ] + x_old[j + _2k1 - 1];
 }
 """)
```

We're done writing our kernel! But this is not a full implementation of the up-sweep, of course. We have to do the rest in Python. Let's get our kernel and begin the implementation. This mostly speaks for itself as it follows the pseudocode exactly; we should recall that we are updating x_old_gpu by copying from x_gpu using [:], which will preserve the memory allocation and merely copy the new data over rather than re-allocate. Also note how we set our block and grid sizes depending on how many threads we have to launch—we try to keep our block sizes as multiples of size 32 (which is our rule-of-thumb in this text, we go into the details why we use 32 specifically in Chapter 11, *Performance Optimization in CUDA*). We should put from __future__ import division at the beginning of our file, since we'll use Python 3-style division in calculating our block and kernel sizes.

One issue to mention is that we are assuming that x is of dyadic length 32 or greater—this can be modified trivially if you wish to have this operate on arrays of other sizes by padding our arrays with zeros, however:

```
up_gpu = up_ker.get_function("up_ker")

def up_sweep(x):
    x = np.float64(x)
    x_gpu = gpuarray.to_gpu(np.float64(x) )
    x_old_gpu = x_gpu.copy()
    for k in range( int(np.log2(x.size) ) ) :
        num_threads = int(np.ceil( x.size / 2**(k+1)))
        grid_size = int(np.ceil(num_threads / 32))
        if grid_size > 1:
            block_size = 32
        else:
            block_size = num_threads
        up_gpu(x_gpu, x_old_gpu, np.int32(k) , block=(block_size,1,1),
grid=(grid_size,1,1))
        x_old_gpu[:] = x_gpu[:]
    x_out = x_gpu.get()
    return(x_out)
```

Now we'll embark on writing the down-sweep. Again, let's start with the kernel, which will have the functionality of the inner `parfor` loop of the pseudocode. It follows similarly as before—again, we'll use two arrays, so using a `temp` variable as in the pseudocode is unnecessary here, and again we use bit-shift operators to obtain the values of 2^k and 2^{k+1}. We calculate j similarly to before:

```
down_ker = SourceModule("""
__global__ void down_ker(double *y, double *y_old, int k)
{
 int j = blockIdx.x*blockDim.x + threadIdx.x;

 int _2k = 1 << k;
 int _2k1 = 1 << (k+1);


 int j = tid*_2k1;

 y[j + _2k - 1 ] = y_old[j + _2k1 - 1];
 y[j + _2k1 - 1] = y_old[j + _2k1 - 1] + y_old[j + _2k - 1];
}
""")

down_gpu = down_ker.get_function("down_ker")
```

We now can write our Python function that will iteratively launch the kernel, which corresponds to the outer `for` loop of the down-sweep phase. This is similar to the Python function for the up-sweep phase. One important distinction from looking at the pseudocode is that we have to iterate from the largest value in the outer `for` loop to the smallest; we can just use Python's `reversed` function to do this. Now we can implement the down-sweep phase:

```
def down_sweep(y):
    y = np.float64(y)
    y[-1] = 0
    y_gpu = gpuarray.to_gpu(y)
    y_old_gpu = y_gpu.copy()
    for k in reversed(range(int(np.log2(y.size)))):
        num_threads = int(np.ceil( y.size / 2**(k+1)))
        grid_size = int(np.ceil(num_threads / 32))
        if grid_size > 1:
            block_size = 32
        else:
            block_size = num_threads
        down_gpu(y_gpu, y_old_gpu, np.int32(k), block=(block_size,1,1),
grid=(grid_size,1,1))
        y_old_gpu[:] = y_gpu[:]
    y_out = y_gpu.get()
    return(y_out)
```

Having implemented both the up-sweep and down-sweep phases, our last task is trivial to complete:

```
def efficient_prefix(x):
        return(down_sweep(up_sweep(x)))
```

We have now fully implemented a host-synchronized version of the work-efficient parallel prefix algorithm! (This implementation is available in the `work-efficient_prefix.py` file in the repository, along with some test code.)

Summary

We started with an implementation of Conway's *Game of Life*, which gave us an idea of how the many threads of a CUDA kernel are organized in a block-grid tensor-type structure. We then delved into block-level synchronization by way of the CUDA function, `__syncthreads()`, as well as block-level thread intercommunication by using shared memory; we also saw that single blocks have a limited number of threads that we can operate over, so we'll have to be careful in using these features when we create kernels that will use more than one block across a larger grid.

We gave an overview of the theory of parallel prefix algorithms, and we ended by implementing a naive parallel prefix algorithm as a single kernel that could operate on arrays limited by a size of 1,024 (which was synchronized with ___syncthreads and performed both the `for` and `parfor` loops internally), and with a work-efficient parallel prefix algorithm that was implemented across two kernels and three Python functions could operate on arrays of arbitrary size, with the kernels acting as the inner `parfor` loops of the algorithm, and with the Python functions effectively operating as the outer `for` loops and synchronizing the kernel launches.

Questions

1. Change the random vector in `simple_scalar_multiply_kernel.py` so that it is of a length of 10,000, and modify the `i` index in the definition of the kernel so that it can be used over multiple blocks in the form of a grid. See if you can now launch this kernel over 10,000 threads by setting block and grid parameters to something like `block=(100,1,1)` and `grid=(100,1,1)`.

2. In the previous question, we launched a kernel that makes use of 10,000 threads simultaneously; as of 2018, there is no NVIDIA GPU with more than 5,000 cores. Why does this still work and give the expected results?

3. The naive parallel prefix algorithm has time complexity O(*log n*) given that we have *n* or more processors for a dataset of size *n*. Suppose that we use a naive parallel prefix algorithm on a GTX 1050 GPU with 640 cores. What does the asymptotic time complexity become in the case that `n >> 640`?

4. Modify `naive_prefix.py` to operate on arrays of arbitrary size (possibly non-dyadic), only bounded by 1,024.

5. The `__syncthreads()` CUDA device function only synchronizes threads across a single block. How can we synchronize across all threads in all blocks across a grid?

6. You can convince yourself that the second prefix sum algorithm really is more work-efficient than the naive prefix sum algorithm with this exercise. Suppose that we have a dataset of size 32. What is the exact number of "addition" operations required by the first and second algorithm in this case?

7. In the implementation of the work-efficient parallel prefix we use a Python function to iterate our kernels and synchronize the results. Why can't we just put a `for` loop inside the kernels with careful use of `__syncthreads()` instead?

8. Why does it make more sense to implement the naive parallel prefix within a single kernel that handles its own synchronization within CUDA C, than it makes more sense to implement the work-efficient parallel prefix using both kernels and Python functions and have the host handle the synchronization?

5
Streams, Events, Contexts, and Concurrency

In the prior chapters, we saw that there are two primary operations we perform from the host when interacting with the GPU:

- Copying memory data to and from the GPU
- Launching kernel functions

We know that *within* a single kernel, there is one level of concurrency among its many threads; however, there is another level of concurrency *over* multiple kernels *and* GPU memory operations that are also available to us. This means that we can launch multiple memory and kernel operations at once, without waiting for each operation to finish. However, on the other hand, we will have to be somewhat organized to ensure that all inter-dependent operations are synchronized; this means that we shouldn't launch a particular kernel until its input data is fully copied to the device memory, or we shouldn't copy the output data of a launched kernel to the host until the kernel has finished execution.

To this end, we have what are known as **CUDA streams**—a **stream** is a sequence of operations that are run in order on the GPU. By itself, a single stream isn't of any use—the point is to gain concurrency over GPU operations issued by the host by using multiple streams. This means that we should interleave launches of GPU operations that correspond to different streams, in order to exploit this notion.

We will be covering this notion of streams extensively in this chapter. Additionally, we will look at **events**, which are a feature of streams that are used to precisely time kernels and indicate to the host as to what operations have been completed within a given stream.

Finally, we will briefly look at CUDA **contexts**. A **context** can be thought of as analogous to a process in your operating system, in that the GPU keeps each context's data and kernel code *walled off* and encapsulated away from the other contexts currently existing on the GPU. We will see the basics of this near the end of the chapter.

The following are the learning outcomes for this chapter:

- Understanding the concepts of device and stream synchronization
- Learning how to effectively use streams to organize concurrent GPU operations
- Learning how to effectively use CUDA events
- Understanding CUDA contexts
- Learning how to explicitly synchronize within a given context
- Learning how to explicitly create and destroy a CUDA context
- Learning how to use contexts to allow for GPU usage among multiple processes and threads on the host

Technical requirements

A Linux or Windows 10 PC with a modern NVIDIA GPU (2016—onward) is required for this chapter, with all necessary GPU drivers and the CUDA Toolkit (9.0–onward) installed. A suitable Python 2.7 installation (such as Anaconda Python 2.7) with the PyCUDA module is also required.

This chapter's code is also available on GitHub:

https://github.com/PacktPublishing/Hands-On-GPU-Programming-with-Python-and-CUDA

 For more information about the prerequisites, check the *Preface* of this book, and for the software and hardware requirements, check the README in https://github.com/PacktPublishing/Hands-On-GPU-Programming-with-Python-and-CUDA.

CUDA device synchronization

Before we can use CUDA streams, we need to understand the notion of **device synchronization**. This is an operation where the host blocks any further execution until all operations issued to the GPU (memory transfers and kernel executions) have completed. This is required to ensure that operations dependent on prior operations are not executed out-of-order—for example, to ensure that a CUDA kernel launch is completed before the host tries to read its output.

In CUDA C, device synchronization is performed with the `cudaDeviceSynchronize` function. This function effectively blocks further execution on the host until all GPU operations have completed. `cudaDeviceSynchronize` is so fundamental that it is usually one of the very first topics covered in most books on CUDA C—we haven't seen this yet, because PyCUDA has been invisibly calling this for us automatically as needed. Let's take a look at an example of CUDA C code to see how this is done manually:

```
// Copy an array of floats from the host to the device.
cudaMemcpy(device_array, host_array, size_of_array*sizeof(float),
cudaMemcpyHostToDevice);
// Block execution until memory transfer to device is complete.
cudaDeviceSynchronize();
// Launch CUDA kernel.
Some_CUDA_Kernel <<< block_size, grid_size >>> (device_array,
size_of_array);
// Block execution until GPU kernel function returns.
cudaDeviceSynchronize();
// Copy output of kernel to host.
cudaMemcpy(host_array,  device_array, size_of_array*sizeof(float),
cudaMemcpyDeviceToHost);
// Block execution until memory transfer to host is complete.
cudaDeviceSynchronize();
```

In this block of code, we see that we have to synchronize with the device directly after every single GPU operation. If we only have a need to call a single CUDA kernel at a time, as seen here, this is fine. But if we want to concurrently launch multiple independent kernels and memory operations operating on different arrays of data, it would be inefficient to synchronize across the entire device. In this case, we should synchronize across multiple streams. We'll see how to do this right now.

Using the PyCUDA stream class

We will start with a simple PyCUDA program; all this will do is generate a series of random GPU arrays, process each array with a simple kernel, and copy the arrays back to the host. We will then modify this to use streams. Keep in mind this program will have no point at all, beyond illustrating how to use streams and some basic performance gains you can get. (This program can be seen in the `multi-kernel.py` file, under the 5 directory in the GitHub repository.)

Of course, we'll start by importing the appropriate Python modules, as well as the `time` function:

```
import pycuda.autoinit
import pycuda.driver as drv
from pycuda import gpuarray
from pycuda.compiler import SourceModule
import numpy as np
from time import time
```

We now will specify how many arrays we wish to process—here, each array will be processed by a different kernel launch. We also specify the length of the random arrays we will generate, as follows:

```
num_arrays = 200
array_len = 1024**2
```

We now have a kernel that operates on each array; all this will do is iterate over each point in the array, and multiply and divide it by 2 for 50 times, ultimately leaving the array intact. We want to restrict the number of threads that each kernel launch will use, which will help us gain concurrency among many kernel launches on the GPU so that we will have each thread iterate over different parts of the array with a `for` loop. (Again, remember that this kernel function will be completely useless for anything other than for learning about streams and synchronization!) If each kernel launch uses too many threads, it will be harder to gain concurrency later:

```
ker = SourceModule("""
__global__ void mult_ker(float * array, int array_len)
{
     int thd = blockIdx.x*blockDim.x + threadIdx.x;
     int num_iters = array_len / blockDim.x;

     for(int j=0; j < num_iters; j++)
     {
         int i = j * blockDim.x + thd;

         for(int k = 0; k < 50; k++)
         {
              array[i] *= 2.0;
              array[i] /= 2.0;
         }
     }
}
""")

mult_ker = ker.get_function('mult_ker')
```

Now, we will generate some random data array, copy these arrays to the GPU, iteratively launch our kernel over each array across 64 threads, and then copy the output data back to the host and assert that the same with NumPy's `allclose` function. We will time the duration of all operations from start to finish by using Python's `time` function, as follows:

```
data = []
data_gpu = []
gpu_out = []

# generate random arrays.
for _ in range(num_arrays):
    data.append(np.random.randn(array_len).astype('float32'))

t_start = time()

# copy arrays to GPU.
for k in range(num_arrays):
    data_gpu.append(gpuarray.to_gpu(data[k]))

# process arrays.
for k in range(num_arrays):
    mult_ker(data_gpu[k], np.int32(array_len), block=(64,1,1),
grid=(1,1,1))

# copy arrays from GPU.
for k in range(num_arrays):
    gpu_out.append(data_gpu[k].get())

t_end = time()

for k in range(num_arrays):
    assert (np.allclose(gpu_out[k], data[k]))

print 'Total time: %f' % (t_end - t_start)
```

We are now prepared to run this program. I will run it right now:

```
PS C:\Users\btuom\examples\5> python .\multi-kernel.py
Total time: 2.976000
```

So, it took almost three seconds for this program to complete. We will make a few simple modifications so that our program can use streams, and then see if we can get any performance gains (this can be seen in the `multi-kernel_streams.py` file in the repository).

First, we note that for each kernel launch we have a separate array of data that it processes, and these are stored in Python lists. We will have to create a separate stream object for each individual array/kernel launch pair, so let's first add an empty list, entitled `streams`, that will hold our stream objects:

```
data = []
data_gpu = []
gpu_out = []
streams = []
```

We can now generate a series of streams that we will use to organize the kernel launches. We can get a stream object from the `pycuda.driver` submodule with the `Stream` class. Since we've imported this submodule and aliased it as `drv`, we can fill up our list with new stream objects, as follows:

```
for _ in range(num_arrays):
    streams.append(drv.Stream())
```

Now, we will have to first modify our memory operations that transfer data to the GPU. Consider the following steps for it:

1. Look for the first loop that copies the arrays to the GPU with the `gpuarray.to_gpu` function. We will want to switch to the asynchronous and stream-friendly version of this function, `gpu_array.to_gpu_async`, instead. (We must now also specify which stream each memory operation should use with the `stream` parameter):

```
for k in range(num_arrays):
    data_gpu.append(gpuarray.to_gpu_async(data[k],
stream=streams[k]))
```

2. We can now launch our kernels. This is exactly as before, only we must specify what stream to use by using the `stream` parameter:

```
for k in range(num_arrays):
    mult_ker(data_gpu[k], np.int32(array_len), block=(64,1,1),
grid=(1,1,1), stream=streams[k])
```

3. Finally, we need to pull our data off the GPU. We can do this by switching the `gpuarray get` function to `get_async`, and again using the `stream` parameter, as follows:

```
for k in range(num_arrays):
    gpu_out.append(data_gpu[k].get_async(stream=streams[k]))
```

We are now ready to run our stream-friendly modified program:

```
PS C:\Users\btuom\examples\5> python .\multi-kernel_streams.py
Total time: 0.945000
```

In this case, we have a triple-fold performance gain, which is not too bad considering the very few numbers of modifications we had to make. But before we move on, let's try to get a deeper understanding as to why this works.

Let's consider the case of two CUDA kernel launches. We will also perform GPU memory operations corresponding to each kernel before and after we launch our kernels, for a total of six operations. We can visualize the operations happening on the GPU with respect to time with a graph as such—moving to the right on the *x*-axis corresponds to time duration, while the *y*-axis corresponds to operations being executed on the GPU at a particular time. This is depicted with the following diagram:

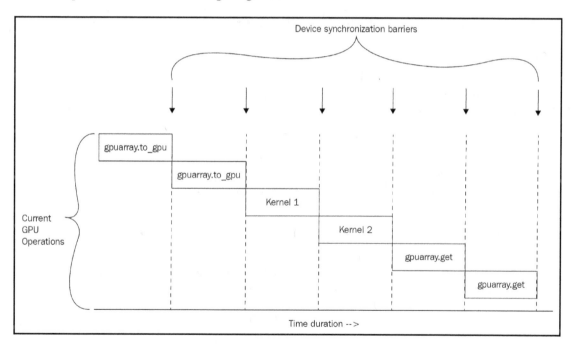

It's not too hard to visualize why streams work so well in performance increase—since operations in a single stream are blocked until only all *necessary* prior operations are competed, we will gain concurrency among distinct GPU operations and make full use of our device. This can be seen by the large overlap of concurrent operations. We can visualize stream-based concurrency over time as follows:

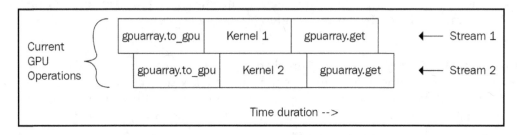

Concurrent Conway's game of life using CUDA streams

We will now see a more interesting application—we will modify the LIFE (Conway's *Game of Life*) simulation from the last chapter, so that we will have four independent windows of animation displayed concurrently. (It is suggested you look at this example from the last chapter, if you haven't yet.)

Let's get a copy of the old LIFE simulation from the last chapter in the repository, which should be under `conway_gpu.py` in the 4 directory. We will now modify this into our new CUDA-stream based concurrent LIFE simulation. (This new streams-based simulation that we will see in a moment is also available in the `conway_gpu_streams.py` file in this chapter's directory, 5.)

Go to the main function at the end of the file. We will set a new variable that indicates how many concurrent animations we will display at once with `num_concurrent` (where N indicates the height/width of the simulation lattice, as before). We will set it to 4 here, but you can feel free to try other values:

```
if __name__ == '__main__':

    N = 128
    num_concurrent = 4
```

We will now need a collection of `num_concurrent` stream objects, and will also need to allocate a collection of input and output lattices on the GPU. We'll of course just store these in lists and initialize the lattices as before. We will set up some empty lists and fill each with the appropriate objects over a loop, as such (notice how we set up a new initial state lattice on each iteration, send it to the GPU, and concatenate it to `lattices_gpu`):

```
streams = []
lattices_gpu = []
newLattices_gpu = []

for k in range(num_concurrent):
    streams.append(drv.Stream())
    lattice = np.int32( np.random.choice([1,0], N*N, p=[0.25,
0.75]).reshape(N, N) )
    lattices_gpu.append(gpuarray.to_gpu(lattice))
    newLattices_gpu.append(gpuarray.empty_like(lattices_gpu[k]))
```

Since we're only doing this loop once during the startup of our program and the virtually all of the computational work will be in the animation loop, we really don't have to worry about actually using the streams we just immediately generated.

We will now set up the environment with Matplotlib using the subplots function; notice how we can set up multiple animation plots by setting the `ncols` parameter. We will have another list structure that will correspond to the images that are required for the animation updates in `imgs`. Notice how we can now set this up with `get_async` and the appropriate corresponding stream:

```
fig, ax = plt.subplots(nrows=1, ncols=num_concurrent)
imgs = []

for k in range(num_concurrent):
    imgs.append( ax[k].imshow(lattices_gpu[k].get_async(stream=streams[k]),
interpolation='nearest') )
```

The last thing to change in the main function is the penultimate line starting with `ani = animation.FuncAnimation`. Let's modify the arguments to the `update_gpu` function to reflect the new lists we are using and add two more arguments, one to pass our `streams` list, plus a parameter to indicate how many concurrent animations there should be:

```
ani = animation.FuncAnimation(fig, update_gpu, fargs=(imgs,
newLattices_gpu, lattices_gpu, N, streams, num_concurrent) , interval=0,
frames=1000, save_count=1000)
```

We now duly make the required modifications to the `update_gpu` function to take these extra parameters. Scroll up a bit in the file and modify the parameters as follows:

```
def update_gpu(frameNum, imgs, newLattices_gpu, lattices_gpu, N,
streams, num_concurrent):
```

We now need to modify this function to iterate `num_concurrent` times and set each element of `imgs` as before, before finally returning the whole `imgs` list:

```
for k in range(num_concurrent):
    conway_ker( newLattices_gpu[k], lattices_gpu[k], grid=(N/32,N/32,1),
block=(32,32,1), stream=streams[k] )
        imgs[k].set_data(newLattices_gpu[k].get_async(stream=streams[k]) )
        lattices_gpu[k].set_async(newLattices_gpu[k], stream=streams[k])

    return imgs
```

Notice the changes we made—each kernel is launched in the appropriate stream, while `get` has been switched to a `get_async` synchronized with the same stream.

Finally, the last line in the loop copies GPU data from one device array to another without any re-allocation. Before, we could use the shorthand slicing operator `[:]` to directly copy the elements between the arrays without re-allocating any memory on the GPU; in this case, the slicing operator notation acts as an alias for the PyCUDA `set` function for GPU arrays. (`set`, of course, is the function that copies one GPU array to another of the same size, without any re-allocation.) Luckily, there is indeed a stream-synchronized also version of this function, `set_async`, but we need to use this specifically to call this function, explicitly specifying the array to copy and the stream to use.

We're now finished and ready to run this. Go to a Terminal and enter `python conway_gpu_streams.py` at the command line to enjoy the show:

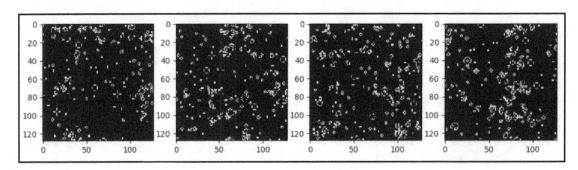

Events

Events are objects that exist *on the GPU*, whose purpose is to act as milestones or progress markers for a stream of operations. Events are generally used to provide measure time duration *on the device side* to precisely time operations; the measurements we have been doing so far have been with host-based Python profilers and standard Python library functions such as `time`. Additionally, events they can also be used to provide a status update for the host as to the state of a stream and what operations it has already completed, as well as for explicit stream-based synchronization.

Let's start with an example that uses no explicit streams and uses events to measure only one single kernel launch. (If we don't explicitly use streams in our code, CUDA actually invisibly defines a default stream that all operations will be placed into).

Here, we will use the same useless multiply/divide loop kernel and header as we did at the beginning of the chapter, and modify most of the following contents. We want a single kernel instance to run a long time for this example, so we will generate a huge array of random numbers for the kernel to process, as follows:

```
array_len = 100*1024**2
data = np.random.randn(array_len).astype('float32')
data_gpu = gpuarray.to_gpu(data)
```

We now construct our events using the `pycuda.driver.Event` constructor (where, of course, `pycuda.driver` has been aliased as `drv` by our prior import statement).

We will create two event objects here, one for the start of the kernel launch, and the other for the end of the kernel launch, (We will always need *two* event objects to measure any single GPU operation, as we will see soon):

```
start_event = drv.Event()
end_event = drv.Event()
```

Now, we are about ready to launch our kernel, but first, we have to mark the `start_event` instance's place in the stream of execution with the event record function. We launch the kernel and then mark the place of `end_event` in the stream of execution, and also with `record`:

```
start_event.record()
mult_ker(data_gpu, np.int32(array_len), block=(64,1,1), grid=(1,1,1))
end_event.record()
```

Events have a binary value that indicates whether they were reached or not yet, which is given by the function query. Let's print a status update for both events, immediately after the kernel launch:

```
print 'Has the kernel started yet? {}'.format(start_event.query())
 print 'Has the kernel ended yet? {}'.format(end_event.query())
```

Let's run this right now and see what happens:

```
PS C:\Users\btuom\examples\5> python .\simple_event_example.py
Has the kernel started yet? False
Has the kernel ended yet? False
```

Our goal here is to ultimately measure the time duration of our kernel execution, but the kernel hasn't even apparently launched yet. Kernels in PyCUDA have launched asynchronously (whether they exist in a specific stream or not), so we have to have to ensure that our host code is properly synchronized with the GPU.

Since `end_event` comes last, we can block further host code execution until the kernel completes by this event object's synchronize function; this will ensure that the kernel has completed before any further lines of host code are executed. Let's add a line a line of code to do this in the appropriate place:

```
end_event.synchronize()

print 'Has the kernel started yet?  {}'.format(start_event.query())

print 'Has the kernel ended yet? {}'.format(end_event.query())
```

Finally, we are ready to measure the execution time of the kernel; we do this with the event object's `time_till` or `time_since` operations to compare to another event object to get the time between these two events in milliseconds. Let's use the `time_till` operation of `start_event` on `end_event`:

```
print 'Kernel execution time in milliseconds: %f ' %
start_event.time_till(end_event)
```

Time duration can be measured between two events that have already occurred on the GPU with the `time_till` and `time_since` functions. Note that these functions always return a value in terms of milliseconds!

Let's try running our program again now:

```
PS C:\Users\btuom\examples\5> python .\simple_event_example.py
Has the kernel started yet? True
Has the kernel ended yet? True
Kernel execution time in milliseconds: 1047.391235
```

(This example is also available in the `simple_event_example.py` file in the repository.)

Events and streams

We will now see how to use event objects with respect to streams; this will give us a highly intricate level of control over the flow of our various GPU operations, allowing us to know exactly how far each individual stream has progressed via the `query` function, and even allowing us to synchronize particular streams with the host while ignoring the other streams.

First, though, we have to realize this—each stream has to have its own dedicated collection of event objects; multiple streams cannot share an event object. Let's see what this means exactly by modifying the prior example, `multi_kernel_streams.py`. After the kernel definition, let's add two additional empty lists—`start_events` and `end_events`. We will fill these lists up with event objects, which will correspond to each stream that we have. This will allow us to time one GPU operation in each stream, since every GPU operation requires two events:

```
data = []
data_gpu = []
gpu_out = []
streams = []
start_events = []
end_events = []

for _ in range(num_arrays):
    streams.append(drv.Stream())
    start_events.append(drv.Event())
    end_events.append(drv.Event())
```

Now, we can time each kernel launch individually by modifying the second loop to use the record of the event at the beginning and end of the launch. Notice that here, since there are multiple streams, we have to input the appropriate stream as a parameter to each event object's `record` function. Also, notice that we can capture the end events in a second loop; this will still allow us to capture kernel execution duration perfectly, without any delay in launching the subsequent kernels. Now consider the following code:

```
for k in range(num_arrays):
    start_events[k].record(streams[k])
    mult_ker(data_gpu[k], np.int32(array_len), block=(64,1,1),
grid=(1,1,1), stream=streams[k])

for k in range(num_arrays):
    end_events[k].record(streams[k])
```

Now we're going to extract the duration of each individual kernel launch. Let's add a new empty list after the iterative assert check, and fill it with the duration by way of the `time_till` function:

```
kernel_times = []
for k in range(num_arrays):
    kernel_times.append(start_events[k].time_till(end_events[k]))
```

Let's now add two `print` statements at the very end, to tell us the mean and standard deviation of the kernel execution times:

```
print 'Mean kernel duration (milliseconds): %f' % np.mean(kernel_times)
print 'Mean kernel standard deviation (milliseconds): %f' %
np.std(kernel_times)
```

We can now run this:

```
PS C:\Users\btuom\examples\5> python .\multi-kernel_events.py
Total time: 1.078000
Mean kernel duration (milliseconds): 71.417903
Mean kernel standard deviation (milliseconds): 6.401030
```

(This example is also available as `multi-kernel_events.py` in the repository.)

We see that there is a relatively low degree of standard deviation in kernel duration, which is good, considering each kernel processes the same amount of data over the same block and grid size—if there were a high degree of deviation, then that would mean that we were making highly uneven usage of the GPU in our kernel executions, and we would have to re-tune parameters to gain a greater level of concurrency.

Contexts

A CUDA **context** is usually described as being analogous to a process in an operating system. Let's review what this means—a process is an instance of a single program running on a computer; all programs outside of the operating system kernel run in a process. Each process has its own set of instructions, variables, and allocated memory, and is, generally speaking, blind to the actions and memory of other processes. When a process ends, the operating system kernel performs a cleanup, ensuring that all memory that the process allocated has been de-allocated, and closing any files, network connections, or other resources the process has made use of. (Curious Linux users can view the processes running on their computer with the command-line `top` command, while Windows users can view them with the Windows Task Manager).

Similar to a process, a context is associated with a single host program that is using the GPU. A context holds in memory all CUDA kernels and allocated memory that is making use of and is blind to the kernels and memory of other currently existing contexts. When a context is destroyed (at the end of a GPU based program, for example), the GPU performs a cleanup of all code and allocated memory within the context, freeing resources up for other current and future contexts. The programs that we have been writing so far have all existed within a single context, so these operations and concepts have been invisible to us.

Let's also remember that a single program starts as a single process, but it can fork itself to run across multiple processes or threads. Analogously, a single CUDA host program can generate and use multiple CUDA contexts on the GPU. Usually, we will create a new context when we want to gain host-side concurrency when we fork new processes or threads of a host process. (It should be emphasized, however, that there is no exact one-to-one relation between host processes and CUDA contexts).

As in many other areas of life, we will start with a simple example. We will first see how to access a program's default context and synchronize across it.

Synchronizing the current context

We're going to see how to explicitly synchronize our device within a context from within Python as in CUDA C; this is actually one of the most fundamental skills to know in CUDA C, and is covered in the first or second chapters in most other books on the topic. So far, we have been able to avoid this topic, since PyCUDA has performed most synchronizations for us automatically with `pycuda.gpuarray` functions such as `to_gpu` or `get`; otherwise, synchronization was handled by streams in the case of the `to_gpu_async` or `get_async` functions, as we saw at the beginning of this chapter.

We will be humble and start by modifying the program we wrote in Chapter 3, *Getting Started with PyCUDA,* which generates an image of the Mandelbrot set using explicit context synchronization. (This is available here as the file `gpu_mandelbrot0.py` under the 3 directory in the repository.)

 We won't get any performance gains over our original Mandelbrot program here; the only point of this exercise is just to help us understand CUDA contexts and GPU synchronization.

Looking at the header, we, of course, see the `import pycuda.autoinit` line. We can access the current context object with `pycuda.autoinit.context`, and we can synchronize in our current context by calling the `pycuda.autoinit.context.synchronize()` function.

Now let's modify the `gpu_mandelbrot` function to handle explicit synchronization. The first GPU-related line we see is this:

`mandelbrot_lattice_gpu = gpuarray.to_gpu(mandelbrot_lattice)`

We can now change this to be explicitly synchronized. We can copy to the GPU asynchronously with `to_gpu_async`, and then synchronize as follows:

```
mandelbrot_lattice_gpu = gpuarray.to_gpu_async(mandelbrot_lattice)
pycuda.autoinit.context.synchronize()
```

We then see the next line allocates memory on the GPU with the `gpuarray.empty` function. Memory allocation in CUDA is, by the nature of the GPU architecture, automatically synchronized; there is no *asynchronous* memory allocation equivalent here. Hence, we keep this line as it was before.

 Memory allocation in CUDA is always synchronized!

We now see the next two lines—our Mandelbrot kernel is launched with an invocation to `mandel_ker`, and we copy the contents of our Mandelbrot `gpuarray` object with an invocation to `get`. We synchronize after the kernel launch, switch `get` to `get_async`, and finally synchronize one last line:

```
mandel_ker( mandelbrot_lattice_gpu, mandelbrot_graph_gpu,
np.int32(max_iters), np.float32(upper_bound))
pycuda.autoinit.context.synchronize()
```

```
mandelbrot_graph = mandelbrot_graph_gpu.get_async()
pycuda.autoinit.context.synchronize()
```

We can now run this, and it will produce a Mandelbrot image to disk, exactly as in Chapter 3, *Getting Started with PyCUDA.*

(This example is also available as gpu_mandelbrot_context_sync.py in the repository.)

Manual context creation

So far, we have been importing pycuda.autoinit at the beginning of all of our PyCUDA programs; this effectively creates a context at the beginning of our program and has it destroyed at the end.

Let's try doing this manually. We will make a small program that just copies a small array to the GPU, copies it back to the host, prints the array, and exits.

We start with the imports:

```
import numpy as np
from pycuda import gpuarray
import pycuda.driver as drv
```

First, we initialize CUDA with the pycuda.driver.init function, which is here aliased as drv:

```
drv.init()
```

Now we choose which GPU we wish to work with; this is necessary for the cases where one has more than one GPU. We can select a specific GPU with pycuda.driver.Device; if you only have one GPU, as I do, you can access it with pycuda.driver.Device(0), as follows:

```
dev = drv.Device(0)
```

We can now create a new context on this device with make_context, as follows:

```
ctx = dev.make_context()
```

Now that we have a new context, this will automatically become the default context. Let's copy an array into the GPU, copy it back to the host, and print it:

```
x = gpuarray.to_gpu(np.float32([1,2,3]))
print x.get()
```

Now we are done. We can destroy the context by calling the `pop` function:

```
ctx.pop()
```

That's it! We should always remember to destroy contexts that we explicitly created with `pop` before our program exists.

(This example can be seen in the `simple_context_create.py` file under this chapter's directory in the repository.)

Host-side multiprocessing and multithreading

Of course, we may seek to gain concurrency on the host side by using multiple processes or threads on the host's CPU. Let's make the distinction right now between a host-side operating system process and thread with a quick overview.

Every host-side program that exists outside the operating system kernel is executed as a process, and can also exist in multiple processes. A process has its own address space, as it runs concurrently with, and independently of, all other processes. A process is, generally speaking, blind to the actions of other processes, although multiple processes can communicate through sockets or pipes. In Linux and Unix, new processes are spawned with the fork system call.

In contrast, a host-side thread exists within a single process, and multiple threads can also exist within a single process. Multiple threads in a single process run concurrently. All threads in the same process share the same address space within the process and have access to the same shared variables and data. Generally, resource locks are used for accessing data among multiple threads, so as to avoid race conditions. In compiled languages such as C, C++, or Fortran, multiple process threads are usually managed with the Pthreads or OpenMP APIs.

Threads are much more lightweight than processes, and it is far faster for an operating system kernel to switch tasks between multiple threads in a single process, than to switch tasks between multiple processes. Normally, an operating system kernel will automatically execute different threads and processes on different CPU cores to establish true concurrency.

A peculiarity of Python is that while it supports multi-threading through the `threading` module, all threads will execute on the same CPU core. This is due to technicalities of Python being an interpreted scripting language, and is related to Python's Global Identifier Lock (GIL). To achieve true multi-core concurrency on the host through Python, we, unfortunately, must spawn multiple processes with the `multiprocessing` module. (Unfortunately, the multiprocessing module is currently not fully functional under Windows, due to how Windows handles processes. Windows users will sadly have to stick to single-core multithreading here if they want to have any form of host-side concurrency.)

We will now see how to use both threads in Python to use GPU based operations; Linux users should note that this can be easily extended to processes by switching references of `threading` to `multiprocessing`, and references to `Thread` to `Process`, as both modules look and act similarly. By the nature of PyCUDA, however, we will have to create a new CUDA context for every thread or process that we will use that will make use of the GPU. Let's see how to do this right now.

Multiple contexts for host-side concurrency

Let's first briefly review how to create a single host thread in Python that can return a value to the host with a simple example. (This example can also be seen in the `single_thread_example.py` file under 5 in the repository.) We will do this by using the `Thread` class in the `threading` module to create a subclass of `Thread`, as follows:

```
import threading
class PointlessExampleThread(threading.Thread):
```

We now set up our constructor. We call the parent class's constructor and set up an empty variable within the object that will be the return value from the thread:

```
def __init__(self):
    threading.Thread.__init__(self)
    self.return_value = None
```

We now set up the run function within our thread class, which is what will be executed when the thread is launched. We'll just have it print a line and set the return value:

```
def run(self):
    print 'Hello from the thread you just spawned!'
    self.return_value = 123
```

We finally have to set up the join function. This will allow us to receive a return value from the thread:

```
def join(self):
    threading.Thread.join(self)
    return self.return_value
```

Now we are done setting up our thread class. Let's start an instance of this class as the NewThread object, spawn the new thread by calling the start method, and then block execution and get the output from the host thread by calling join:

```
NewThread = PointlessExampleThread()
NewThread.start()
thread_output = NewThread.join()
print 'The thread completed and returned this value: %s' % thread_output
```

Now let's run this:

```
PS C:\Users\btuom\examples\5> python .\single_thread_example.py
Hello from the thread you just spawned!
The thread completed and returned this value: 123
```

Now, we can expand this idea among multiple concurrent threads on the host to launch concurrent CUDA operations by way of multiple contexts and threading. We will now look at one last example. Let's re-use the pointless multiply/divide kernel from the beginning of this chapter and launch it within each thread that we spawn.

First, let's look at the imports. Since we are making explicit contexts, remember to remove pycuda.autoinit and add an import threading at the end:

```
import pycuda
import pycuda.driver as drv
from pycuda import gpuarray
from pycuda.compiler import SourceModule
import numpy as np
from time import time
import threading
```

We will use the same array size as before, but this time we will have a direct correspondence between the number of the threads and the number of the arrays. Generally, we don't want to spawn more than 20 or so threads on the host, so we will only go for 10 arrays. So, consider now the following code:

```
num_arrays = 10
array_len = 1024**2
```

Now, we will store our old kernel as a string object; since this can only be compiled within a context, we will have to compile this in each thread individually:

```
kernel_code = """
__global__ void mult_ker(float * array, int array_len)
{
    int thd = blockIdx.x*blockDim.x + threadIdx.x;
    int num_iters = array_len / blockDim.x;
  for(int j=0; j < num_iters; j++)
    {
    int i = j * blockDim.x + thd;
    for(int k = 0; k < 50; k++)
    {
        array[i] *= 2.0;
        array[i] /= 2.0;
    }
  }
 }
}
"""
```

Now we can begin setting up our class. We will make another subclass of `threading.Thread` as before, and set up the constructor to take one parameter as the input array. We will initialize an output variable with `None`, as we did before:

```
class KernelLauncherThread(threading.Thread):
    def __init__(self, input_array):
        threading.Thread.__init__(self)
        self.input_array = input_array
        self.output_array = None
```

We can now write the `run` function. We choose our device, create a context on that device, compile our kernel, and extract the kernel function reference. Notice the use of the `self` object:

```
def run(self):
    self.dev = drv.Device(0)
    self.context = self.dev.make_context()
    self.ker = SourceModule(kernel_code)
    self.mult_ker = self.ker.get_function('mult_ker')
```

We now copy the array to the GPU, launch the kernel, and copy the output back to the host. We then destroy the context:

```
self.array_gpu = gpuarray.to_gpu(self.input_array)
self.mult_ker(self.array_gpu, np.int32(array_len), block=(64,1,1),
grid=(1,1,1))
self.output_array = self.array_gpu.get()
self.context.pop()
```

Finally, we set up the join function. This will return `output_array` to the host:

```
def join(self):
    threading.Thread.join(self)
    return self.output_array
```

We are now done with our subclass. We will set up some empty lists to hold our random test data, thread objects, and thread output values, similar to before. We will then generate some random arrays to process and set up a list of kernel launcher threads that will operate on each corresponding array:

```
data = []
gpu_out = []
threads = []
for _ in range(num_arrays):
    data.append(np.random.randn(array_len).astype('float32'))
for k in range(num_arrays):
 threads.append(KernelLauncherThread(data[k]))
```

We will now launch each thread object, and extract its output into the `gpu_out` list by using `join`:

```
for k in range(num_arrays):
    threads[k].start()

for k in range(num_arrays):
    gpu_out.append(threads[k].join())
```

Finally, we just do a simple assert on the output arrays to ensure they are the same as the input:

```
for k in range(num_arrays):
    assert (np.allclose(gpu_out[k], data[k]))
```

This example can be seen in the `multi-kernel_multi-thread.py` file in the repository.

Summary

We started this chapter by learning about device synchronization and the importance of synchronization of operations on the GPU from the host; this allows dependent operations to allow antecedent operations to finish before proceeding. This concept has been hidden from us, as PyCUDA has been handling synchronization for us automatically up to this point. We then learned about CUDA streams, which allow for independent sequences of operations to execute on the GPU simultaneously without synchronizing across the entire GPU, which can give us a big performance boost; we then learned about CUDA events, which allow us to time individual CUDA kernels within a given stream, and to determine if a particular operation in a stream has occurred. Next, we learned about contexts, which are analogous to processes in a host operating system. We learned how to synchronize across an entire CUDA context explicitly and then saw how to create and destroy contexts. Finally, we saw how we can generate multiple contexts on the GPU, to allow for GPU usage among multiple threads or processes on the host.

Questions

1. In the launch parameters for the kernel in the first example, our kernels were each launched over 64 threads. If we increase the number of threads to and beyond the number of cores in our GPU, how does this affect the performance of both the original to the stream version?

2. Consider the CUDA C example that was given at the very beginning of this chapter, which illustrated the use of `cudaDeviceSynchronize`. Do you think it is possible to get some level of concurrency among multiple kernels without using streams and only using `cudaDeviceSynchronize`?

3. If you are a Linux user, modify the last example that was given to operate over processes rather than threads.

4. Consider the `multi-kernel_events.py` program; we said it is good that there was a low standard deviation of kernel execution durations. Why would it be bad if there were a high standard deviation?

5. We only used 10 host-side threads in the last example. Name two reasons why we have to use a relatively small number of threads or processes for launching concurrent GPU operations on the host.

6
Debugging and Profiling Your CUDA Code

In this chapter, we will finally learn how to debug and profile our GPU code using several different methods and tools. While we can easily debug pure Python code using IDEs such as Spyder and PyCharm, we can't use these tools to debug the actual GPU code, remembering that the GPU code itself is written in CUDA-C with PyCUDA providing an interface. The first and easiest method for debugging a CUDA kernel is the usage of `printf` statements, which we can actually call directly in the middle of a CUDA kernel to print to the standard output. We will see how to use `printf` in the context of CUDA and how to apply it effectively for debugging.

Next, we will fill in some of the gaps in our CUDA-C programming so that we can directly write CUDA programs within the NVIDIA Nsight IDE, which will allow us to make test cases in CUDA-C for some of the code we have been writing. We will take a look at how to compile CUDA-C programs, both from the command line with `nvcc` and also with the Nsight IDE. We will then see how to debug within Nsight and use Nsight to understand the CUDA lockstep property. Finally, we will have an overview of the NVIDIA command line and Visual Profilers for profiling our code.

The learning outcomes for this chapter include the following:

- Using `printf` effectively as a debugging tool for CUDA kernels
- Writing complete CUDA-C programs outside of Python, especially for creating test cases for debugging
- Compiling CUDA-C programs on the command line with the `nvcc` compiler
- Developing and debugging CUDA programs with the NVIDIA Nsight IDE
- Understanding the CUDA warp lockstep property and why we should avoid branch divergence within a single CUDA warp
- Learn to effectively use the NVIDIA command line and Visual Profilers for GPU code

Technical requirements

A Linux or Windows 10 PC with a modern NVIDIA GPU (2016—onward) is required for this chapter, with all necessary GPU drivers and the CUDA Toolkit (9.0–onward) installed. A suitable Python 2.7 installation (such as Anaconda Python 2.7) with the PyCUDA module is also required.

This chapter's code is also available on GitHub at `https://github.com/PacktPublishing/Hands-On-GPU-Programming-with-Python-and-CUDA`.

 For more information about the prerequisites, check the *Preface* of this book, and for the software and hardware requirements, check the README in `https://github.com/PacktPublishing/Hands-On-GPU-Programming-with-Python-and-CUDA`.

Using printf from within CUDA kernels

It may come as a surprise, but we can actually print text to the standard output from directly within a CUDA kernel; not only that, each individual thread can print its own output. This will come in particularly handy when we are debugging our kernels, as we may need to monitor the values of particular variables or computations at particular points in our code and it will also free us from the shackles of using a debugger to go through step by step. Printing output from a CUDA kernel is done with none other than the most fundamental function in all of C/C++ programming, the function that most people will learn when they write their first `Hello world` program in C: `printf`. Of course, `printf` is the standard function that prints a string to the standard output, and is really the equivalent in the C programming language of Python's `print` function.

Let's now briefly review how to use `printf` before we see how to use it in CUDA. The first thing to remember is that `printf` always takes a string as its first parameter; so printing "Hello world!" in C is done with `printf("Hello world!\n");`. (Of course, \n indicates "new line" or "return", which moves the output in the Terminal to the next line.) `printf` can also take a variable number of parameters in the case that we want to print any constants or variables from directly within C: if we want to print the `123` integers to the output, we do this with `printf("%d", 123);` (where %d indicates that an integer follows the string.)

Similarly, we use `%f`, `%e`, or `%g` to print floating-point values (where `%f` is the decimal notation, `%e` is the scientific notation, and `%g` is the shortest representation whether decimal or scientific). We can even print several values in a row, remembering to place these specifiers in the correct order: `printf("%d is a prime number, %f is close to pi, and %d is even.\n", 17, 3.14, 4);` will print "17 is a prime number, 3.14 is close to pi, and 4 is even." on the Terminal.

Now, nearly halfway through this book, we will finally embark on creating our first parallel `Hello world` program in CUDA! We start by importing the appropriate modules into Python and then write our kernel. We will start out by printing the thread and grid identification of each individual thread (we will only launch this in one-dimensional blocks and grids, so we only need the x values):

```
ker = SourceModule('''
__global__ void hello_world_ker()
{
    printf("Hello world from thread %d, in block %d!\\n", threadIdx.x,
blockIdx.x);
```

Let's stop for a second and note that we wrote \\n rather than \n. This is due to the fact that the triple quote in Python itself will interpret \n as a "new line", so we have to indicate that we mean this literally by using a double backslash so as to pass the \n directly into the CUDA compiler.

We will now print some information about the block and grid dimensions, but we want to ensure that it is printed after every thread has already finished its initial `printf` command. We can do this by putting in `__syncthreads();` to ensure each individual thread will be synchronized after the first `printf` function is executed.

Now, we only want to print the block and grid dimensions to the terminal only once; if we just place `printf` statements here, every single thread will print out the same information. We can do this by having only one specified thread print to the output; let's go with the 0th thread of the 0th block, which is the only thread that is guaranteed to exist no matter the block and grid dimensionality we choose. We can do this with a C `if` statement:

```
if(threadIdx.x == 0 && blockIdx.x == 0)
{
```

We will now print the dimensionality of our block and grid and close up the `if` statement, and that will be the end of our CUDA kernel:

```
printf("-----------------------------------\\n");
printf("This kernel was launched over a grid consisting of %d blocks,\\n",
gridDim.x);
printf("where each block has %d threads.\\n", blockDim.x);
}
}
''')
```

We will now extract the kernel and then launch it over a grid consisting of two blocks, where each block has five threads:

```
hello_ker = ker.get_function("hello_world_ker")
hello_ker( block=(5,1,1), grid=(2,1,1) )
```

Let's run this right now (this program is also available in `hello-world_gpu.py` under 6 in the repository):

```
PS C:\Users\btuom\examples\6> python .\hello-world_gpu.py
Hello world from thread 0, in block 1!
Hello world from thread 1, in block 1!
Hello world from thread 2, in block 1!
Hello world from thread 3, in block 1!
Hello world from thread 4, in block 1!
Hello world from thread 0, in block 0!
Hello world from thread 1, in block 0!
Hello world from thread 2, in block 0!
Hello world from thread 3, in block 0!
Hello world from thread 4, in block 0!
-----------------------------------
This kernel was launched over a grid consisting of 2 blocks,
where each block has 5 threads.
```

Using printf for debugging

Let's go over an example to see how we can approach debugging a CUDA kernel with `printf` with an example before we move on. There is no exact science to this method, but it is a skill that can be learned through experience. We will start with a CUDA kernel that is for matrix-matrix multiplication, but that has several bugs in it. (The reader is encouraged to go through the code as we go along, which is available as the `broken_matrix_ker.py` file in the 6 directories within the repository.)

Let's briefly review matrix-matrix multiplication before we continue. Suppose we have two matrices $N \times N$, A and B, and we multiply these together to get another matrix, C, of the same size as follows: $AB = C$. We do this by iterating over all tuples $i, j \in \{0, \ldots, N - 1\}$ and setting the value of $C[i, j]$ to the dot product of the ith row of A and the jth column of B: $C[i, j] = A[i, :] \cdot B[:, j]$.

In other words, we set each i, j element in the output matrix C as follows:

$$C[i, j] = \sum_{k=0}^{N-1} A[i, k] B[k, j] \text{ for } i, j \in \{0, \ldots, N - 1\}$$

Suppose we already wrote a kernel that is to perform matrix-matrix multiplication, which takes in two arrays representing the input matrices, an additional pre allocated float array that the output will be written to, and an integer that indicates the height and width of each matrix (we will assume that all matrices are the same size and square-shaped). These matrices are all to be represented as one-dimensional `float *` arrays in a row-wise one-dimensional layout. Furthermore, this will be implemented so that each CUDA thread will handle a single row/column tuple in the output matrix.

We make a small test case and check it against the output of the matrix multiplication in CUDA, and it fails as an assertion check on two 4 x 4 matrices, as follows:

```
test_a = np.float32( [xrange(1,5)] * 4 )
test_b = np.float32([xrange(14,10, -1)]*4 )
output_mat = np.matmul(test_a, test_b)

test_a_gpu = gpuarray.to_gpu(test_a)
test_b_gpu = gpuarray.to_gpu(test_b)
output_mat_gpu = gpuarray.empty_like(test_a_gpu)

matrix_ker(test_a_gpu, test_b_gpu, output_mat_gpu, np.int32(4),
block=(2,2,1), grid=(2,2,1))

assert( np.allclose(output_mat_gpu.get(), output_mat) )
```

We will run this program right now, and unsurprisingly get the following output:

```
PS C:\Users\btuom\examples\6> python .\broken_matrix_ker.py
Traceback (most recent call last):
  File ".\broken_matrix_ker.py", line 64, in <module>
    assert( np.allclose(output_mat_gpu.get(), output_mat) )
AssertionError
PS C:\Users\btuom\examples\6>
```

Let's now look at the CUDA C code, which consists of a kernel and a device function:

```
ker = SourceModule('''
// row-column dot-product for matrix multiplication
__device__ float rowcol_dot(float *matrix_a, float *matrix_b, int row, int
col, int N)
{
 float val = 0;

 for (int k=0; k < N; k++)
 {
     val += matrix_a[ row + k*N ] * matrix_b[ col*N + k];
 }
 return(val);
}


// matrix multiplication kernel that is parallelized over row/column
tuples.

__global__ void matrix_mult_ker(float * matrix_a, float * matrix_b, float *
output_matrix, int N)
{
 int row = blockIdx.x + threadIdx.x;
 int col = blockIdx.y + threadIdx.y;

 output_matrix[col + row*N] = rowcol_dot(matrix_a, matrix_b, col, row, N);
}
''')
```

Our goal is to place `printf` invocations intelligently throughout our CUDA code so that we can monitor a number of appropriate values and variables in the kernel and device function; we should also be sure to print out the thread and block numbers alongside these values at every `printf` invocation.

Let's start at the entry point of our kernel. We see two variables, `row` and `col`, so we should check these right away. Let's put the following line right after we set them (since this is parallelized over two dimensions, we should print the x and y values of `threadIdx` and `blockIdx`):

```
printf("threadIdx.x,y: %d,%d blockIdx.x,y: %d,%d -- row is %d, col is
%d.\\n", threadIdx.x, threadIdx.y, blockIdx.x, blockIdx.y, row, col);
```

Running the code again, we get this output:

```
PS C:\Users\btuom\examples\6> python .\broken_matrix_ker.py
threadIdx.x,y: 0,0 blockIdx.x,y: 1,0 -- row is 1, col is 0.
threadIdx.x,y: 1,0 blockIdx.x,y: 1,0 -- row is 2, col is 0.
threadIdx.x,y: 0,1 blockIdx.x,y: 1,0 -- row is 1, col is 1.
threadIdx.x,y: 1,1 blockIdx.x,y: 1,0 -- row is 2, col is 1.
threadIdx.x,y: 0,0 blockIdx.x,y: 1,1 -- row is 1, col is 1.
threadIdx.x,y: 1,0 blockIdx.x,y: 1,1 -- row is 2, col is 1.
threadIdx.x,y: 0,1 blockIdx.x,y: 1,1 -- row is 1, col is 2.
threadIdx.x,y: 1,1 blockIdx.x,y: 1,1 -- row is 2, col is 2.
threadIdx.x,y: 0,0 blockIdx.x,y: 0,0 -- row is 0, col is 0.
threadIdx.x,y: 1,0 blockIdx.x,y: 0,0 -- row is 1, col is 0.
threadIdx.x,y: 0,1 blockIdx.x,y: 0,0 -- row is 0, col is 1.
threadIdx.x,y: 1,1 blockIdx.x,y: 0,0 -- row is 1, col is 1.
threadIdx.x,y: 0,0 blockIdx.x,y: 0,1 -- row is 0, col is 1.
threadIdx.x,y: 1,0 blockIdx.x,y: 0,1 -- row is 1, col is 1.
threadIdx.x,y: 0,1 blockIdx.x,y: 0,1 -- row is 0, col is 2.
threadIdx.x,y: 1,1 blockIdx.x,y: 0,1 -- row is 1, col is 2.
Traceback (most recent call last):
  File ".\broken_matrix_ker.py", line 64, in <module>
    assert( np.allclose(output_mat_gpu.get(), output_mat) )
AssertionError
PS C:\Users\btuom\examples\6>
```

There are two things that are immediately salient: that there are repeated values for row and column tuples (every individual tuple should be represented only once), and that the row and column values never exceed two, when they both should reach three (since this unit test is using 4 x 4 matrices). This should indicate to us that we are calculating the row and column values wrongly; indeed, we are forgetting to multiply the `blockIdx` values by the `blockDim` values to find the objective row/column values. We fix this as follows:

```
int row = blockIdx.x*blockDim.x + threadIdx.x;
int col = blockIdx.y*blockDim.y + threadIdx.y;
```

If we run the program again, though, we still get an assertion error. Let's keep our original `printf` invocation in place, so we can monitor the values as we continue. We see that there is an invocation to a device function in the kernel, `rowcol_dot`, so we decide to look into there. Let's first ensure that the variables are being passed into the device function correctly by putting this `printf` invocation at the beginning:

```
printf("threadIdx.x,y: %d,%d blockIdx.x,y: %d,%d -- row is %d, col is %d, N
is %d.\\n", threadIdx.x, threadIdx.y, blockIdx.x, blockIdx.y, row, col, N);
```

When we run our program, even more lines will come out, however, we will see one that says—`threadIdx.x,y: 0,0 blockIdx.x,y: 1,0 -- row is 2, col is 0.` and yet another that says—`threadIdx.x,y: 0,0 blockIdx.x,y: 1,0 -- row is 0, col is 2, N is 4.` By the `threadIdx` and `blockIdx` values, we see that this is the same thread in the same block, but with the `row` and `col` values reversed. Indeed, when we look at the invocation of the `rowcol_dot` device function, we see that `row` and `col` are indeed reversed from that in the declaration of the device function. We fix this, but when we run the program again, we get yet another assertion error.

Let's place another `printf` invocation in the device function, within the `for` loop; this, of course, is the *dot product* that is to perform a dot product between rows of matrix A with columns of matrix B. We will check the values of the matrices we are multiplying, as well as k; we will also only look at the values of the very first thread, or else we will get an incoherent mess of an output:

```
if(threadIdx.x == 0 && threadIdx.y == 0 && blockIdx.x == 0 && blockIdx.y ==
0)
            printf("Dot-product loop: k value is %d, matrix_a value is %f,
matrix_b is %f.\\n", k, matrix_a[ row + k*N ], matrix_b[ col*N + k]);
```

Let's look at the values of the A and B matrices that are set up for our unit tests before we continue:

```
In [2]: print test_a
[[ 1.   2.   3.   4.]
 [ 1.   2.   3.   4.]
 [ 1.   2.   3.   4.]
 [ 1.   2.   3.   4.]]

In [3]: print test_b
[[ 14.   13.   12.   11.]
 [ 14.   13.   12.   11.]
 [ 14.   13.   12.   11.]
 [ 14.   13.   12.   11.]]

In [4]:
```

We see that both matrices vary when we switch between columns but are constant when we change between rows. Therefore, by the nature of matrix multiplication, the values of matrix A should vary across k in our `for` loop, while the values of B should remain constant. Let's run the program again and check the pertinent output:

```
Dot-product loop: k value is 0, matrix_a value is 1.000000, matrix_b is 14.000000.
Dot-product loop: k value is 1, matrix_a value is 1.000000, matrix_b is 13.000000.
Dot-product loop: k value is 2, matrix_a value is 1.000000, matrix_b is 12.000000.
Dot-product loop: k value is 3, matrix_a value is 1.000000, matrix_b is 11.000000.
```

So, it appears that we are not accessing the elements of the matrices in a correct way; remembering that these matrices are stored in a row-wise format, we modify the indices so that their values are accessed in the proper manner:

```
val += matrix_a[ row*N + k ] * matrix_b[ col + k*N];
```

Running the program again will yield no assertion errors. Congratulations, you just debugged a CUDA kernel using the only `printf`!

Filling in the gaps with CUDA-C

We will now go through the very basics of how to write a full-on CUDA-C program. We'll start small and just translate the *fixed* version of the little matrix multiplication test program we just debugged in the last section to a pure CUDA-C program, which we will then compile from the command line with NVIDIA's `nvcc` compiler into a native Windows or Linux executable file (we will see how to use the Nsight IDE in the next section, so we will just be doing this with only a text editor and the command line for now). Again, the reader is encouraged to look at the code we are translating from Python as we go along, which is available as the `matrix_ker.py` file in the repository.

Now, let's open our favorite text editor and create a new file entitled `matrix_ker.cu`. The extension will indicate that this is a CUDA-C program, which can be compiled with the `nvcc` compiler.

CUDA-C program and library source code filenames always use the `.cu` file extension.

Let's start at the beginning—as Python uses the `import` keyword at the beginning of a program for libraries, we recall the C language uses `#include`. We will need to include a few import libraries before we continue.

Let's start with these:

```
#include <cuda_runtime.h>
#include <stdio.h>
#include <stdlib.h>
```

Let's briefly think about what we need these for: `cuda_runtime.h` is the header file that has the declarations of all of the particular CUDA datatypes, functions, and structures that we will need for our program. We will need to include this for any pure CUDA-C program that we write. `stdio.h`, of course, gives us all of the standard I/O functions for the host such as `printf`, and we need `stdlib.h` for using the `malloc` and `free` dynamic memory allocation functions on the host.

 Remember to always put `#include <cuda_runtime.h>` at the beginning of every pure CUDA-C program!

Now, before we continue, we remember that we will ultimately have to check the output of our kernel with a correct known output, as we did with NumPy's `allclose` function. Unfortunately, we don't have a standard or easy-to-use numerical math library in C as Python has with NumPy. More often than not, it's just easier to write your own equivalent function if it's something simple, as in this case. This means that we will now explicitly have to make our own equivalent to NumPy's `allclose`. We will do so as such: we will use the `#define` macro in C to set up a value called `_EPSILON`, which will act as a constant to indicate the minimum value between the output and expected output to be considered the same, and we will also set up a macro called `_ABS`, which will tell us the absolute difference between two numbers. We do so as follows:

```
#define _EPSILON 0.001
#define _ABS(x) ( x > 0.0f ? x : -x )
```

We can now create our own version of `allclose`. This will take in two float pointers and an integer value, `len`. We loop through both arrays and check them: if any points differ by more than `_EPSILON`, we return -1, otherwise we return 0 to indicate that the two arrays do indeed match.

We note one thing: since we are using CUDA-C, we precede the definition of the function with `__host__`, to indicate that this function is intended to be run on the CPU rather than on the GPU:

```
__host__ int allclose(float *A, float *B, int len)
{
```

```
int returnval = 0;
for (int i = 0; i < len; i++)
{
  if ( _ABS(A[i] - B[i]) > _EPSILON )
  {
    returnval = -1;
    break;
  }
}
return(returnval);
}
```

We now can cut and paste the device and kernel functions exactly as they appear in our Python version here:

```
__device__ float rowcol_dot(float *matrix_a, float *matrix_b, int row, int col, int N)
{
  float val = 0;
  for (int k=0; k < N; k++)
  {
        val += matrix_a[ row*N + k ] * matrix_b[ col + k*N];
  }
  return(val);
}

__global__ void matrix_mult_ker(float * matrix_a, float * matrix_b, float * output_matrix, int N)
{

    int row = blockIdx.x*blockDim.x + threadIdx.x;
    int col = blockIdx.y*blockDim.y + threadIdx.y;

  output_matrix[col + row*N] = rowcol_dot(matrix_a, matrix_b, row, col, N);
}
```

Again, in contrast with __host__, notice that the CUDA device function is preceded by __device__, while the CUDA kernel is preceded by __global__.

Now, as in any C program, we will need to write the main function, which will run on the host, where we will set up our test case and from which we explicitly launch our CUDA kernel onto GPU. Again, in contrast to vanilla C, we will have explicitly to specify that this is also to be run on the CPU with __host__:

```
__host__ int main()
{
```

The first thing we will have to do is select and initialize our GPU. We do so with `cudaSetDevice` as follows:

```
cudaSetDevice(0);
```

`cudaSetDevice(0)` will select the default GPU. If you have multiple GPUs installed in your system, you can select and use them instead with `cudaSetDevice(1)`, `cudaSetDevice(2)`, and so on.

We will now set up `N` as in Python to indicate the height/width of our matrix. Since our test case will consist only of 4 x 4 matrices, we set it to 4. Since we will be working with dynamically allocated arrays and pointers, we will also have to set up a value that will indicate the number of bytes our test matrices will require. The matrices will consist of N x N floats, and we can determine the number of bytes required by a float with the `sizeof` keyword in C:

```
int N = 4;
int num_bytes = sizeof(float)*N*N;
```

We now set up our test matrices as such; these will correspond exactly to the `test_a` and `test_b` matrices that we saw in our Python test program (notice how we use the `h_` prefix to indicate that these arrays are stored on the host, rather than on the device):

```
float h_A[] = { 1.0, 2.0, 3.0, 4.0, \
                1.0, 2.0, 3.0, 4.0, \
                1.0, 2.0, 3.0, 4.0, \
                1.0, 2.0, 3.0, 4.0 };

float h_B[] = { 14.0, 13.0, 12.0, 11.0, \
                14.0, 13.0, 12.0, 11.0, \
                14.0, 13.0, 12.0, 11.0, \
                14.0, 13.0, 12.0, 11.0 };
```

We now set up another array, which will indicate the expected output of the matrix multiplication of the prior test matrices. We will have to calculate this explicitly and put these values into our C code. Ultimately, we will compare this to the GPU output at the end of the program, but let's just set it up and get it out of the way:

```
float h_AxB[] = { 140.0, 130.0, 120.0, 110.0, \
                  140.0, 130.0, 120.0, 110.0, \
                  140.0, 130.0, 120.0, 110.0, \
                  140.0, 130.0, 120.0, 110.0 };
```

We now declare some pointers for arrays that will live on the GPU, and for that we will copy the values of h_A and h_B and pointer to the GPU's output. Notice how we just use standard float pointers for this. Also, notice the prefix d_— this is another standard CUDA-C convention that indicates that these will exist on the device:

```
float * d_A;
float * d_B;
float * d_output;
```

Now, we will allocate some memory on the device for d_A and d_B with cudaMalloc, which is almost the same as malloc in C; this is what PyCUDA gpuarray functions such as empty or to_gpu have been calling us invisibly to allocate memory arrays on the GPU throughout this book:

```
cudaMalloc((float **) &d_A, num_bytes);
cudaMalloc((float **) &d_B, num_bytes);
```

Let's think a bit about how this works: in C functions, we can get the address of a variable by preceding it with an ampersand (&); if you have an integer, x, we can get its address with &x. &x will be a pointer to an integer, so its type will be int *. We can use this to set values of parameters into a C function, rather than use only pure return values.

Since cudaMalloc sets the pointer through a parameter rather than with the return value (in contrast to the regular malloc), we have to use the ampersand operator, which will be a pointer to a pointer, as it is a pointer to a float pointer as here (float **). We have to typecast this value explicitly with the parenthesis since cudaMalloc can allocate arrays of any type. Finally, in the second parameter, we have to indicate how many bytes to allocate on the GPU; we already set up num_bytes previously to be the number of bytes we will need to hold a 4 x 4 matrix consisting of floats, so we plug this in and continue.

We can now copy the values from h_A and h_B to d_A and d_B respectively with two invocations of the function cudaMemcpy, as follows:

```
cudaMemcpy(d_A, h_A, num_bytes, cudaMemcpyHostToDevice);
cudaMemcpy(d_B, h_B, num_bytes, cudaMemcpyHostToDevice);
```

cudaMemcpy always takes a destination pointer as the first argument, a source pointer as the second, the number of bytes to copy as the third argument, and a final parameter. The last parameter will indicate if we are copying from the host to the GPU with cudaMemcpyHostToDevice, from the GPU to the host with cudaMemcpyDeviceToHost, or between two arrays on the GPU with cudaMemcpyDeviceToDevice.

We will now allocate an array to hold the output of our matrix multiplication on the GPU with another invocation of `cudaMalloc`:

```
cudaMalloc((float **) &d_output, num_bytes);
```

Finally, we will have to have some memory set up on the host that will store the output of the GPU when we want to check the output of our kernel. Let's set up a regular C float pointer and allocate memory with `malloc` as we would normally:

```
float * h_output;
h_output = (float *) malloc(num_bytes);
```

Now, we are almost ready to launch our kernel. CUDA uses a data structure called `dim3` to indicate block and grid sizes for kernel launches; we will set these up as such, since we want a grid with a dimension of 2 x 2 and blocks that are also of a dimension of 2 x 2:

```
dim3 block(2,2,1);
dim3 grid(2,2,1);
```

We are now ready to launch our kernel; we use the triple-triangle brackets to indicate to the CUDA-C compiler the block and grid sizes that the kernel should be launched over:

```
matrix_mult_ker <<< grid, block >>> (d_A, d_B, d_output, N);
```

Now, of course, before we can copy the output of the kernel back to the host, we have to ensure that the kernel has finished executing. We do this by calling `cudaDeviceSynchronize`, which will block the host from issuing any more commands to the GPU until the kernel has finished execution:

```
cudaDeviceSynchronize();
```

We now can copy the output of our kernel to the array we've allocated on the host:

```
cudaMemcpy(h_output, d_output, num_bytes, cudaMemcpyDeviceToHost);
```

Again, we synchronize:

```
cudaDeviceSynchronize();
```

Before we check the output, we realize that we no longer need any of the arrays we allocated on the GPU. We free this memory by calling `cudaFree` on each array:

```
cudaFree(d_A);
cudaFree(d_B);
cudaFree(d_output);
```

We're done with the GPU, so we call `cudaDeviceReset`:

```
cudaDeviceReset();
```

Now, we finally check the output we copied onto the host with the `allclose` function we wrote at the beginning of this chapter. If the actual output doesn't match the expected output, we print an error and return −1, otherwise, we print that it does match and we return 0. We then put a closing bracket on our program's `main` function:

```
if (allclose(h_AxB, h_output, N*N) < 0)
{
    printf("Error! Output of kernel does not match expected output.\n");
    free(h_output);
    return(-1);
}
else
{
    printf("Success! Output of kernel matches expected output.\n");
    free(h_output);
    return(0);
}
}
```

Notice that we make one final invocation to the standard C free function since we have allocated memory to `h_output` , in both cases.

We now save our file, and compile it into a Windows or Linux executable file from the command line with `nvcc matrix_ker.cu -o matrix_ker`. This should output a binary executable file, `matrix_ker.exe` (in Windows) or `matrix_ker` (in Linux). Let's try compiling and running it right now:

```
PS C:\Users\btuom\examples\6> nvcc matrix_ker.cu -o matrix_ker
matrix_ker.cu
   Creating library matrix_ker.lib and object matrix_ker.exp
PS C:\Users\btuom\examples\6> .\matrix_ker.exe
Success!  Output of kernel matches expected output.
PS C:\Users\btuom\examples\6>
```

Congratulations, you've just created your first pure CUDA-C program! (This example is available as `matrix_ker.cu` in the repository, under 7.)

Using the Nsight IDE for CUDA-C development and debugging

Let's now learn how to use the Nsight IDE for developing CUDA-C programs. We will see how to import the program we just wrote, and compile and debug it from within Nsight. Note that there are differences between the Windows and Linux versions of Nsight, since it is effectively a plugin of the Visual Studio IDE under Windows and in the Eclipse IDE under Linux. We will cover both in the following two subsections; feel free to skip whatever operating system does not apply to you here.

Using Nsight with Visual Studio in Windows

Open up Visual Studio, and click on **File**, then choose **New | Project....** A window will pop up where you set the type of project: choose the **NVIDIA** drop-down item, and then choose **CUDA 9.2**:

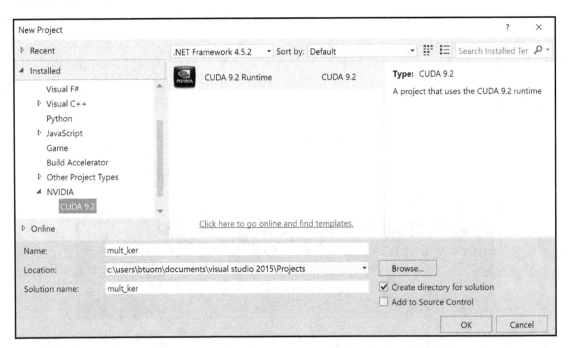

Give the project some appropriate name and then click **OK**. A project should appear in the solution explorer window with a simple premade CUDA test program, consisting of one source file, `kernel.cu`, which consists of a simple parallel add kernel with test code. If you want to see whether this compiles and runs, click the green right-pointing arrow at the top marked **Local Windows Debugger**. A Terminal should pop up with some text output from the kernel and then close immediately.

> If you have problems with a Windows Terminal-based application closing after you run it from Visual Studio, try adding `getchar()`; to the end of the main function, which will keep the Terminal open until you press a key. (Alternatively, you can also use a debugger breakpoint at the end of the program.)

Now, let's add the CUDA-C program we just wrote. In the **Solution Explorer** window, right-click `kernel.cu`, and click **Remove** on `kernel.cu`. Now, right-click on the project name, and choose **Add**, and then choose **Existing item**. We will now be able to select an existing file, so find where the path is to `matrix_ker.cu` and add it to the project. Click on the green arrow marked **Local Windows Debugger** at the top of the IDE and the program should compile and run, again in a Windows Terminal. So, that's it—we can set up and compile a complete CUDA program in Visual Studio now, just from those few steps.

Let's now see how to debug our CUDA kernel. Let's start by adding one breakpoint to our code at the entry point of the kernel `matrix_mult_ker`, where we set the value of `row` and `col`. We can add this breakpoint by clicking on the gray column left of the line numbers on the window; a red dot should appear there for every breakpoint we add. (You can ignore any red squiggly lines that the Visual Studio editor may place under your code; this is due to the fact that CUDA is not a *native* language to Visual Studio):

```
37
38      // matrix multiplication kernel that is parallelized over row/column tuples.
39      __global__ void matrix_mult_ker(float * matrix_a, float * matrix_b, float * output_matrix, int N)
40      {
41
42          int row = blockIdx.x*blockDim.x + threadIdx.x;
43          int col = blockIdx.y*blockDim.y + threadIdx.y;
44
45          output_matrix[col + row*N] = rowcol_dot(matrix_a, matrix_b, row, col, N);
46      }
47
```

We can now start debugging. From the top menu, choose the **Nsight** drop-down menu and choose **Start CUDA Debugging**. There may be two options here, **Start CUDA Debugging (Next-Gen)** and **Start CUDA Debugging (Legacy)**. It doesn't matter which one, but you may have issues with **Next-Gen** depending on your GPU; in that case, choose **Legacy**.

Your program should start up, and the debugger should halt at the breakpoint in our kernel that we just set. Let's press *F10* to step over the line, and now see if the `row` variable gets set correctly. Let's look at the **Locals** window in the **Variable Explorer**:

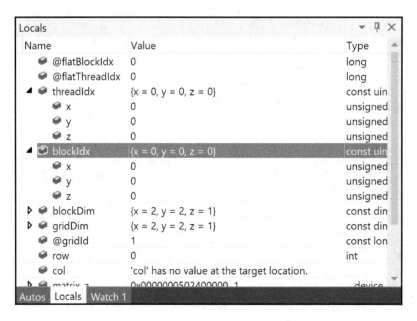

We can see that we are currently in the very first thread in the very first block in the grid by checking the values of `threadIdx` and `blockIdx`; `row` is set to `0`, which does indeed correspond to the correct value. Now, let's check the value of row for some different thread. To do this, we have to switch the **thread focus** in the IDE; we do this by clicking the **Nsight** drop-down menu above, then choosing **Windows|CUDA Debug Focus...**. A new menu should appear allowing you to choose a new thread and block. Change thread from **0, 0, 0** to **1, 0, 0** in the menu, and click **OK**:

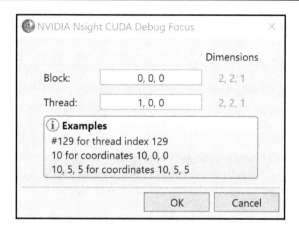

When you check the variables again, you should see the correct value is set for `row` for this thread:

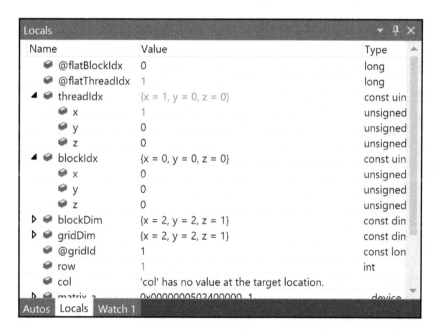

In a nutshell, that is how you debug with Nsight in Visual Studio. We now have the basics of how to debug a CUDA program from Nsight/Visual Studio in Windows, and we can use all of the regular conventions as we would for debugging a regular Windows program as with any other IDE (setting breakpoints, starting the debugger, continue/resume, step over, step in, and step out). Namely, the main difference is you have to know how to switch between CUDA threads and blocks to check variables, otherwise, it's pretty much the same.

Using Nsight with Eclipse in Linux

We will now see how to use Nsight in Linux. You can open Nsight from either your desktop by selecting it or you can run it from a command line with the `nsight` command. The Nsight IDE will open. From the top of the IDE, click on **File**, then choose **New...** from the drop-down menu, and from there choose **New CUDA C/C++ Project**. A new window will appear, and from here choose **CUDA Runtime Project**. Give the project some appropriate name, and then click **Next**. You'll be prompted to give further settings options, but the defaults will work fine for our purposes for now. (Be sure to note where the source folder and project paths will be located in the third and fourth screens here.) You'll get to a final screen, where you can press **Finish** to create the project:

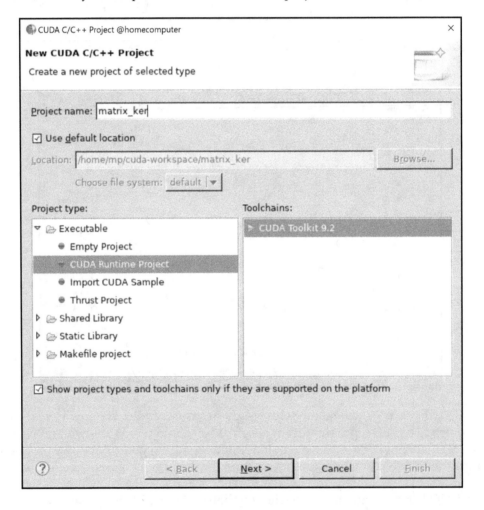

Finally, you'll end up at a project view with your new project and some placeholder code open; as of CUDA 9.2, this will consist of a reciprocal kernel example.

We can now import our code. Either you can just use the editor in Nsight to delete all of the code in the default source file and cut and paste it in, or you can manually delete the file from the project's source directory, manually copy the `matrix_ker.cu` file into the source directory, and then choose to refresh the source directory view in Nsight by selecting it and then pressing *F5*. You can now build the project with *Ctrl + B*, and run it with *F11*. The output of our program should appear within the IDE itself within the **Console** subwindow, as follows:

We can now set a breakpoint within our CUDA code; let's set it at the entry point of our kernel where the **row** value is set. We set the cursor onto that row in the Eclipse editor, and then press *Ctrl + Shift + B* to set it.

We can now begin debugging by pressing *F11* (or clicking the **bug** icon). The program should be paused at the very beginning of the `main` function, so press *F8* to *resume* to the first breakpoint. You should see the first line in our CUDA kernel highlighted with an arrow pointing to it in the IDE; let's step over the current line by pressing *F6*, which will ensure that the **row** has been set.

Now, we can easily switch between different threads and blocks in our CUDA grid to check the current values that they hold as follows: from the top of the IDE, click on the **Window** drop-down menu, then click **Show view**, and then choose **CUDA**. A window with the currently running kernel should open, and from here you can see a list of all of the blocks that this kernel is running over.

Click on the first one and from here you will be able to see all of the individual threads that are running within the block:

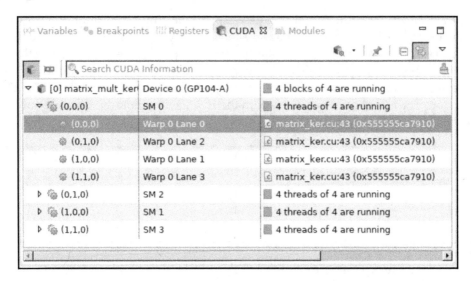

Now, we can look at the variable corresponding to the very first thread in the very first block by clicking on the **Variables** tab—here, **row** should be **0**, as expected:

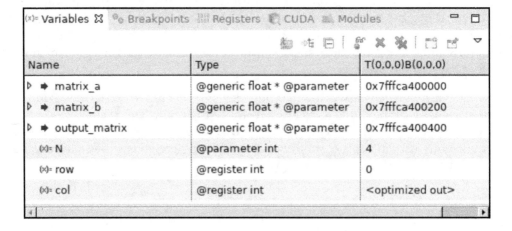

Now, we can check the values for a different thread by again going to the **CUDA** tab, choosing the appropriate thread, and switching back. Let's stay in the same block, but choose thread **(1, 0, 0)** this time, and check the value of **row** again:

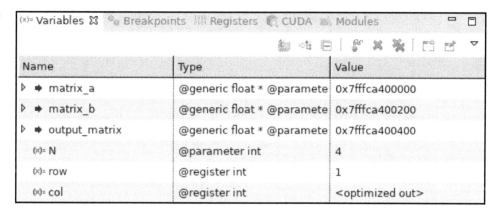

We see that the value of **row** is now **1**, as we expect.

We now have the basics of how to debug a CUDA program from Nsight/Eclipse in Linux, and we can use all of the regular conventions as you would for debugging a regular Linux program as with any other IDE (setting breakpoints, starting the debugger, continue/resume, step over, step in, and step out). Namely, the main difference here is we have to know how to switch between CUDA threads and blocks to check variables, otherwise, it's pretty much the same.

Using Nsight to understand the warp lockstep property in CUDA

We will now use Nsight to step through some code to help us better understand some of the CUDA GPU architecture, and how **branching** within a kernel is handled. This will give us some insight about how to write more efficient CUDA kernels. By branching, we mean how the GPU handles control flow statements such as `if`, `else`, or `switch` within a CUDA kernel. In particular, we are interested in how **branch divergence** is handled within a kernel, which is what happens when one thread in a kernel satisfies the conditions to be an `if` statement, while another doesn't and is an `else` statement: they are divergent because they are executing different pieces of code.

Let's write a small CUDA-C program as an experiment: we will start with a small kernel that prints one output if its `threadIdx.x` value is even and another if it is odd. We then write a `main` function that will launch this kernel over one single block consisting of 32 different threads:

```
#include <cuda_runtime.h>
#include <stdio.h>

__global__ void divergence_test_ker()
{
    if( threadIdx.x % 2 == 0)
        printf("threadIdx.x %d : This is an even thread.\n", threadIdx.x);
    else
        printf("threadIdx.x %d : This is an odd thread.\n", threadIdx.x);
}

__host__ int main()
{
    cudaSetDevice(0);
    divergence_test_ker<<<1, 32>>>();
    cudaDeviceSynchronize();
    cudaDeviceReset();
}
```

(This code is also available as `divergence_test.cu` in the repository.)

If we compile and run this from the command line, we might naively expect there to be an interleaved sequence of strings from even and odd threads; or maybe they will be randomly interleaved—since all of the threads run concurrently and branch about the same time, this would make sense.

Instead, every single time we run this, we always get this output:

```
PS C:\Users\btuom\examples\6> .\divergence_test.exe
threadIdx.x 0 : This is an even thread.
threadIdx.x 2 : This is an even thread.
threadIdx.x 4 : This is an even thread.
threadIdx.x 6 : This is an even thread.
threadIdx.x 8 : This is an even thread.
threadIdx.x 10 : This is an even thread.
threadIdx.x 12 : This is an even thread.
threadIdx.x 14 : This is an even thread.
threadIdx.x 16 : This is an even thread.
threadIdx.x 18 : This is an even thread.
threadIdx.x 20 : This is an even thread.
threadIdx.x 22 : This is an even thread.
threadIdx.x 24 : This is an even thread.
threadIdx.x 26 : This is an even thread.
threadIdx.x 28 : This is an even thread.
threadIdx.x 30 : This is an even thread.
threadIdx.x 1 : This is an odd thread.
threadIdx.x 3 : This is an odd thread.
threadIdx.x 5 : This is an odd thread.
threadIdx.x 7 : This is an odd thread.
threadIdx.x 9 : This is an odd thread.
threadIdx.x 11 : This is an odd thread.
threadIdx.x 13 : This is an odd thread.
threadIdx.x 15 : This is an odd thread.
threadIdx.x 17 : This is an odd thread.
threadIdx.x 19 : This is an odd thread.
threadIdx.x 21 : This is an odd thread.
threadIdx.x 23 : This is an odd thread.
threadIdx.x 25 : This is an odd thread.
threadIdx.x 27 : This is an odd thread.
threadIdx.x 29 : This is an odd thread.
threadIdx.x 31 : This is an odd thread.
PS C:\Users\btuom\examples\6>
```

All of the strings corresponding to even threads are printed first, while all of the odd strings are printed second. Perhaps the Nsight debugger can shed some light on this; let's import this little program into an Nsight project as we did in the last section, putting a breakpoint at the first if statement in our kernel. We will then do a *step over*, so that the debugger stops where the first printf statement is. Since the default thread in Nsight is **(0,0,0)**, this should have satisfied the first if statement so it will be stuck there until the debugger continues.

Let's switch over to an odd thread, say **(1,0,0)**, and see where it is in our program now:

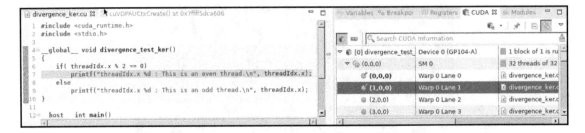

Very strange! Thread **(1,0,0)** is also at the same place in execution as thread **(0,0,0)**. Indeed, if we check every single other odd thread here, it will be stuck in the same place—at a `printf` statement that all of the odd threads should have skipped right past.

What gives? This is known as the **warp lockstep property**. A **warp** in the CUDA architecture is a unit of 32 "lanes" within which our GPU executes kernels and grids over, where each lane will execute a single thread. A major limitation of warps is that all threads executing on a single warp must step through the same exact code in **lockstep**; this means that not every thread does indeed run the same code, but just ignores steps that are not applicable to it. (This is called lockstep because it's like a group of soldiers marching *lockstep* in unison—whether they want to march, or not!)

The lockstep property implies that if one single thread running on a warp diverges from all 31 other threads in a single `if` statement, all 31 other threads have their execution delayed until this single anomalous thread finishes and returns from its solitary `if` divergence. This is a property that you should always keep in mind when writing kernels, and why branch divergence should be minimized as much as possible as a general rule in CUDA programming.

Using the NVIDIA nvprof profiler and Visual Profiler

We will end with a brief overview of the command-line Nvidia `nvprof` profiler. In contrast to the Nsight IDE, we can freely use any Python code that we have written—we won't be compelled here to write full-on, pure CUDA-C test function code.

We can do a basic profiling of a binary executable program with the `nvprof program` command; we can likewise profile a Python script by using the `python` command as the first argument, and the script as the second as follows: `nvprof python program.py`. Let's profile the simple matrix-multiplication CUDA-C executable program that we wrote earlier, with `nvprof matrix_ker`:

```
          Type  Time(%)      Time     Calls       Avg       Min       Max  Name
GPU activities:   42.94%   2.3360us         2   1.1680us     896ns   1.4400us  [CUDA memcpy HtoD]
                  41.18%   2.2400us         1   2.2400us   2.2400us   2.2400us  matrix_mult_ker(float*, float*, float*, int)
                  15.88%     864ns         1     864ns     864ns     864ns  [CUDA memcpy DtoH]
    API calls:    72.42%   139.27ms         3   46.422ms   7.7580us   139.25ms  cudaMalloc
                  25.66%   49.351ms         1   49.351ms   49.351ms   49.351ms  cudaDeviceReset
                   1.46%   2.8053ms        88   31.878us     484ns   1.5375ms  cuDeviceGetAttribute
                   0.15%   290.91us         3   96.969us   14.060us   260.85us  cudaFree
                   0.14%   266.18us         3   88.727us   73.212us   111.52us  cudaMemcpy
                   0.06%   119.27us         1   119.27us   119.27us   119.27us  cuDeviceGetName
                   0.05%   101.33us         2   50.666us   11.152us   90.181us  cudaDeviceSynchronize
                   0.02%   38.787us         1   38.787us   38.787us   38.787us  cuDeviceTotalMem
                   0.02%   29.576us         1   29.576us   29.576us   29.576us  cudaLaunchKernel
                   0.01%   21.818us         1   21.818us   21.818us   21.818us  cudaSetDevice
                   0.00%   8.7280us         3   2.9090us     485ns   7.2730us  cuDeviceGetCount
                   0.00%   8.7270us         1   8.7270us   8.7270us   8.7270us  cuDeviceGetPCIBusId
                   0.00%   3.3940us         2   1.6970us     485ns   2.9090us  cuDeviceGet
```

We see that this is very similar to the output of the Python cProfiler module that we first used to analyze a Mandelbrot algorithm way back in Chapter 1, *Why GPU Programming?*—only now, this exclusively tells us only about all of the CUDA operations that were executed. So, we can use this when we specifically want to optimize on the GPU, rather than concern ourselves with any of the Python or other commands that executed on the host. (We can further analyze each individual CUDA kernel operation with block and grid size launch parameters if we add the command-line option, `--print-gpu-trace`.)

Let's look at one more trick to help us *visualize* the execution time of all of the operations of a program; we will use `nvprof` to dump a file that can then be read by the NVIDIA Visual Profiler, which will show this to us graphically. Let's do this using an example from the last chapter, `multi-kernel_streams.py` (this is available in the repository under 5). Let's recall that this was one of our introductory examples to the idea of CUDA streams, which allow us to execute and organize multiple GPU operations concurrently. Let's dump the output to a file with the `.nvvp` file suffix with the `-o` command-line option as follows: `nvprof -o m.nvvp python multi-kernel_streams.py`. We can now load this file into the NVIDIA Visual Profiler with the `nvvp m.nvvp` command.

We should see a timeline across all CUDA streams as such (remembering that the name of the kernel used in this program is called `mult_ker`):

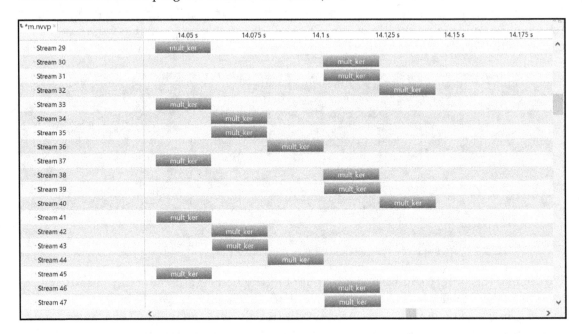

Not only can we see all kernel launches, but also memory allocations, memory copies, and other operations. This can be useful for getting an intuitive and visual understanding of how your program is using your GPU over time.

Summary

We started out in this chapter by seeing how `printf` can be used within a CUDA kernel to output data from individual threads; we saw in particular how useful this can be for debugging code. We then covered some of the gaps in our knowledge in CUDA-C, so that we can write full test programs that we can compile into proper executable binary files: there is a lot of overhead here that was hidden from us before that we have to be meticulous about. Next, we saw how to create and compile a project in the Nsight IDE and how to use it for debugging. We saw how to stop at any breakpoint we set in a CUDA kernel and switch between individual threads to see the different local variables. We also used the Nsight debugger to learn about the warp lockstep property and why it is important to avoid branch divergence in CUDA kernels. Finally, we had a very brief overview of the NVIDIA command-line `nvprof` profiler and Visual Profiler for analyzing our GPU code.

Questions

1. In the first CUDA-C program that we wrote, we didn't use a `cudaDeviceSynchronize` command after the calls we made to allocate memory arrays on the GPU with `cudaMalloc`. Why was this not necessary? (Hint: Review the last chapter.)

2. Suppose we have a single kernel that is launched over a grid consisting of two blocks, where each block has 32 threads. Suppose all of the threads in the first block execute an `if` statement, while all of the threads in the second block execute the corresponding `else` statement. Will all of the threads in the second block have to "lockstep" through the commands in the `if` statement as the threads in the first block are actually executing them?

3. What if we executed a similar piece of code, only over a grid consisting of one single block executed over 64 threads, where the first 32 threads execute an `if` and the second 32 execute an `else` statement?

4. What can the `nvprof` profiler measure for us that Python's cProfiler cannot?

5. Name some contexts where we might prefer to use `printf` to debug a CUDA kernel and other contexts where it might be easier to use Nsight to debug a CUDA kernel.

6. What is the purpose of the `cudaSetDevice` command in CUDA-C?

7. Why do we have to use `cudaDeviceSynchronize` after every kernel launch or memory copy in CUDA-C?

7
Using the CUDA Libraries with Scikit-CUDA

In this chapter, we will be taking a tour of three of the standard CUDA libraries intended for streamlined numerical and scientific computation. The first that we will look at is **cuBLAS**, which is NVIDIA's implementation of the **Basic Linear Algebra Subprograms** (**BLAS**) specification for CUDA. (cuBLAS is NVIDIA's answer to various optimized, CPU-based implementations of BLAS, such as the free/open source OpenBLAS or Intel's proprietary Math Kernel Library.) The next library that we will look at is **cuFFT**, which can perform virtually every variation of the **fast Fourier transform** (**FFT**) on the GPU. We'll look at how we can use cuFFT for filtering in image processing in particular. We will then look at **cuSolver**, which can perform more involved linear algebra operations than those featured in cuBLAS, such as **singular value decomposition** (**SVD**) or Cholesky factorization.

So far, we have been primarily dealing with one single Python module that acted as our gateway to CUDA—PyCUDA. While PyCUDA is a very powerful and versatile Python library, its main purpose is to provide a gateway to program, compile, and launch CUDA kernels, rather than provide an interface to the CUDA libraries. To this end, fortunately, there is a free Python module available that provides a user-friendly wrapper interface to these libraries. This is called Scikit-CUDA.

While you don't have to know PyCUDA or even understand GPU programming to appreciate Scikit-CUDA, it is conveniently compatible with PyCUDA; Scikit-CUDA, for instance, can operate easily with PyCUDA's `gpuarray` class, and this allows you to easily pass data between our own CUDA kernel routines and Scikit-CUDA. Additionally, most routines will also work with PyCUDA's stream class, which will allow us to properly synchronize our own custom CUDA kernels with Scikit-CUDA's wrappers.

Please note that, besides these three listed libraries, Scikit-CUDA also provides wrappers for the proprietary CULA library, as well as for the open source MAGMA library. Both have a lot of overlap with the functionality provided by the official NVIDIA libraries. Since these libraries are not installed by default with a standard CUDA installation, we will opt to not cover them in this chapter. Interested readers can learn more about CULA and MAGMA at `http://www.culatools.com` and `http://icl.utk.edu/magma/`, respectively.

 It is suggested that readers take a look at the official documentation for Scikit-CUDA, which is available here: `https://media.readthedocs.org/pdf/scikit-cuda/latest/scikit-cuda.pdf`.

The learning outcomes for this chapter are as follows:

- To learn how to install Scikit-CUDA
- To understand the basic purposes and differences between the standard CUDA libraries
- To learn how to use low-level cuBLAS functions for basic linear algebra
- To learn how to use the SGEMM and DGEMM operations to measure the performance of a GPU in FLOPS
- To learn how to use cuFFT to perform 1D or 2D FFT operations on the GPU
- To learn how to create a 2D convolutional filter using the FFT, and apply it to simple image processing
- To understand how to perform a Singular Value Decomposition (SVD) with cuSolver
- To learn how to use cuSolver's SVD algorithm to perform basic principal component analysis

Technical requirements

A Linux or Windows 10 PC with a modern NVIDIA GPU (2016—onward) is required for this chapter, with all of the necessary GPU drivers and the CUDA Toolkit (9.0–onward) installed. A suitable Python 2.7 installation (such as Anaconda Python 2.7) that includes the PyCUDA module is also required.

This chapter's code is also available on GitHub, and can be found at `https://github.com/PacktPublishing/Hands-On-GPU-Programming-with-Python-and-CUDA`.

For more information about the prerequisites, check out the preface of this book. For more information about the software and hardware requirements, check out the README file at `https://github.com/PacktPublishing/Hands-On-GPU-Programming-with-Python-and-CUDA`.

Installing Scikit-CUDA

It is suggested that you install the latest stable version of Scikit-CUDA directly from GitHub: `https://github.com/lebedov/scikit-cuda`.

Unzip the package into a directory, and then open up the command line here and install the module by typing `python setup.py install` into the command line. You may then run the unit tests to ensure that a correct installation has been performed with `python setup.py test`. (This method is suggested for both Windows and Linux users.) Alternatively, Scikit-CUDA can be installed directly from the PyPI repository with `pip install scikit-cuda`.

Basic linear algebra with cuBLAS

We will start this chapter by learning how to use Scikit-CUDA's cuBLAS wrappers. Let's spend a moment discussing BLAS. BLAS (Basic Linear Algebra Subroutines) is a specification for a basic linear algebra library that was first standardized in the 1970s. BLAS functions are broken down into several categories, which are referred to as *levels*.

Level 1 BLAS functions consist of operations purely on vectors—vector-vector addition and scaling (also known as $ax+y$ operations, or AXPY), dot products, and norms. Level 2 BLAS functions consist of general matrix-vector operations (GEMV), such as matrix multiplication of a vector, while level 3 BLAS functions consist of "general matrix-matrix" (GEMM) operations, such as matrix-matrix multiplication. Originally, these libraries were written entirely in FORTRAN in the 1970s, so you should take into account that there are some seemingly archaic holdovers in usage and naming that may seem cumbersome to new users today.

cuBLAS is NVIDIA's own implementation of the BLAS specification, which is of course optimized to make full use of the GPU's parallelism. Scikit-CUDA provides wrappers for cuBLAS that are compatible with PyCUDA `gpuarray` objects, as well as with PyCUDA streams. This means that we can couple and interface these functions with our own custom CUDA-C kernels by way of PyCUDA, as well as synchronize these operations over multiple streams.

Level-1 AXPY with cuBLAS

Let's start with a basic level-1 $ax + y$ (or AXPY) operation with cuBLAS. Let's stop for a moment and review a bit of linear algebra and think about what this means. Here, a is considered to be a scalar; that is, a real number, such as -10, 0, 1.345, or 100. x and y are considered to be vectors in some vector space, $\mathbb{R}^n$. This means that x and y are n-tuples of real numbers, so in the case of $\mathbb{R}^3$, these could be values such as [1,2,3] or [-0.345, 8.15, -15.867]. ax means the scaling of x by a, so if a is 10 and x is the first prior value, then ax is each individual value of x multiplied by a; that is, [10, 20, 30]. Finally, the sum $ax + y$ means that we add each individual value in each slot of both vectors to produce a new vector, which would be as follows (assuming that y is the second vector given)—[9.655, 28.15, 14.133].

Let's do this in cuBLAS now. First, let's import the appropriate modules:

```
import pycuda.autoinit
from pycuda import gpuarray
import numpy as np
```

Now let's import cuBLAS:

```
from skcuda import cublas
```

We can now set up our vector arrays and copy them to the GPU. Note that we are using 32-bit (single precision) floating point numbers:

```
a = np.float32(10)
x = np.float32([1,2,3])
y = np.float32([-.345,8.15,-15.867])
x_gpu = gpuarray.to_gpu(x)
y_gpu = gpuarray.to_gpu(y)
```

We now have to create a **cuBLAS context**. This is similar in nature to CUDA contexts, which we discussed in Chapter 5, *Streams, Events, Contexts, and Concurrency*, only this time it is used explicitly for managing cuBLAS sessions. The `cublasCreate` function creates a cuBLAS context and gives a handle to it as its output. We will need to hold onto this handle for as long as we intend to use cuBLAS in this session:

```
cublas_context_h = cublas.cublasCreate()
```

We can now use the `cublasSaxpy` function. The S stands for single precision, which is what we will need since we are working with 32-bit floating point arrays:

```
cublas.cublasSaxpy(cublas_context_h, x_gpu.size, a, x_gpu.gpudata, 1,
y_gpu.gpudata, 1)
```

Let's discuss what we just did. Also, let's keep in mind that this is a direct wrapper to a low-level C function, so the input may seem more like a C function than a true Python function. In short, this performed an "AXPY" operation, ultimately putting the output data into the `y_gpu` array. Let's go through each input parameter one by one.

The first input is always the CUDA context handle. We then have to specify the size of the vectors, since this function will be ultimately operating on C pointers; we can do this by using the `size` parameter of a gpuarray. Having typecasted our scalar already to a NumPy `float32` variable, we can pass the `a` variable right over as the scalar parameter. We then hand the underlying C pointer of the `x_gpu` array to this function using the `gpudata` parameter. Then we specify the **stride** of the first array as 1: the stride specifies how many steps we should take between each input value. (In contrast, if you were using a vector from a column in a row-wise matrix, you would set the stride to the width of the matrix.) We then put in the pointer to the `y_gpu` array, and set its stride to 1 as well.

We are done with our computation; now we have to explicitly destroy our cuBLAS context:

```
cublas.cublasDestroy(cublas_context)
```

We can now verify whether this is close with NumPy's `allclose` function, like so:

```
print 'This is close to the NumPy approximation: %s' % np.allclose(a*x + y
, y_gpu.get())
```

Again, notice that the final output was put into the `y_gpu` array, which was also an input.

> Always remember that BLAS and CuBLAS functions act in-place to save time and memory from a new allocation call. This means that an input array will also be used as an output!

We just saw how to perform an `AXPY` operation using the `cublasSaxpy` function.

Let's discuss the prominent upper case S. Like we mentioned previously, this stands for single precision that is, 32-bit real floating point values (`float32`). If we want to operate on arrays of 64-bit real floating point values, (`float64` in NumPy and PyCUDA), then we would use the `cublasDaxpy` function; for 64-bit single precision complex values (`complex64`), we would use `cublasCaxpy`, while for 128-bit double precision complex values (`complex128`), we would use `cublasZaxpy`.

We can tell what type of data a BLAS or CuBLAS function operates on by checking the letter preceding the rest of the function name. Functions that use single precision reals are always preceded with S, double precision reals with D, single precision complex with C, and double precision complex with Z.

Other level-1 cuBLAS functions

Let's look at a few other level-1 functions. We won't go over their operation in depth, but the steps are similar to the ones we just covered: create a cuBLAS context, call the function with the appropriate array pointers (which is accessed with the `gpudata` parameter from a PyCUDA `gpuarray`), and set the strides accordingly. Another thing to keep in mind is that if the output of a function is a single value as opposed to an array (for example, a dot product function), the function will directly output this value to the host rather than within an array of memory that has to be pulled off the GPU. (We will only cover the single precision real versions here, but the corresponding versions for other datatypes can be used by replacing the S with the appropriate letter.)

We can perform a dot product between two single precision real `gpuarrays`, `v_gpu`, and `w_gpu`. Again, the 1s are there to ensure that we are using stride-1 in this calculation! Again, recall that a dot product is the sum of the point-wise multiple of two vectors:

```
dot_output = cublas.cublasSdot(cublas_context_h, v_gpu.size, v_gpu.gpudata,
1, w_gpu.gpudata, 1)
```

We can also perform the L2-norm of a vector like so (recall that for a vector, x, this is its L2-norm, or length, which is calculated with the $(|x_1|^2 + |x_2|^2 + \cdots + |x_n|^2)^{1/2}$ formula):

```
l2_output = cublas.cublasSnrm2(cublas_context_h, v_gpu.size, v_gpu.gpudata,
1)
```

Level-2 GEMV in cuBLAS

Let's look at how to do a GEMV matrix-vector multiplication. This is defined as the following operation for an m x n matrix A, an n-dimensional vector x, a m-dimensional vector y, and for the scalars *alpha* and *beta*:

$$y \leftarrow \alpha Ax + \beta y$$

Now let's look at how the function is laid out before we continue:

```
cublasSgemv(handle, trans, m, n, alpha, A, lda, x, incx, beta, y, incy)
```

Let's go through these inputs one-by-one:

- `handle` refers to the cuBLAS context handle.
- `trans` refers to the structure of the matrix—we can specify whether we want to use the original matrix, a direct transpose, or a conjugate transpose (for complex matrices). This is important to keep in mind because this function will expect that the matrix A is stored in **column-major** format.
- `m` and `n` are the number of rows and columns of the matrix A that we want to use.
- `alpha` is the floating-point value for α.
- A is the *m x n* matrix *A*.
- `lda` indicates the leading dimension of the matrix, where the total size of the matrix is actually `lda` x n. This is important in the column-major format because if `lda` is larger than m, this can cause problems for cuBLAS when it tries to access the values of A since its underlying structure of this matrix is a one-dimensional array.
- We then have x and its stride, `incx`; x is the underlying C pointer of the vector being multiplied by A. Remember, x will have to be of size n; that is, the number of columns of A.
- `beta`, which is the floating-point value for β.
- Finally, we have y and its stride `incy` as the last parameters. We should remember that y should be of size m, or the number of rows of A.

Let's test this by generating a 10 x 100 matrix of random values A, and a vector x of 100 random values. We'll initialize y as a matrix of 10 zeros. We will set alpha to 1 and beta to 0, just to get a direct matrix multiplication with no scaling:

```
m = 10
n = 100
alpha = 1
beta = 0
A = np.random.rand(m,n).astype('float32')
x = np.random.rand(n).astype('float32')
y = np.zeros(m).astype('float32')
```

We will now have to get A into **column-major** (or column-wise) format. NumPy stores matrices as **row-major** (or row-wise) by default, meaning that the underlying one-dimensional array that is used to store a matrix iterates through all of the values of the first row, then all of the values of the second row, and so on. You should remember that a transpose operation swaps the columns of a matrix with its rows. However, the result will be that the new one-dimensional array underlying the transposed matrix will represent the original matrix in a column-major format. We can make a copy of the transposed matrix of A with A.T.copy() like so, and copy this as well as x and y to the GPU:

```
A_columnwise = A.T.copy()
A_gpu = gpuarray.to_gpu(A_columnwise)
x_gpu = gpuarray.to_gpu(x)
y_gpu = gpuarray.to_gpu(y)
```

Since we now have the column-wise matrix stored properly on the GPU, we can set the trans variable to not take the transpose by using the _CUBLAS_OP dictionary:

```
trans = cublas._CUBLAS_OP['N']
```

Since the size of the matrix is exactly the same as the number of rows that we want to use, we now set lda as m. The strides for the *x* and *y* vectors are, again, 1. We now have all of the values we need set up, and can now create our CuBLAS context and store its handle, like so:

```
lda = m
incx = 1
incy = 1
handle = cublas.cublasCreate()
```

We can now launch our function. Remember that A, x, and y are actually PyCUDA gpuarray objects, so we have to use the gpudata parameter to input into this function. Other than doing this, this is pretty straightforward:

```
cublas.cublasSgemv(handle, trans, m, n, alpha, A_gpu.gpudata, lda,
x_gpu.gpudata, incx, beta, y_gpu.gpudata, incy)
```

We can now destroy our cuBLAS context and check the return value to ensure that it is correct:

```
cublas.cublasDestroy(handle)
print 'cuBLAS returned the correct value: %s' % np.allclose(np.dot(A,x),
y_gpu.get())
```

Level-3 GEMM in cuBLAS for measuring GPU performance

We will now look at how to perform a **general matrix-matrix multiplication** (**GEMM**) with CuBLAS. We will actually try to make something a little more utilitarian than the last few examples we saw in cuBLAS—we will use this as a performance metric for our GPU to determine the number of **Floating Point Operations Per Second** (**FLOPS**) it can perform, which will be two separate values: the case of single precision, and that of double precision. Using GEMM is a standard technique for evaluating the performance of computing hardware in FLOPS, as it gives a much better understanding of sheer computational power than using pure clock speed in MHz or GHz.

 If you need a brief review, recall that we covered matrix-matrix multiplication in depth in the last chapter. If you forgot how this works, it's strongly suggested that you review this chapter before you move on to this section.

First, let's see how a GEMM operation is defined:

$$C \leftarrow \alpha AB + \beta C$$

This means that we perform a matrix multiplication of *A* and *B*, scale the result by *alpha*, and then add this to the *C* matrix that we have scaled by *beta*, placing the final result in *C*.

Let's think about how many floating point operations are executed to get the final result of a real-valued GEMM operation, assuming that *A* is an *m* x *k* (where *m* is rows and *k* is columns) matrix, *B* is a *k* x *n* matrix, and *C* is an *m* x *n* matrix. First, let's figure out how many operations are required for computing *AB*. Let's take a single column of *A* and multiply it by *B*: this will amount to *k* multiplies and *k* - 1 adds for each of the *m* rows in *A*, which means that this is *km + (k-1)m* total operations over *m* rows. There are *n* columns in *B*, so computing *AB* will total to *kmn + (k-1)mn = 2kmn - mn* operations. Now, we use *alpha* to scale *AB*, which will be *mn* operations, since that is the size of the matrix *AB*; similarly, scaling *C* by *beta* is another *mn* operation. Finally, we add these two resulting matrices, which is yet another *mn* operation. This means that we will have a total of *2kmn - mn + 3mn* = *2kmn + 2mn = 2mn(k+1)* floating point operations in a given GEMM operation.

Now the only thing we have to do is run a timed GEMM operation, taking note of the different sizes of the matrices, and divide *2kmn + 2mn* by the total time duration to calculate the FLOPS of our GPU. The resulting number will be very large, so we will represent this in terms of GFLOPS – that is, how many billions (10^9) of operations that can be computed per second. We can compute this by multiplying the FLOPS value by 10^{-9}.

Now we are ready to start coding this up. Let's start with our import statements, as well as the `time` function:

```
import pycuda.autoinit
from pycuda import gpuarray
import numpy as np
from skcuda import cublas
from time import time
```

Now we will set the `m`, `n`, and `k` variables for our matrix sizes. We want our matrices to be relatively big so that the time duration is sufficiently large so as to avoid divide by 0 errors. The following values should be sufficient for any GPU released up to mid-2018 or earlier; users with newer cards may consider increasing these values:

```
m = 5000
n = 10000
k = 10000
```

We will now write a function that computes the GFLOPS for both single and double precision. We will set the input value to `'D'` if we wish to use double precision, or `'S'` otherwise:

```
def compute_gflops(precision='S'):

if precision=='S':
    float_type = 'float32'
elif precision=='D':
    float_type = 'float64'
else:
    return -1
```

Now let's generate some random matrices that are of the appropriate precision that we will use for timing. The GEMM operations act similarly to the GEMV operation we saw before, so we will have to transpose these before we copy them to the GPU. (Since we are just doing timing, this step isn't necessary, but it's good practice to remember this.)

We will set up some other necessary variables for GEMM, whose purpose should be self-explanatory at this point (`transa`, `lda`, `ldb`, and so on):

```
A = np.random.randn(m, k).astype(float_type)
B = np.random.randn(k, n).astype(float_type)
C = np.random.randn(m, n).astype(float_type)
A_cm = A.T.copy()
B_cm = B.T.copy()
C_cm = C.T.copy()
A_gpu = gpuarray.to_gpu(A_cm)
B_gpu = gpuarray.to_gpu(B_cm)
```

```
C_gpu = gpuarray.to_gpu(C_cm)
alpha = np.random.randn()
beta = np.random.randn()
transa = cublas._CUBLAS_OP['N']
transb = cublas._CUBLAS_OP['N']
lda = m
ldb = k
ldc = m
```

We can now start the timer! First, we will create a cuBLAS context:

```
t = time()
handle = cublas.cublasCreate()
```

We will now launch GEMM. Keep in mind that there are two versions for the real case: `cublasSgemm` for single precision and `cublasDgemm` for double precision. We can execute the appropriate function using a little Python trick: we will write a string with `cublas%sgemm` with the appropriate parameters, and then replace the `%s` with D or S by appending `% precision` to the string. We will then execute this string as Python code with the `exec` function, like so:

```
exec('cublas.cublas%sgemm(handle, transa, transb, m, n, k, alpha,
A_gpu.gpudata, lda, B_gpu.gpudata, ldb, beta, C_gpu.gpudata, ldc)' %
precision)
```

We can now destroy the cuBLAS context and get the final time for our computation:

```
cublas.cublasDestroy(handle)
t = time() - t
```

Then we need to compute the GFLOPS using the equation we derived and return it as the output of this function:

```
gflops = 2*m*n*(k+1)*(10**-9) / t
return gflops
```

Now we can set up our main function. We will output the GFLOPS in both the single and double precision cases:

```
if __name__ == '__main__':
    print 'Single-precision performance: %s GFLOPS' % compute_gflops('S')
    print 'Double-precision performance: %s GFLOPS' % compute_gflops('D')
```

Now let's do a little homework before we run this program—go to `https://www.` `techpowerup.com` and search for your GPU, and then take note of two things—the single precision floating point performance and the double precision floating point performance. I am using a GTX 1050 right now, and it's listing claims that it has 1,862 GFLOPS performance in single precision, and 58.20 GFLOPS performance in double precision. Let's run this program right now and see if this aligns with the truth:

```
In [3]: run cublas_gemm_flops.py
Single-precision performance: 1748.4264918 GFLOPS
Double-precision performance: 61.7956005349 GFLOPS
```

Lo and behold, it does!

> This program is also available as the `cublas_gemm_flops.py` file under the directory in this book's repository.

Fast Fourier transforms with cuFFT

Now let's look at how we can do some basic **fast Fourier transforms** (**FFT**) with cuFFT. First, let's briefly review what exactly a Fourier transform is. If you have taken an advanced Calculus or Analysis class, you might have seen the Fourier transform defined as an integral formula, like so:

$$\hat{f}(\xi) = \int_{-\infty}^{\infty} f(x)e^{-2\pi i x \xi} dx$$

What this does is take f as a time domain function over x. This gives us a corresponding frequency domain function over "ξ". This turns out to be an incredibly useful tool that touches virtually all branches of science and engineering.

Let's remember that the integral can be thought of as a sum; likewise, there is a corresponding discrete, finite version of the Fourier Transform called the **discrete Fourier transform (DFT)**. This operates on vectors of a finite length and allows them to be analyzed or modified in the frequency domain. The DFT of an n-dimensional vector x is defined as follows:

$$\hat{x}[k] = \sum_{n=0}^{N-1} x[n] \cdot e^{-\frac{2\pi i}{N}kn}$$

In other words, we can multiply a vector, x, by the complex N x N matrix $\left[e^{-\frac{2\pi i}{N}kn}\right]_{k,n=0}^{N-1}$ (here, k corresponds to row number, while n corresponds to column number) to find its DFT. We should also note the inverse formula that lets us retrieve x from its DFT (replace y with the DFT of x here, and the output will be the original x):

$$\check{y}[n] = \frac{1}{N} \sum_{k=0}^{N-1} y[k] \cdot e^{\frac{2\pi i}{N}kn}$$

Normally, computing a matrix-vector operation is of computational complexity $O(N^2)$ for a vector of length N. However, due to symmetries in the DFT matrix, this can always be reduced to $O(N \log N)$ by using an FFT. Let's look at how we can use an FFT with CuBLAS, and then we will move on to a more interesting example.

A simple 1D FFT

Let's start by looking at how we can use cuBLAS to compute a simple 1D FFT. First, we will briefly discuss the cuFFT interface in Scikit-CUDA.

There are two submodules here that we can access the cuFFT library with, `cufft` and `fft`. `cufft` consists of a collection of low-level wrappers for the cuFFT library, while `fft` provides a more user-friendly interface; we will be working solely with `fft` in this chapter.

Let's start with the appropriate imports, remembering to include the Scikit-CUDA `fft` submodule:

```
import pycuda.autoinit
from pycuda import gpuarray
import numpy as np
from skcuda import fft
```

We now will set up some random array and copy it to the GPU. We will also set up an empty GPU array that will be used to store the FFT (notice that we are using a real float32 array as an input, but the output will be a complex64 array, since the Fourier transform is always complex-valued):

```
x = np.asarray(np.random.rand(1000), dtype=np.float32 )
x_gpu = gpuarray.to_gpu(x)
x_hat = gpuarray.empty_like(x_gpu, dtype=np.complex64)
```

We will now set up a cuFFT plan for the forward FFT transform. This is an object that cuFFT uses to determine the shape, as well as the input and output data types of the transform:

```
plan = fft.Plan(x_gpu.shape,np.float32,np.complex64)
```

We will also set up a plan for the inverse FFT plan object. Notice that this time we go from `complex64` to real `float32`:

```
inverse_plan = fft.Plan(x.shape, in_dtype=np.complex64,
out_dtype=np.float32)
```

Now, we must take the forward FFT from `x_gpu` into `x_hat`, and the inverse FFT from `x_hat` back into `x_gpu`. Notice that we set `scale=True` in the inverse FFT; we do this to indicate to cuFFT to scale the inverse FFT by 1/N:

```
fft.fft(x_gpu, x_hat, plan)
fft.ifft(x_hat, x_gpu, inverse_plan, scale=True)
```

We now will check `x_hat` against a NumPy FFT of x, and `x_gpu` against x itself:

```
y = np.fft.fft(x)
print 'cuFFT matches NumPy FFT: %s' % np.allclose(x_hat.get(), y,
atol=1e-6)
print 'cuFFT inverse matches original: %s' % np.allclose(x_gpu.get(), x,
atol=1e-6)
```

If you run this, you will see that `x_hat` does not match `y`, yet, inexplicably, `x_gpu` matches `x`. How is this possible? Well, let's remember that x is real; if you look at how the Discrete Fourier Transform is computed, you can prove mathematically that the outputs of a real vector will repeat as their complex conjugates after N/2. While the NumPy FFT fully computes these values anyway, cuFFT saves time by only computing the first half of the outputs when it sees that the input is real, and it sets the remaining outputs to 0. You should verify that this is the case by checking the preceding variables.

Thus, if we change the first print statement in the preceding code to only compare the first N/2 outputs between CuFFT and NumPy, then this will return true:

```
print 'cuFFT matches NumPy FFT: %s' % np.allclose(x_hat.get()[0:N//2],
y[0:N//2], atol=1e-6)
```

Using an FFT for convolution

We will now look at how we can use an FFT to perform **convolution**. Let's review what exactly convolution is, first: given two one-dimensional vectors, x and y, their convolution is defined as follows:

$$(x * y)[n] = \sum_{m=-\infty}^{\infty} x[m]y[n-m]$$

This is of interest to us because if x is some long, continuous signal, and y only has a small amount of localized non-zero values, then y will act as a filter on x; this has many applications in itself. First, we can use a filter to smooth the signal x (as is common in digital signal processing and image processing). We can also use it to collect samples of the signal x so as to represent the signal or compress it (as is common in the field of data compression or compressive sensing), or use filters to collect features for signal or image recognition in machine learning. This idea forms the basis for convolutional neural networks).

Of course, computers cannot handle infinitely long vectors (at least, not yet), so we will be considering **circular convolution**. In circular convolution, we are dealing with two length *n*-vectors whose indices below 0 or above n-1 will wrap around to the other end; that is to say, $x[-1] = x[n-1]$, $x[-2] = x[n-2]$, $x[n] = x[0]$, $x[n+1] = x[1]$, and so on. We define circular convolution of x and y like so:

$$(x * y)[n] = \sum_{m=0}^{N-1} x[m]y[n-m]$$

It turns out that we can perform a circular convolution using an FFT quite easily; we can do this by performing an FFT on x and y, point-wise-multiplying the outputs, and then performing an inverse FFT on the final results. This result is known as the **convolution theorem**, which can also be expressed as follows:

$$(x * y)[n] = \tilde{\hat{x}}\hat{y}[n]$$

We will be doing this over two dimensions, since we wish to apply the result to signal processing. While we have only seen the math for FFTs and convolution along one dimension, two-dimensional convolution and FFTs work very similarly to their one-dimensional counterparts, only with some more complex indexing. We will opt to skip over this, however, so that we can get directly into the application.

Using cuFFT for 2D convolution

Now we are going to make a small program that performs **Gaussian filtering** on an image using cuFFT-based two-dimensional convolution. Gaussian filtering is an operation that smooths a rough image using what is known as a Gaussian filter. This is named as such because it is based on the Gaussian (normal) distribution in statistics. This is how the Gaussian filter is defined over two dimensions with a standard deviation of σ:

$$G(x, y) = \frac{1}{\sqrt{2\pi\sigma^2}} e^{-\frac{x^2 + y^2}{2\sigma^2}}$$

When we convolve a discrete image with a filter, we sometimes refer to the filter as a **convolution kernel**. Oftentimes, image processing engineers will just call this a plain kernel, but since we don't want to confuse these with CUDA kernels, we will always use the full term, convolution kernel. We will be using a discrete version of the Gaussian filter as our convolution kernel here.

Let's start with the appropriate imports; notice that we will use the Scikit-CUDA submodule `linalg` here. This will provide a higher-level interface for us than cuBLAS. Since we're working with images here, we will also import Matplotlib's `pyplot` submodule. Also note that we will use Python 3-style division here, from the first line; this means that if we divide two integers with the / operator, then the return value will be a float without typecasting (we perform integer division with the // operator):

```
from __future__ import division
import pycuda.autoinit
from pycuda import gpuarray
```

```
import numpy as np
from skcuda import fft
from skcuda import linalg
from matplotlib import pyplot as plt
```

Let's jump right in and start writing the convolution function. This will take in two NumPy arrays of the same size, x and y. We will typecast these to complex64 arrays, and then return -1 if they are not of the same size:

```
def cufft_conv(x , y):
    x = x.astype(np.complex64)
    y = y.astype(np.complex64)

    if (x.shape != y.shape):
        return -1
```

We will now set up our FFT plan and inverse FFT plan objects:

```
plan = fft.Plan(x.shape, np.complex64, np.complex64)
inverse_plan = fft.Plan(x.shape, np.complex64, np.complex64)
```

Now we can copy our arrays to the GPU. We will also set up some empty arrays of the appropriate sizes to hold the FFTs of these arrays, plus one additional array that will hold the output of the final convolution, out_gpu:

```
x_gpu = gpuarray.to_gpu(x)
y_gpu = gpuarray.to_gpu(y)

x_fft = gpuarray.empty_like(x_gpu, dtype=np.complex64)
y_fft = gpuarray.empty_like(y_gpu, dtype=np.complex64)
out_gpu = gpuarray.empty_like(x_gpu, dtype=np.complex64)
```

We now can perform our FFTs:

```
fft.fft(x_gpu, x_fft, plan)
fft.fft(y_gpu, y_fft, plan)
```

We will now perform pointwise (Hadamard) multiplication between x_fft and y_fft with the linalg.multiply function. We will set overwrite=True so as to write the final value into y_fft:

```
linalg.multiply(x_fft, y_fft, overwrite=True)
```

Now we will call the inverse FFT, outputting the final result into `out_gpu`. We transfer this value to the host and return it:

```
fft.ifft(y_fft, out_gpu, inverse_plan, scale=True)
conv_out = out_gpu.get()
return conv_out
```

We are not done yet. Our convolution kernel will be much smaller than our input image, so we will have to adjust the sizes of our two 2D arrays (both the convolution kernel and the image) so that they are equal and perform the pointwise multiplication between them. Not only should we ensure that they are equal, but we also need to ensure that we perform **zero padding** on the arrays and that we appropriately center the convolution kernel. Zero padding means that we add a buffer of zeros on the sides of the images so as to prevent a wrap-around error. If we are using an FFT to perform our convolution, remember that it is a circular convolution, so the edges will literally always wrap-around. When we are done with our convolution, we can remove the buffer from the outside of the image to get the final output image.

Let's create a new function called `conv_2d` that takes in a convolution kernel, `ker`, and an image, `img`. The padded image size will be (`2*ker.shape[0] + img.shape[0]`, `2*ker.shape[1] + img.shape[1]`). Let's set up the padded convolution kernel first. We will create a 2D array of zeros of this size, and then set the upper-left submatrix as our convolution kernel, like so:

```
def conv_2d(ker, img):

    padded_ker = np.zeros( (img.shape[0] + 2*ker.shape[0], img.shape[1] +
2*ker.shape[1] )).astype(np.float32)
    padded_ker[:ker.shape[0], :ker.shape[1]] = ker
```

We will now have to shift our convolution kernel so that its center is precisely at the coordinate (0,0). We can do this with the NumPy `roll` command:

```
padded_ker = np.roll(padded_ker, shift=-ker.shape[0]//2, axis=0)
padded_ker = np.roll(padded_ker, shift=-ker.shape[1]//2, axis=1)
```

Now we need to pad the input image:

```
padded_img = np.zeros_like(padded_ker).astype(np.float32)
padded_img[ker.shape[0]:-ker.shape[0], ker.shape[1]:-ker.shape[1]] = img
```

Now we have two arrays of the same size that are appropriately formatted. We can now use our `cufft_conv` function that we just wrote here:

```
out_ = cufft_conv(padded_ker, padded_img)
```

We now can remove the zero buffer outside of our image. We then return the result:

```
output = out_[ker.shape[0]:-ker.shape[0], ker.shape[1]:-ker.shape[1]]

return output
```

We are not yet done. Let's write some small functions to set up our Gaussian filter, and then we can move on to applying this to an image. We can write the basic filter itself with a single line using a lambda function:

```
gaussian_filter = lambda x, y, sigma : (1 / np.sqrt(2*np.pi*(sigma**2))
)*np.exp( -(x**2 + y**2) / (2 * (sigma**2) ))
```

We can now write a function that uses this filter to output a discrete convolution kernel. The convolution kernel will be of height and length `2*sigma + 1`, which is fairly standard:

 Notice that we normalize the values of our Gaussian kernel by summing its values into `total_` and dividing it.

```
def gaussian_ker(sigma):
    ker_ = np.zeros((2*sigma+1, 2*sigma+1))
    for i in range(2*sigma + 1):
        for j in range(2*sigma + 1):
            ker_[i,j] = gaussian_filter(i - sigma, j - sigma, sigma)
    total_ = np.sum(ker_.ravel())
    ker_ = ker_ / total_
    return ker_
```

We are now ready to test this on an image! As our test case, we will use Gaussian filtering to blur a color JPEG image of this book's editor, *Akshada Iyer*. (This image is available under the Chapter07 directory in the GitHub repository with the file name akshada.jpg.) We will use Matplotlib's imread function to read the image; this is stored as an array of unsigned 8-bit integers ranging from 0 to 255 by default. We will typecast this to an array of floats and normalize it so that all of the values will range from 0 to 1.

 Note to the readers of the print edition of this text: although the print edition of this text is in greyscale, this a color image.

We will then set up an empty array of zeros that will store the blurred image:

```
if __name__ == '__main__':
    akshada = np.float32(plt.imread('akshada.jpg')) / 255
    akshada_blurred = np.zeros_like(akshada)
```

Let's set up our convolution kernel. Here, a standard deviation of 15 should be enough:

```
ker = gaussian_ker(15)
```

We can now blur the image. Since this is a color image, we will have to apply Gaussian filtering to each color layer (red, green, and blue) individually; this is indexed by the third dimension in the image arrays:

```
for k in range(3):
    akshada_blurred[:,:,k] = conv_2d(ker, akshada[:,:,k])
```

Now let's look at the **Before** and **After** images side-by-side by using some Matplotlib tricks:

```
fig, (ax0, ax1) = plt.subplots(1,2)
fig.suptitle('Gaussian Filtering', fontsize=20)
ax0.set_title('Before')
ax0.axis('off')
ax0.imshow(akshada)
ax1.set_title('After')
ax1.axis('off')
ax1.imshow(akshada_blurred)
plt.tight_layout()
plt.subplots_adjust(top=.85)
plt.show()
```

We can now run the program and observe the effects of Gaussian filtering:

 This program is available in the Chapter07 directory in a file called conv_2d.py in the repository for this book.

Using cuSolver from Scikit-CUDA

We will now look at how we can use cuSolver from Scikit-CUDA's linalg submodule. Again, this provides a high-level interface for both cuBLAS and cuSolver, so we don't have to get caught up in the small details.

As we noted in the introduction, cuSolver is a library that's used for performing more advanced linear algebra operations than cuBLAS, such as the Singular Value Decomposition, LU/QR/Cholesky factorization, and eigenvalue computations. Since cuSolver, like cuBLAS and cuFFT, is another vast library, we will only take the time to look at one of the most fundamental operations in data science and machine learning—SVD.

Please refer to NVIDIA's official documentation on cuSOLVER if you would like further information on this library: `https://docs.NVIDIA.com/cuda/cusolver/index.html`.

Singular value decomposition (SVD)

SVD takes any m x n matrix A, and then returns three matrices in return—U, Σ, and V. Here, U is an m x m unitary matrix, Σ is an m x n diagonal matrix, and V is an n x n unitary matrix. By *unitary*, we mean that a matrix's columns form an orthonormal basis; by *diagonal*, we mean that all values in the matrix are zero, except for possibly the values along its diagonal.

The significance of the SVD is that this decomposes A into these matrices so that we have $A = U\Sigma V^{T}$; moreover, the values along the diagonal of Σ will all be positive or zero, and are known as the singular values. We will see some applications of this soon, but you should keep in mind that the computational complexity of SVD is of the order O(mn^2)—for large matrices, it is definitely a good idea to use a GPU, since this algorithm is parallelizable.

We'll now look at how we can compute the SVD of a matrix. Let's make the appropriate import statements:

```
import pycuda.autoinit
from pycuda import gpuarray
import numpy as np
from skcuda import linalg
```

We will now generate a relatively large random matrix and transfer it to the GPU:

```
a = np.random.rand(1000,5000).astype(np.float32)
a_gpu = gpuarray.to_gpu(a)
```

We can now execute the SVD. This will have three outputs corresponding to the matrices that we just described. The first parameter will be the matrix array we just copied to the GPU. Then we need to specify that we want to use cuSolver as our backend for this operation:

```
U_d, s_d, V_d = linalg.svd(a_gpu,  lib='cusolver')
```

Now let's copy these arrays from the GPU to the host:

```
U = U_d.get()
s = s_d.get()
V = V_d.get()
```

s is actually stored as a one-dimensional array; we will have to create a zero matrix of size 1000 x 5000 and copy these values along the diagonal. We can do this with the NumPy diag function, coupled with some array slicing:

```
S = np.zeros((1000,5000))
S[:1000,:1000] = np.diag(s)
```

We can now matrix-multiply these values on the host with the NumPy dot function to verify that they match up to our original array:

```
print 'Can we reconstruct a from its SVD decomposition? : %s' %
np.allclose(a, np.dot(U, np.dot(S, V)), atol=1e-5)
```

Since we are using only float32s and our matrix is relatively large, a bit of numerical error was introduced; we had to set the "tolerance" level (atol) a little higher than usual here, but it's still small enough to verify that the two arrays are sufficiently close.

Using SVD for Principal Component Analysis (PCA)

Principal Component Analysis (PCA) is a tool that's used primarily for dimensionality reduction. We can use this to look at a dataset and find which dimensions and linear subspaces are the most salient. While there are several ways to implement this, we will show you how to perform PCA using SVD.

We'll do this as follows—we will work with a dataset that exists in 10 dimensions. We will start by creating two vectors that are heavily weighted in the front, and 0 otherwise:

```
vals = [ np.float32([10,0,0,0,0,0,0,0,0,0]) ,
np.float32([0,10,0,0,0,0,0,0,0,0]) ]
```

We will then add 9,000 additional vectors: 6,000 of these will be the same as the first two vectors, only with a little added random white noise, and the remaining 3,000 will just be random white noise:

```
for i in range(3000):
    vals.append(vals[0] + 0.001*np.random.randn(10))
    vals.append(vals[1] + 0.001*np.random.randn(10))
    vals.append(0.001*np.random.randn(10))
```

We will now typecast the `vals` list to a `float32` NumPy array. We take the mean over the rows and subtract this value from each row. (This is a necessary step for PCA.) We then transpose this matrix, since cuSolver requires that input matrices have fewer or equal rows compared to the columns:

```
vals = np.float32(vals)
vals = vals - np.mean(vals, axis=0)
v_gpu = gpuarray.to_gpu(vals.T.copy())
```

We will now run cuSolver, just like we did previously, and copy the output values off of the GPU:

```
U_d, s_d, V_d = linalg.svd(v_gpu, lib='cusolver')

u = U_d.get()
s = s_d.get()
v = V_d.get()
```

Now we are ready to begin our investigative work. Let's open up IPython and take a closer look at u and s. First, let's look at s; its values are actually the square roots of the **principal values**, so we will square them and then take a look:

```
In [3]: print s**2
[   3.00100688e+05   1.00011516e+05   9.27482639e-03   9.26916022e-03
     9.21287015e-03   9.14533995e-03   9.02440213e-03   8.79677106e-03
     8.72804411e-03   8.61862674e-03]
```

You will notice that the first two principal values are of the order 10^5, while the remaining components are of the order 10^{-3}. This tells us there is only really a two-dimensional subspace that is even relevant to this data at all, which shouldn't be surprising. These are the first and second values, which will correspond to the first and second principal components that is, the corresponding vectors. Let's take a look at these vectors, which will be stored in U:

```
In [4]: print u[:,0]
[ -7.07105637e-01   7.07107902e-01  -3.11021381e-06  -1.28881106e-06
  -2.04502885e-06   1.54779946e-06  -2.50539756e-06   3.35367849e-06
  -1.68121846e-06   3.36088988e-07]

In [5]: print u[:,1]
[ -7.07107902e-01  -7.07105637e-01  -5.94599987e-06   1.07432527e-07
   3.17310139e-07  -6.16845739e-07  -9.59202112e-07  -8.96491883e-07
   2.71546742e-06   6.28509406e-06]
```

You will notice that these two vectors are very heavily weighted in the first two entries, which are of the order 10^{-1}; the remaining entries are all of the order 10^{-6} or lower, and are comparably irrelevant. This is what we should have expected, considering how biased we made our data in the first two entries. That, in a nutshell, is the idea behind PCA.

Summary

We started this chapter by looking at how to use the wrappers for the cuBLAS library from Scikit-CUDA; we have to keep many details in mind here, such as when to use column-major storage, or if an input array will be overwritten in-place. We then look at how to perform one- and two-dimensional FFTs with cuFFT from Scikit-CUDA, and how to create a simple convolutional filter. We then showed you how to apply this for a simple Gaussian blurring effect on an image. Finally, we looked at how to perform a singular value decomposition (SVD) on the GPU with cuSolver, which is normally a very computationally onerous operation, but which parallelizes fairly well onto the GPU. We ended this chapter by looking at how to use the SVD for basic PCA.

Questions

1. Suppose you get a job translating some old legacy FORTRAN BLAS code to CUDA. You open a file and see a function called SBLAH, and another called ZBLEH. Can you tell what datatypes these two functions use without looking them up?
2. Can you alter the cuBLAS level-2 GEMV example to work by directly copying the matrix A to the GPU, without taking the transpose on the host to set it column-wise?
3. Use cuBLAS 32-bit real dot-product (`cublasSdot`) to implement matrix-vector multiplication using one row-wise matrix and one stride-1 vector.
4. Implement matrix-matrix multiplication using `cublasSdot`.
5. Can you implement a method to precisely measure the GEMM operations in the performance measurement example?
6. In the example of the 1D FFT, try typecasting x as a `complex64` array, and then switching the FFT and inverse FFT plans to be `complex64` valued in both directions. Then confirm whether `np.allclose(x, x_gpu.get())` is true without checking the first half of the array. Why do you think this works now?
7. Notice that there is a dark edge around the blurred image in the convolution example. Why is this in the blurred image but not in the original? Can you think of a method that you can use to mitigate this?

8
The CUDA Device Function Libraries and Thrust

In the last chapter, looking at a fairly broad overview of the libraries that are available in CUDA through the Scikit-CUDA wrapper module. We will now look at a few other libraries that we will have to use directly from within CUDA C proper, without the assistance of wrappers like those in Scikit-CUDA. We will start by looking at two standard libraries that consist of device functions that we may invoke from any CUDA C kernel cuRAND and the CUDA Math API. By the end of learning how to use these libraries, we will know how to use these libraries in the context of Monte Carlo integration. Monte Carlo integration is a well-known randomized method that provides estimates for the values of definite integrals from calculus. We will first look at a basic example of how to implement a simple Monte Carlo method with cuRAND to do a basic estimate of the value of Pi (as in the well-known constant, $\pi=3.14159...$), and then we'll embark on a more ambitious project where we will construct a Python class that can perform definite integration on any arbitrary mathematical function, and use the Math API for creating such functions. We'll also look at how to effectively use some ideas from metaprogramming in our design of this class.

We will then take another look at writing some pure CUDA programs with the help of the Thrust C++ library. Thrust is a library that provides C++ template containers, similar to those in the C++ Standard Template Library (STL). This will enable us to manipulate CUDA C arrays from C++ in a more natural way that is closer to PyCUDA's `gpuarray` and the STL's vector container. This will save us from having to constantly use pointers, such as *mallocs* and *frees*, that plagued us before in CUDA C.

In this chapter, we will look at the following topics:

- Understanding the purpose that a seed has in generating lists of pseudo-random numbers
- Using cuRAND device functions for generating random numbers in a CUDA kernel

- Understanding the concept of Monte Carlo integration
- Using dictionary-based string formatting in Python for metaprogramming
- Using the CUDA Math API device function library
- Understanding what a functor is
- Using the Thrust vector container when programming in pure CUDA C

Technical requirements

A Linux or Windows 10 PC with a modern NVIDIA GPU (2016—onward) is required for this chapter, with all of the necessary GPU drivers and the CUDA Toolkit (9.0–onward) installed. A suitable Python 2.7 installation (such as Anaconda Python 2.7) with the PyCUDA module is also required.

This chapter's code is also available on GitHub, and can be found at `https://github.com/PacktPublishing/Hands-On-GPU-Programming-with-Python-and-CUDA`.

 For more information about the prerequisites for this chapter, check the preface of this book. For the software and hardware requirements, check out the README at `https://github.com/PacktPublishing/Hands-On-GPU-Programming-with-Python-and-CUDA`.

The cuRAND device function library

Let's start with cuRAND. This is a standard CUDA library that is used for generating pseudo-random values within a CUDA kernel on a thread-by-thread basis, which is initialized and invoked by calling device functions from each individual thread within a kernel. Let's emphasize again that this is a **pseudo-random** sequence of values—since the digital hardware is always deterministic and never random or arbitrary, we use algorithms to generate a sequence of apparently random values from an initial **seed value**. Usually, we can set the seed value to a truly random value (such as the clock time in milliseconds), which will yield us with a nicely arbitrary sequence of *random* values. These generated random values have no correlation with prior or future values in the sequence generated by the same seed, although there can be correlations and repeats when you combine values generated from different seeds. For this reason, you have to be careful that the values you wish to be mutually *random* are generated by the same seed.

Let's start by looking at the function prototype for `curand_init`, which we will initialize with an appropriate seed:

```
__device__ void curand_init ( unsigned long long seed, unsigned long long
sequence, unsigned long long offset, curandState_t *state)
```

Here, all of the inputs are unsigned long, which in C is an unsigned (non-negative valued) 64-bit integer. First, we can see the `seed`, which is, of course, the seed value. Generally speaking, you'll set this with the clock value or some variation. We then see a value called `sequence` and as we stated previously, values generated by cuRAND will only be truly mathematically mutually random if they are generated by the same seed value. So, if we have multiple threads using the same seed value, we use `sequence` to indicate which sub-sequence of random numbers of length 2^{190} for the current thread to use, while we use `offset` to indicate at which point to start within this sub-sequence; this will generate values in each thread that are all mathematically mutually random with no correlation. Finally, the last parameter is for a pointer to a `curandState_t` object; this keeps track of where we are in the sequence of pseudo-random numbers.

After you initialize a class object, you will then generate random values from the appropriate random distribution by calling the appropriate device function. The two most common distributions are uniform and normal (Gaussian). A uniform distribution (`curand_uniform`, in cuRAND) is a function that outputs values that are all equally probable over a given range: that is to say, for a uniform distribution over 0 to 1, there is a 10% chance that a value will fall between 0 and 0.1, or between 0.9 to 1, or between any two points that are spaced .1 away from each other. The normal distribution (`curand_normal`, in cuRAND) has values that are centered at a particular mean, which will be distributed according to the well-known bell-shaped curve that is defined by the distribution's standard deviation. (The default mean of `curand_normal` is 0 and the standard deviation is 1 in cuRAND, so this will have to be shifted and scaled manually for other values.) Another well-known distribution supported by cuRAND is the Poisson distribution (`curand_poisson`), which is used for modeling the occurrences of random events over time.

We will be primarily looking at how to use cuRAND in the context of uniform distributions in the next section, due to their applicability to Monte Carlo integration. Readers interested in learning how to use more features in cuRAND are encouraged to look at the official documentation from NVIDIA.

Estimating π with Monte Carlo

First, we will apply our new knowledge of cuRAND to perform an estimate of the well-known mathematical constant π, or Pi, which is, of course, the never-ending irrational number 3.14159265358979...

To get an estimate, though, we need to take a moment to think about what this means. Let's think about a circle. Remember that the radius of a circle is the length from the center of the circle to any point in the circle; usually, this is designated with R. The diameter is defined as $D = 2R$, and the circumference C is the length around the circle. Pi is then defined as $\pi = C / D$. We can use Euclidean geometry to find a formula for the area of the circle, which turns out being $A = \pi R^2$. Now, let's think about a circle with radius R being circumscribed in a square with all sides of length $2R$:

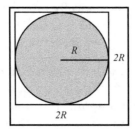

So, of course, we know that the area of the square is $(2R)^2 = 4R^2$. Let's consider $R=1$, so that we have known that the area of the circle is exactly π, while the area of the square is exactly 4. Let's make a further assumption and state that both the circle and square are centered at (0,0) in the Cartesian plane. Now, let's take a completely random value within the square, (x,y), and see if it falls within the circle. How can we do this? By applying the Pythagorean formula: we do this by checking whether $x^2 + y^2$ is less than or equal to 1. Let's designate the total number of random points we choose with *iters*, and the number of hits with *hits*.

Let's do a little bit more thinking about this: the probability of picking a point within the circle should be proportionate to the area of the circle divided by the area of the rectangle; here, this is π / 4. However, if we choose a very large value of random points, notice that we will get the following approximation:

$$\pi \approx 4 \frac{hits}{iters}$$

This is exactly how we will estimate π! The number of iterations we will have to do will be very high before we can come up with a decent estimate of Pi, but notice how nicely parallelizable this is: we can check the "hits" in different threads, splitting the total number of iterations among different threads. At the end of the day, we can just sum up the total number of hits among all of the threads to get our estimate.

We can now begin to write a program to make our Monte Carlo estimate. Let's first import the usual Python modules that we will need for a PyCUDA program, with one addition from SymPy:

 SymPy is used for perfect *symbolic* computations that are to be made in Python so that when we have very large integers, we can use the Rational function to make a much more accurate floating-point estimate of a division.

```
import pycuda.autoinit
import pycuda.driver as drv
from pycuda import gpuarray
from pycuda.compiler import SourceModule
import numpy as np
from sympy import Rational
```

Now, we have to do something a little different than normal when we build our kernel: we need to set the option no_extern_c=True in SourceModule. This modifies how the code is compiled so that our code can properly link with C++ code, as required by the cuRAND library. We then begin writing our kernel and include the appropriate header:

```
ker = SourceModule(no_extern_c=True, source='''
#include <curand_kernel.h>
```

Now, let's include a macro for the Pythagorean distance. Since we are just checking if this value is equal to or below 1, we can, therefore, omit the square root. We will be using a lot of unsigned 64-bit integers, so let's make another macro to save us from typing unsigned long long over and over:

```
#define _PYTHAG(a,b) (a*a + b*b)
#define ULL unsigned long long
```

We can now set up our kernel. By the nature of PyCUDA, this will have to be compiled to the interface as a bonafide C function rather than as a C++ function. We do this with an extern "C" block:

```
extern "C" {
```

We can now define our kernel. We will have two parameters: one for `iters`, which is the total number of iterations for each thread, and another for an array that will hold the total number of hits for each thread. We will need a `curandState` object for this:

```
__global__ void estimate_pi(ULL iters, ULL * hits)
{
    curandState cr_state;
```

Let's hold the global thread ID in an integer called `tid`:

```
int tid = blockIdx.x * blockDim.x + threadIdx.x;
```

`clock()` is a device function that outputs the current time down to the millisecond. We can add `tid` to the output of `clock()` to get a unique seed for each thread. We don't need to use different subsequences or offsets, so let's set them both to 0. We will also carefully typecast everything here to 64-bit unsigned integers:

```
curand_init( (ULL) clock() + (ULL) tid, (ULL) 0, (ULL) 0, &cr_state);
```

Let's set up the x and y values to hold a random point in the rectangle:

```
float x, y;
```

We will then iterate `iters` times to see how many hits in the circle we get. We generate these with `curand_uniform(&cr_state)`. Notice that we can generate them over 0 to 1, rather than from -1 to 1, since the squaring of these in the `_PYTHAG` macro will remove any negative values:

```
for(ULL i=0; i < iters; i++)
  {
      x = curand_uniform(&cr_state);
      y = curand_uniform(&cr_state);

      if(_PYTHAG(x,y) <= 1.0f)
          hits[tid]++;
  }
```

We can now end and close off our kernel, as well as the `extern "C"` block with another final } bracket:

```
return;
}
}
''')
```

Now, let's get the Python wrapper function to our kernel with `get_function`. We will also set up the block and grid sizes: 32 threads per block, and 512 blocks per grid. Let's calculate the total number of threads and set up an array on the GPU to hold all of the hits (initialized to 0s, of course):

```
pi_ker = ker.get_function("estimate_pi")
threads_per_block = 32
blocks_per_grid = 512
total_threads = threads_per_block * blocks_per_grid
hits_d = gpuarray.zeros((total_threads,),dtype=np.uint64)
```

Let's set up the total number of iterations per thread to 2^{24}:

```
iters = 2**24
```

We can now launch the kernel as usual:

```
pi_ker(np.uint64(iters), hits_d, grid=(blocks_per_grid,1,1),
block=(threads_per_block,1,1))
```

Now, let's sum over the number of hits in the array, which gives us the total number of hits. Let's also calculate the total number of iterations among all of the threads in the array:

```
total_hits = np.sum( hits_d.get() )
total = np.uint64(total_threads) * np.uint64(iters)
```

We can now make our estimate with `Rational`, like so:

```
est_pi_symbolic =  Rational(4)*Rational(int(total_hits), int(total) )
```

We can now convert this into a floating point value:

```
est_pi = np.float(est_pi_symbolic.evalf())
```

Let's check our estimate against NumPy's constant value, `numpy.pi`:

```
print "Our Monte Carlo estimate of Pi is : %s" % est_pi
print "NumPy's Pi constant is: %s " % np.pi
print "Our estimate passes NumPy's 'allclose' : %s" % np.allclose(est_pi,
np.pi)
```

We are now done. Let's run this from IPython and check it out (This program is also available as the `monte_carlo_pi.py` file under `Chapter08` in this book's repository.):

```
In [25]: run monte_carlo_pi.py
Our Monte Carlo estimate of Pi is : 3.14159237769
NumPy's Pi constant is: 3.14159265359
Our estimate passes NumPy's 'allclose' : True
```

The CUDA Math API

Now, we will take a look at the **CUDA Math API**. This is a library that consists of device functions similar to those in the standard C `math.h` library that can be called from individual threads in a kernel. One difference here is that single and double valued floating-point operations are overloaded, so if we use `sin(x)` where x is a float, the sin function will yield a 32-bit float as the output, while if x were a 64-bit double, then the output of `sin` would also be a 64-bit value (Usually, this is the proper name for a 32-bit function, but it has an f at the end, such as `sinf`). There are also additional **instrinsic** functions. Intrinsic functions are less accurate but faster math functions that are built into the NVIDIA CUDA hardware; generally, they have similar names to the original function, except that they are preceded with two underscores—therefore, the intrinsic, 32-bit sin function is `__sinf`.

A brief review of definite integration

Now, we're going to use some object-oriented programming in Python to set up a class that we can use to evaluate definite integrals of functions using a Monte Carlo method. Let's stop for a moment and talk about what we mean: suppose we have a mathematical function (as in the type you might see in a calculus class) that we call *f(x)*. When we graph this out on the Cartesian plane between points *a* and *b*, it may look something like this:

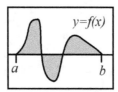

Now, let's review exactly what definite integration means—let's denote the first gray area in this graph as *I*, the second gray area as *II*, and the third gray area as *III*. Notice that the second gray area here is below zero. The definite integral of *f* here, from *a* to *b*, will be the value *I - II + III*, and we will denote this mathematically as $\int_a^b f(x)dx$. In general, the definite integral from *a* to *b* is just the sum of all of the total "positive" area bounded by the *f* function and x-axis with y > 0 between *a* and *b*, minus all of the "negative" area bounded by the *f* function and the x-axis with y < 0 between *a* and *b*.

There are many ways to calculate or estimate the definite integral of a function between two points. One that you may have seen in a calculus class is to find a closed-form solution: find the anti-derivative of *f*, *F*, and calculate *F(b) - F(a)*. In many areas, though, we won't be able to find an exact anti-derivative, and we will have to determine the definite integral numerically. This is exactly the idea behind Monte Carlo integration: we evaluate *f* at many, many random points between *a* and *b*, and then use those to make an estimate of the definite integral.

Computing definite integrals with the Monte Carlo method

We are now going to use the CUDA Math API for representing an arbitrary mathematical function, *f*, while using the cuRAND library to implement the Monte Carlo integral. We will do this with **metaprogramming**: we will use Python to generate the code for a device function from a code template, which will plug into an appropriate Monte Carlo kernel for integration.

 The idea here is that it will look and act similarly to some of the metaprogramming tools we've seen with PyCUDA, such as `ElementwiseKernel`.

Let's start by importing the appropriate modules into our new project:

```
import pycuda.autoinit
import pycuda.driver as drv
from pycuda import gpuarray
from pycuda.compiler import SourceModule
import numpy as np
```

We're going to use a trick in Python called **dictionary based string formatting**. Let's go over this for a minute before we continue. Suppose we are writing a chunk of CUDA C code, and we are unsure of whether we want a particular collection of variables to be float or double; perhaps it looks like this: `code_string="float x, y; float * z;"`. We might actually want to format the code so that we can switch between floats and doubles on the fly. Let's change all references from `float` in the string to `%(precision)s`—`code_string="%(precision)s x, y; %(precision)s * z;"`. We can now set up an appropriate dictionary that will swap `%(presision)s` with `double`, which is, `code_dict = {'precision' : 'double'}`, and get the new double string with `code_double = code_string % code_dict`. Let's take a look:

```
In [1]: code_string="%(precision)s x, y; %(precision)s * z;"

In [2]: code_dict = {'precision' : 'double'}

In [3]: code_double = code_string % code_dict

In [4]: print code_double
double x, y; double * z;
```

Now, let's think for a moment about how we want our new Monte Carlo integrator to work. We will also have it take a string that is a math equation that is written using the CUDA Math API to define the function we want to integrate. We can then fit this string into the code using the dictionary trick we just learned, and use this to integrate arbitrary functions. We will also use the template to switch between `float` and `double` precision, as per the user's discretion.

We can now begin our CUDA C code:

```
MonteCarloKernelTemplate = '''
#include <curand_kernel.h>
```

We will keep the unsigned 64-bit integer macro from before, `ULL`. Let's define some new macros for a reciprocal of x (`_R`), and for squaring (`_P2`):

```
#define ULL unsigned long long
#define _R(z) ( 1.0f / (z) )
#define _P2(z) ( (z) * (z) )
```

Now, let's define a device function that our equation string will plug into. We will use the `math_function` value when we have to swap the text from a dictionary. We will have another value called p, for precision (which will either be a `float` or `double`). We'll call this device function f. We'll put an `inline` in the declaration of the function, which will save us a little time from branching when this is called from the kernel:

```
__device__ inline %(p)s f(%(p)s x)
{
    %(p)s y;
    %(math_function)s;
    return y;
}
```

Now, let's think about how this will work— We declare a 32 or 64-bit floating point value called y, call `math_function`, and then return y. `math_function`, which will only make sense if it's some code that acts on the input parameter x and sets some value to y, such as y = `sin(x)`. Let's keep this in mind and continue.

We will now begin writing our Monte Carlo integration kernel. Let's remember that we have to make our CUDA kernel visible from plain C with the `extern "C"` keyword. We will then set up our kernel.

First, we will indicate how many random samples each thread in the kernel should take with `iters`; we then indicate the lower bound of integration (*b*) with `lo` and the upper bound (*a*) with `hi`, and pass in an array, `ys_out`, to store the collection of partial integrals for each thread (we will later sum over `ys_out` to get the value of the complete definite integral from `lo` to `hi` on the host side). Again, notice how we are referring to the precision as p:

```
extern "C" {
__global__ void monte_carlo(int iters, %(p)s lo, %(p)s hi, %(p)s * ys_out)
{
```

We will need a `curandState` object for generating random values. We will also need to find the global thread ID and the total number of threads. Since we are working with a one-dimensional mathematical function, it makes sense to set up our block and grid parameters in one dimension, x, as well:

```
curandState cr_state;
int tid = blockIdx.x * blockDim.x + threadIdx.x;
int num_threads = blockDim.x * gridDim.x;
```

We will now calculate the amount of area there is between `lo` and `hi` that a single thread will process. We'll do this by dividing up the entire length of the integration (which will be `hi - lo`) by the total number of threads.:

 Again, note how we are using templating tricks so that this value can be multi-precision.

```
%(p)s t_width = (hi - lo) / ( %(p)s ) num_threads;
```

Recall that we have a parameter called `iters`; this indicates how many random values each thread will sample. We need to know what the density of the samples is in a little bit; that is, the average number of samples per unit distance. We calculate it like so, remembering to typecast the integer `iters` into a floating-point value:

```
%(p)s density = ( ( %(p)s ) iters ) / t_width;
```

Recall that we are dividing the area we are integrating over by the number of threads. This means that each thread will have its own start and end point. Since we are dividing up the lengths fairly for each thread, we calculate this like so:

```
%(p)s t_lo = t_width*tid + lo;
 %(p)s t_hi = t_lo + t_width;
```

We can now initialize cuRAND like we did previously, making sure that each thread is generating random values from its own individual seed:

```
curand_init( (ULL) clock() + (ULL) tid, (ULL) 0, (ULL) 0, &cr_state);
```

Before we start sampling, we will need to set up some additional floating point values. `y` will hold the final value for the integral estimate from `t_lo` to `t_hi`, and `y_sum` will hold the sum of all of the sampled values. We will also use the `rand_val` variable to hold the raw random value we generate, and `x` to store the scaled random value from the area that we will be sampling from:

```
%(p)s y, y_sum = 0.0f;
%(p)s rand_val, x;
```

Now, let's loop to the sample values from our function, adding the values into y_sum. The one salient thing to notice is the %(p_curand)s at the end of curand_uniform—the 32-bit floating point version of this function is curand_uniform, while the 64-bit version is curand_uniform_double. We will have to swap this with either _double or an empty string later, depending on what level of precision we go with here. Also, notice how we scale rand_val so that x falls between t_lo and t_hi, remembering that random uniform distributions in cuRAND only yields values between 0 and 1:

```
for (int i=0; i < iters; i++)
{
    rand_val = curand_uniform%(p_curand)s(&cr_state);
    x = t_lo + t_width * rand_val;
    y_sum += f(x);
}
```

We can now calculate the value of the subintegral from t_lo to t_hi by dividing y_sum by density:

```
y = y_sum / density;
```

We output this value into the array and close off our CUDA kernel, as well as the extern "C", with the final closing bracket. We're done writing CUDA C, so we will close off this section with a triple-quote:

```
ys_out[tid] = y;
    }
}
'''
```

We will now do something a little different—we're going to set up a class to handle our definite integrals. Let's call it MonteCarloIntegrator. We will start, of course, by writing the constructor, that is, the __init__ function. This is where we will input the object reference, self. Let's set up the default value for math_function to be 'y = sin(x)', with the default precision as 'd', for double. We'll also set the default value for lo as 0 and hi as the NumPy approximation of π. Finally, we'll have values for the number of random samples each thread will take (samples_per_thread), and the grid size that we will launch our kernel over (num_blocks).

Let's start this function by storing the text string math_function within the self object for later use:

```
def __init__(self, math_function='y = sin(x)', precision='d', lo=0,
hi=np.pi, samples_per_thread=10**5, num_blocks=100):
        self.math_function = math_function
```

Now, let's set up the values related to our choice of floating-point precision that we will need for later, particularly for setting up our template dictionary. We will also store the `lo` and `hi` values within the object. Let's also be sure to raise exception errors if the user inputs an invalid datatype, or if `hi` is actually smaller than `lo`:

```
if precision in [None, 's', 'S', 'single', np.float32]:
    self.precision = 'float'
    self.numpy_precision = np.float32
    self.p_curand = ''
elif precision in ['d','D', 'double', np.float64]:
    self.precision = 'double'
    self.numpy_precision = np.float64
    self.p_curand = '_double'
else:
    raise Exception('precision is invalid datatype!')

if (hi - lo <= 0):
    raise Exception('hi - lo <= 0!')
else:
    self.hi = hi
    self.lo = lo
```

We can now set up our code template dictionary:

```
MonteCarloDict = {'p' : self.precision, 'p_curand' : self.p_curand,
'math_function' : self.math_function}
```

We can now generate the actual final code using dictionary-based string formatting, and compile. Let's also turn off warnings from the `nvcc` compiler by setting `options=['-w']` in `SourceModule`:

```
self.MonteCarloCode = MonteCarloKernelTemplate % MonteCarloDict

self.ker = SourceModule(no_extern_c=True , options=['-w'],
source=self.MonteCarloCode)
```

We will now set up a function reference in our object to our compiled kernel with `get_function`. Let's save the remaining two parameters within our object before we continue:

```
self.f = self.ker.get_function('monte_carlo')
self.num_blocks = num_blocks
self.samples_per_thread = samples_per_thread
```

Now, while we will need different instantiations of `MonteCarloIntegrator` objects to evaluate definite integrals of different mathematical functions or floating point precision, we might want to evaluate the same integral over different `lo` and `hi` bounds, change the number of threads/grid size, or alter the number of samples we take at each thread. Thankfully, these are easy alterations to make, and can all be made at runtime.

We'll set up a specific function for evaluating the integral of a given object. We will set the default values of these parameters to be those that we stored during the call to the constructor:

```
def definite_integral(self, lo=None, hi=None, samples_per_thread=None,
num_blocks=None):
    if lo is None or hi is None:
        lo = self.lo
        hi = self.hi
    if samples_per_thread is None:
        samples_per_thread = self.samples_per_thread
    if num_blocks is None:
        num_blocks = self.num_blocks
        grid = (num_blocks,1,1)
    else:
        grid = (num_blocks,1,1)

    block = (32,1,1)
    num_threads = 32*num_blocks
```

We can finish this function off by setting up an empty array to store the partial sub-integrals and launching the kernel. We then need to sum over the sub-integrals to get the final value, which we return:

```
self.ys = gpuarray.empty((num_threads,) , dtype=self.numpy_precision)

self.f(np.int32(samples_per_thread), self.numpy_precision(lo),
self.numpy_precision(hi), self.ys, block=block, grid=grid)

self.nintegral = np.sum(self.ys.get() )

return np.sum(self.nintegral)
```

We are ready to try this out. Let's just set up a class with the default values—this will integrate `y = sin(x)` from 0 to π. If you remember calculus, the anti-derivative of *sin(x)* is *-cos(x)*, so we can evaluate the definite integral like so:

$$\int_0^\pi sin(x)dx = [-cos(x)]\Big|_0^\pi = -cos(\pi) + cos(0) = 2$$

Therefore, we should get a numerical value close to 2. Let's see what we get:

```
In [2]: sin_integral = MonteCarloIntegrator()

In [3]: sin_integral.definite_integral()
Out[3]: 2.0000000334270522
```

Writing some test cases

Now, we will finally get to see how to use the CUDA Math API to write some test cases for our class by way of the `math_function` parameter. These will be fairly straightforward if you have any experience with the C/C++ standard math library. Again, these functions are overloaded so that we don't have to change the names of anything when we switch between single and double precision.

We've already seen one example, namely $y = sin(x)$. Let's try something a little more ambitious:

$$y = log(x)sin^2(x)$$

We will integrate this function from $a=11.733$ to $b=18.472$, and then check the output of our Monte Carlo integrator against the known value of this integral from another source. Here, Mathematica indicates that the value of this definite integral is 8.9999, so we will check against that.

Now, let's think of how to represent this function: here, *log* refers to the base-*e* logarithm (also known as *ln*), and this is just `log(x)` in the Math API. We already set up a macro for squaring, so we can represent $sin^2(x)$ as `_P2(sin(x))`. We can now represent the entire function with `y = log(x)*_P2(sin(x))`.

Let's use the following equation, integrating from $a=.9$ to $b=4$:

$$y = \frac{1}{1 + sinh(2x)log^2(x)}$$

Remembering that `_R` is the macro we set up for a reciprocal, we can write the function with the Math API like so:

```
'y = _R( 1 + sinh(2*x)*_P2(log(x)) )'
```

Before we move on, let's note that Mathematica tells us that the value of this definite integral is .584977.

Let's check on one more function. Let's be a little ambitious and say that it's this:

$$y = \frac{cosh(x)sin(x)}{\sqrt{x^3 + sin^2(x)}}$$

We can represent this as `'y = (cosh(x)*sin(x))/ sqrt( pow(x,3) + _P2(sin(x)))'`; naturally `sqrt` is the square root in the denominator, and `pow` allows us to take a value of arbitrary power. Of course, `sin(x)` is *sin(x)* and `cosh(x)` is *cosh(x)*. We integrate this from *a*=1.85 to *b*=4.81; Mathematica tells us that the true value of this integral is -3.34553.

We are now ready to check some test cases and verify that our Monte Carlo integral is working! Let's iterate over a list, whose first value is a string indicating the function (using the Math API), the second value indicates the lower bound of integration, the third indicates the upper bound of integration, and the last value indicates the expected value that was calculated with Mathematica:

```
if __name__ == '__main__':

    integral_tests = [('y =log(x)*_P2(sin(x))', 11.733 , 18.472, 8.9999),
('y = _R( 1 + sinh(2*x)*_P2(log(x)) )', .9, 4, .584977), ('y =
(cosh(x)*sin(x))/ sqrt( pow(x,3) + _P2(sin(x)))', 1.85, 4.81, -3.34553) ]
```

We can now iterate over this list and see how well our algorithm works compared to Mathematica:

```
for f, lo, hi, expected in integral_tests:
    mci = MonteCarloIntegrator(math_function=f, precision='d', lo=lo,
hi=hi)
    print 'The Monte Carlo numerical integration of the function\n \t f: x
-> %s \n \t from x = %s to x = %s is : %s ' % (f, lo, hi,
mci.definite_integral())
    print 'where the expected value is : %s\n' % expected
```

Let's run this right now:

```
In [2]: run monte_carlo_integrator.py
The Monte Carlo numerical integration of the function
        f: x -> y =log(x)*_P2(sin(x))
        from x = 11.733 to x = 18.472 is : 8.9999892677
where the expected value is : 8.9999

The Monte Carlo numerical integration of the function
        f: x -> y = _R( 1 + sinh(2*x)*_P2(log(x)) )
        from x = 0.9 to x = 4 is : 0.584976671612
where the expected value is : 0.584977

The Monte Carlo numerical integration of the function
        f: x -> y = (cosh(x)*sin(x))/ sqrt( pow(x,3) + _P2(sin(x)))
        from x = 1.85 to x = 4.81 is : -3.34553137474
where the expected value is : -3.34553
```

 This is also available as the `monte_carlo_integrator.py` file under the `Chapter08` directory in this book's repository.

The CUDA Thrust library

We will now look at the CUDA Thrust Library. This library's central feature is a high-level vector container that is similar C++'s own vector container. While this may sound trivial, this will allow us to program in CUDA C with less reliance on pointers, mallocs, and frees. Like the C++ vector container, Thrust's vector container handles the resizing and concatenation of elements automatically, and with the magic of C++ destructors, *freeing* is also handled automatically when a Thrust vector object goes out of scope.

Thrust actually provides two vector containers: one for the host-side, and one for the device-side. The host-side Thrust vector is more or less identical to the STL vector, with the main difference being that it can interact more easily with the GPU. Let's write a little bit of code in proper CUDA C to get a feel for how this works.

Let's start with the include statements. We'll be using the headers for both the host and device side vectors, and we'll also include the C++ `iostream` library, which will allow us to perform basic I/O operations on the Terminal:

```
#include <thrust/host_vector.h>
#include <thrust/device_vector.h>
#include <iostream>
```

Let's just use the standard C++ namespace (this is so that we don't have to type in the `std::` resolution operator when checking the output):

```
using namespace std;
```

We will now make our main function and set up an empty Thrust vector on the host side. Again, these are C++ templates, so we have to choose the datatype upon declaration with the < > brackets. We will set this up to be an array of integers:

```
int main(void)
{
 thrust::host_vector<int> v;
```

Now, let's append some integers to the end of v by using `push_back`, exactly how we would do so with a regular STL vector:

```
v.push_back(1);
v.push_back(2);
v.push_back(3);
v.push_back(4);
```

We will now iterate through all of the values in the vector, and output each value:

 The output here should be `v[0] == 1` through `v[3] == 4`.

```
for (int i = 0; i < v.size(); i++)
    cout << "v[" << i << "] == " << v[i] << endl;
```

This may have seemed trivial so far. Let's set up a Thrust vector on the GPU and then copy the contents from v:

```
thrust::device_vector<int> v_gpu = v;
```

Yes, that's all—only one line, and we're done. All of the content of v on the host will now be copied to v_gpu on the device! (If this doesn't amaze you, please take another look at Chapter 6, *Debugging and Profiling Your CUDA Code*, and think about how many lines this would have taken us before.)

Let's try using `push_back` on our new GPU vector, and see if we can concatenate another value to it:

```
v_gpu.push_back(5);
```

We will now check the contents of v_gpu, like so:

```
for (int i = 0; i < v_gpu.size(); i++)
    std::cout << "v_gpu[" << i << "] == " << v_gpu[i] << std::endl;
```

 This part should output v_gpu[0] == 1 through v_gpu[4] == 5.

Again, thanks to the destructors of these objects, we don't have to do any cleanup in the form of freeing any chunks of allocated memory. We can now just return from the program, and we are done:

```
    return 0;
}
```

Using functors in Thrust

Let's see how we can use a concept known as **functors** in Thrust. In C++, a **functor** is a class or struct object that looks and acts like a function; this lets us use something that looks and acts like a function, but can hold some parameters that don't have to be set every time it is used.

Let's start a new Thrust program with the appropriate include statements, and use the standard namespace:

```
#include <thrust/host_vector.h>
#include <thrust/device_vector.h>
#include <iostream>
using namespace std;
```

Now, let's set up a basic functor. We will use a struct to represent this, rather than class. This will be a weighted multiplication function, and we will store the weight in a float called w. We will make a constructor that sets up the weight with a default value of 1:

```
struct multiply_functor {
  float w;
  multiply_functor(float _w = 1) : w(_w) {}
```

We will now set up our functor with the `operator()` keyword; this will indicate to the compiler to treat the following block of code as the `default` function for objects of this type. Remember that this will be running on the GPU as a device function, so we precede the whole thing with `__device__`. We indicate the inputs with parentheses and output the appropriate value, which is just a scaled multiple. Now, we can close off the definition of our struct with `};`:

```
    __device__ float operator() (const float & x, const float & y) {
        return w * x * y;
    }
};
```

Now, let's use this to make a basic dot product function; recall that this requires a pointwise multiplication between two arrays, followed by a `reduce` type sum. Let's start by declaring our function and creating a new vector, z, that will hold the values of the point-wise multiplication:

```
float dot_product(thrust::device_vector<float> &v,
thrust::device_vector<float> &w ), thrust::device_vector<float> &z)
{
  thrust::device_vector<float> z(v.size());
```

We will now use Thrust's `transform` operation, which will act on the inputs of v and w point-wise, and output into z. Notice how we input the functor into the last slot of transform; by using the plain closed parentheses like so, it will use the default value of the constructor (w = 1) so that this will act as a normal, non-weighted/scaled dot product:

```
thrust::transform(v.begin(), v.end(), w.begin(), z.begin(),
multiply_functor());
```

We can now sum over z with Thrust's reduce function. Let's just return the value:

```
return thrust::reduce(z.begin(), z.end());
}
```

We're done. Now, let's write some test code—we'll just take the dot product of the vectors [1,2,3] and [1,1,1], which will be easy for us to check. (This will be 6.)

Let's just set up the first vector, v, using `push_back`:

```
int main(void)
{
    thrust::device_vector<float> v;
    v.push_back(1.0f);
    v.push_back(2.0f);
    v.push_back(3.0f);
```

We can now declare a vector, w, to be of size 3, and we can set its default values to 1 using Thrust's fill function, like so:

```
thrust::device_vector<float> w(3);
thrust::fill(w.begin(), w.end(), 1.0f);
```

Let's do a check to make sure that our values are set correctly by outputting their values to cout:

```
for (int i = 0; i < v.size(); i++)
  cout << "v[" << i << "] == " << v[i] << endl;

for (int i = 0; i < w.size(); i++)
  cout << "w[" << i << "] == " << w[i] << endl;
```

Now, we can check the output of our dot product, and then return from the program:

```
cout << "dot_product(v , w) == " << dot_product(v,w) << endl;
return 0;
}
```

Let's compile this (from the command line in both Linux or Windows by using nvcc thrust_dot_product.cu -o thrust_dot_product) and run it:

```
PS C:\Users\btuom\examples\8> .\thrust_dot_product.exe
v[0] == 1
v[1] == 2
v[2] == 3
w[0] == 1
w[1] == 1
w[2] == 1
dot_product(v , w) == 6
```

 The code for this is also available in the thrust_dot_product.cu file in the Chapter08 directory in this book's repository.

Summary

In this chapter, we looked at how to initialize a stream of random numbers in cuRAND by choosing the appropriate seed. Since computers are deterministic devices, they can only generate lists of pseudo-random numbers, so our seed should be something truly random; generally, adding a thread ID to the clock time in milliseconds will work well enough for most purposes.

We then looked at how we can use the uniform distribution from cuRAND to do a basic estimate of Pi. Then we took on a more ambitious project of creating a Python class that can compute definite integrals of arbitrary functions; we used some ideas from metaprogramming coupled with the CUDA Math API to define these `arbitrary` functions. Finally, we had a brief overview of the CUDA Thrust library, which is generally used for writing pure CUDA C programs outside of Python. Thrust most notably provides a `device_vector` container that is similar to the standard C++ `vector`. This reduces some of the cognitive overhead from using pointers in CUDA C.

Finally, we looked at a brief example of how to use Thrust with an appropriate functor to do simple `point-wise` and `reduce` operations, in the form of the implementation of a simple dot product function.

Questions

1. Try rewriting the Monte Carlo integration examples (in the __main__ function in `monte_carlo_integrator.py`) to use the CUDA `instrinsic` functions. How does the accuracy compare to before?

2. We only used the uniform distribution in all of our cuRAND examples. Can you name one possible use or application of using the normal (Gaussian) random distribution in GPU programming?

3. Suppose that we use two different seeds to generate a list of 100 pseudo-random numbers. Should we ever concatenate these into a list of 200 numbers?

4. In the last example, try adding __host__ before __device__ in the definition of our `operator()` function in the `multiply_functor` struct. Now, see if you can directly implement a host-side dot-product function using this functor without any further modifications.

5. Take a look at the `strided_range.cu` file in the Thrust `examples` directory. Can you think of how to use this to implement a general matrix-matrix multiplication using Thrust?

6. What is the importance of the `operator()` function when defining a functor?

9
Implementation of a Deep Neural Network

We will now use our accumulated knowledge of GPU programming to implement our very own deep neural network (DNN) with PyCUDA. DNNs have attracted a lot of interest in the last decade, as they provide a robust and elegant model for machine learning (ML). DNNs was also one of the first applications (outside of rendering graphics) that were able to show the true power of GPUs by leveraging their massive parallel throughput, which ultimately helped NVIDIA rise to become a major player in the field of artificial intelligence.

In the course of this book, we have mostly been covering individual topics in a *bubble* on a chapter-by-chapter basis—here, we will build on many of the subjects we have learned about thus far for our very own implementation of a DNN. While there are several open source frameworks for GPU-based DNNs currently available to the general public—for example, Google's TensorFlow and Keras, Microsoft's CNTK, Facebook's Caffe2, and PyTorch—it is very instructive to go through an implementation of one from scratch, which will give us a greater insight and appreciation of the underlying technologies required for DNNs. We have a lot of material to cover here, so we'll cut right to the chase after a brief introduction to some of the basic concepts.

In this chapter, we will be looking at the following:

- Understanding what an **artificial neuron** (**AN**) is
- Understanding how many ANs can be combined together in a **deep neural network** (**DNN**)
- Implementing a DNN from scratch in CUDA and Python
- Understanding how cross-entropy loss can be used to evaluate the output of a neural network
- Implementing gradient descent to train an NN
- Learning how to train and test an NN on a small dataset

Technical requirements

A Linux or Windows 10 PC with a modern NVIDIA GPU (2016—onward) is required for this chapter, with all of the necessary GPU drivers and the CUDA Toolkit (9.0–onward) installed. A suitable Python 2.7 installation (such as Anaconda Python 2.7) with the PyCUDA module is also required.

This chapter's code is also available on GitHub at `https://github.com/PacktPublishing/Hands-On-GPU-Programming-with-Python-and-CUDA`.

> For more information about the prerequisites for this chapter, check out the preface of this book. For the software and hardware requirements, check out the README file in `https://github.com/PacktPublishing/Hands-On-GPU-Programming-with-Python-and-CUDA`.

Artificial neurons and neural networks

Let's briefly go over some of the basics of **machine learning (ML)** and **neural networks (NNs)**. In Machine Learning, our goal is to take a collection of data with a particular set of labeled classes or characteristics and use these examples to train our system to predict the values of future data. We call a program or function that predicts classes or labels of future data based on prior training data a **classifier**.

There are many types of classifiers, but here we will be focusing on NNs. The idea behind NNs is that they (allegedly) work in a way that is similar to the human brain, in that they learn and classify data using a collection of **artificial neurons (ANs)**, all connected together to form a particular structure. Let's step back for a moment, though, and look at what an individual AN is. In mathematics, this is just an *affine* function from the linear space $\mathbf{R}^n$ to $\mathbf{R}$, like so:

$$AN(\vec{x}) = \vec{w} \cdot \vec{x} + b \text{ where } \vec{x}, \vec{w} \in \mathbb{R}^n, b \in \mathbb{R}$$

We can see that this can be characterized as a dot product between a constant weight vector w and an input vector x, with an additional bias constant b added to the end. (Again, the only *input* into this function here is x; the other values are constants!)

Now, individually a single AN is fairly useless (and stupid), as their *intelligence* only emerges when acting in cooperation with a large number of other ANs. Our first step is to stack a collection of m similar ANs on top of each other so as to form what we will call a **dense layer (DL)**. This is dense because each neuron will process every single input value from x – each AN will take in an array or vector value from $\mathbf{R}^n$ and output a single value in $\mathbf{R}$. Since there are m neurons, this means that we can say their output collectively is in the space $\mathbf{R}^m$. We will notice that if we stack the weights for each neuron in our layer, so as to form an $m \times n$ matrix of weights, we can then just calculate the output of each neuron with a matrix multiplication followed by the addition of the appropriate biases:

$$DL(\vec{x}) = W\vec{x} + \vec{b}, \text{ where } \vec{x} \in \mathbb{R}^n, W = \begin{bmatrix} \vec{w_0}^T \\ \vdots \\ \vec{w_{m-1}}^T \end{bmatrix} \in \mathbb{R}^{m \times n}, \vec{b} = \begin{bmatrix} b_0 \\ \vdots \\ b_{m-1} \end{bmatrix} \in \mathbb{R}^m$$

Now, let's suppose that we want to build an NN classifier that can classify k different classes; we can create a new additional dense layer that takes in the m values from the prior dense layer, and outputs k values. Supposing that we have the appropriate weight and bias values for each layer (which are certainly not trivial to find), and that we also have the appropriate **activation function** set up after each layer (which we will define later), this will act as a classifier between our k distinct classes, giving us the probability of x falling into each respective class based on the outputs of the final layer. Of course, we're getting way ahead of ourselves here, but that is, in a nutshell, how an NN works.

Now, it seems like we can just keep connecting dense layers to each other into long chains to achieve classifications. This is what is known as a DNN. When we have a layer that is not directly connected to the inputs or outputs, that is known as a hidden layer. The strength of a DNN is that the additional layers allow the NN to capture abstractions and subtleties of the data that a shallow NN could not pick up on.

Implementing a dense layer of artificial neurons

Now, let's implement the most important building block of an NN, the **dense layer**. Let's start by declaring a CUDA kernel, like so:

```
__global__ void dense_eval(int num_outputs, int num_inputs, int relu, int
sigmoid, float * w, float * b, float * x, float *y, int batch_size, int
w_t, int b_t, float delta)
```

Let's go over the inputs, one by one. `num_outputs`, of course, indicates the total number of outputs this layer has; this is exactly the number of neurons in the layer. `num_inputs` tells us the size of the input data. Setting a positive value for `relu` and `sigmoid` will indicate that we should use the corresponding activation function on the output of this layer, which we will define later. `w` and `b` are arrays containing the weights and biases of this layer, while `x` and `y` will act as our inputs and outputs. Oftentimes, we wish to classify more than one piece of data at a time. We can indicate this by setting `batch_size` to be the number of points we wish to predict. Finally, `w_t`, `b_t`, and `delta` will be used in the training process to determine the appropriate weights and biases for this layer by means of **gradient descent**. (We will see more on gradient descent in a later section.)

Now, let's start writing our kernel. We will parallelize the computations over each output, so we will set an integer `i` to be the global thread ID to this end, and have any unnecessary extra threads which happen to be running this kernel to just not do anything with the appropriate `if` statement:

```
{
  int i = blockDim.x*blockIdx.x + threadIdx.x;

  if (i < num_outputs)
  {
```

Now, let's iterate over each data point in the batch with the appropriate `for` loop:

```
for(int k=0; k < batch_size; k++)
{
```

We will multiply and accumulate the 32-bit floats from the weights and inputs into a 64-bit double `temp` and then add the appropriate bias point. We will then typecast this back to a 32-bit float and put the value in the output array, and then close off the loop over `k`:

```
double temp = 0.0f;
  for (int j = 0; j < num_inputs; j++)
  {
     temp += ((double) w[(num_inputs)*i + j ] ) * ( (double) x[k*num_inputs +
j]);
  }
  temp += (double) b[i];
  y[k * num_outputs + i] = (float) temp;
}
```

TIP

Multiply and accumulate types of operations are generally subject to a great loss of numerical precision. This can be mitigated by using a temporary variable of higher precision to store values in the course of the operation, and then typecasting this variable back to the original precision after the operation is completed.

To train an NN, we will ultimately have to calculate the derivative (from calculus) of our NN with respect to each weight and bias within each individual layer, which is with respect to a particular batch of inputs. Remember that the derivative of a mathematical function f at the value x can be estimated as $f(x + \delta) - f(x) / \delta$, where delta ($\delta$) is some sufficiently small positive value. We will use the input values w_t and b_t to indicate to the kernel whether we want to calculate the derivative with respect to a particular weight or bias; otherwise, we will set these input values to a negative value to evaluate only for this layer. We will also set delta to be an appropriately small value for the calculation of the derivative, and use this to increment the value of the appropriate bias or weight:

```
if( w_t >= 0 && i == (w_t / num_inputs))
  {
  int j = w_t % num_inputs;
  for(int k=0; k < batch_size; k++)
    y[k*num_outputs + i] += delta*x[k*num_inputs+j];
  }
if( b_t >= 0 && i == b_t )
  {
    for(int k=0; k < batch_size; k++)
    y[k*num_outputs + i] += delta;
  }
```

Now, we will add some code for what is known as the **rectified linear unit** (or **ReLU**) and **sigmoid activation functions**. These are used for processing the immediate output of a dense neural layer. ReLU just sets all negative values to 0, while acting as an identity for positive inputs, while sigmoid just computes the value of the `sigmoid` function on each value ($1 / (1 + e^{-x})$). ReLU (or any other activation function) is used between hidden layers in an NN as a means to make the entire NN act as a nonlinear function; otherwise, the entire NN would constitute a trivial (and inefficiently computed) matrix operation. (While there are many other nonlinear activation functions that can be used between layers, ReLU has been found to be a particularly effective function for training.) Sigmoid is used as a final layer in an NN intended for **labeling**, that is, one that may assign multiple labels for a given input, as opposed to assigning an input to a single class.

Let's go up a little bit in the file, before we even begin to define this CUDA kernel, and define these operations as C macros. We will also remember to put in the CUDA-C code we've just written while we are at it:

```
DenseEvalCode = '''
#define _RELU(x) ( ((x) > 0.0f) ? (x) : 0.0f )
#define _SIGMOID(x) ( 1.0f / (1.0f + expf(-(x)) ))
```

Now, we will use the kernel inputs `relu` and `sigmoid` to indicate whether we should use these additional layers; we will take a positive input from these to indicate that they should be used, respectively. We can add this, close off our kernel, and compile it into a usable Python function:

```
if(relu > 0 || sigmoid > 0)
for(int k=0; k < batch_size; k++)
  {
    float temp = y[k * num_outputs + i];
    if (relu > 0)
     temp = _RELU(temp);
    if (sigmoid > 0)
     temp = _SIGMOID(temp);
    y[k * num_outputs + i] = temp;
  }
 }
 return;
}
'''
eval_mod = SourceModule(DenseEvalCode)
eval_ker = eval_mod.get_function('dense_eval')
```

Now, let's go to the beginning of the file and set up the appropriate import statements. Notice that we will include the `csv` module, which will be used for processing data inputs for testing and training:

```
from __future__ import division
import pycuda.autoinit
import pycuda.driver as drv
from pycuda import gpuarray
from pycuda.compiler import SourceModule
from pycuda.elementwise import ElementwiseKernel
import numpy as np
from Queue import Queue
import csv
import time
```

Now, let's continue setting up our dense layer; we will want to wrap this within a Python class for ease of use, which will make our lives much easier when we start connecting these dense layers together into a full-blown NN. We'll call `class DenseLayer` and start by writing a constructor. Most of the inputs and setup here should be self-explanatory: we should definitely add an option to load weights and biases from a pre-trained network, and we'll also include the option to specify a default *delta* value as well as a default stream. (If no weights or biases are given, weights are initialized to random values, while all biases are set to 0.) We will also specify whether to use ReLU or sigmoid layers here, as well. Toward the end, notice how we set up the block and grid sizes:

```python
class DenseLayer:
    def __init__(self, num_inputs=None, num_outputs=None, weights=None,
b=None, stream=None, relu=False, sigmoid=False, delta=None):
        self.stream = stream

        if delta is None:
            self.delta = np.float32(0.001)
        else:
            self.delta = np.float32(delta)

        if weights is None:
            weights = np.random.rand(num_outputs, num_inputs) - .5
            self.num_inputs = np.int32(num_inputs)
        self.num_outputs = np.int32(num_outputs)

        if type(weights) != pycuda.gpuarray.GPUArray:
            self.weights = gpuarray.to_gpu_async(np.array(weights,
            dtype=np.float32) , stream = self.stream)
        else:
            self.weights = weights

        if num_inputs is None or num_outputs is None:
            self.num_inputs = np.int32(self.weights.shape[1])
            self.num_outputs = np.int32(self.weights.shape[0])

        else:
            self.num_inputs = np.int32(num_inputs)
            self.num_outputs = np.int32(num_outputs)

        if b is None:
            b = gpuarray.zeros((self.num_outputs,),dtype=np.float32)

        if type(b) != pycuda.gpuarray.GPUArray:
            self.b = gpuarray.to_gpu_async(np.array(b,
            dtype=np.float32) , stream = self.stream)
        else:
            self.b = b
```

```
self.relu = np.int32(relu)
self.sigmoid = np.int32(sigmoid)

self.block = (32,1,1)
self.grid = (int(np.ceil(self.num_outputs / 32)), 1,1)
```

Now, we will set up a function in this class to evaluate inputs from this layer; we will meticulously check the input (x) to determine if it is already on the GPU (transferring it over to a gpuarray if not), and we will let the user specify a preallocated gpuarray for output (y), manually allocating an output array if one is not specified. We will also check the delta and w_t/b_t values for the case of training, as well as batch_size. We will then run the kernel on the x input with outputs going into y, and finally return y as the output value:

```
def eval_(self, x, y=None, batch_size=None, stream=None, delta=None, w_t =
None, b_t = None):

if stream is None:
    stream = self.stream

if type(x) != pycuda.gpuarray.GPUArray:
    x = gpuarray.to_gpu_async(np.array(x,dtype=np.float32),
stream=self.stream)

if batch_size is None:
    if len(x.shape) == 2:
        batch_size = np.int32(x.shape[0])
    else:
        batch_size = np.int32(1)

if delta is None:
    delta = self.delta

delta = np.float32(delta)

if w_t is None:
    w_t = np.int32(-1)

if b_t is None:
    b_t = np.int32(-1)

if y is None:
    if batch_size == 1:
        y = gpuarray.empty((self.num_outputs,), dtype=np.float32)
    else:
        y = gpuarray.empty((batch_size, self.num_outputs),
dtype=np.float32)
```

```
    eval_ker(self.num_outputs, self.num_inputs, self.relu, self.sigmoid,
 self.weights, self.b, x, y, np.int32(batch_size), w_t, b_t, delta ,
 block=self.block, grid=self.grid , stream=stream)

   return y
```

There we go. We have fully implemented a dense layer!

Implementation of the softmax layer

We will now look at how we can implement a **softmax layer**. As we have already
discussed, a sigmoid layer is used for assigning labels to a class—that is, if you want to
have multiple nonexclusive characteristics that you want to infer from an input, you should
use a sigmoid layer. A **softmax layer** is used when you only want to assign a single class to
a sample by inference—this is done by computing a probability for each possible class (with
probabilities over all classes, of course, summing to 100%). We can then select the class with
the highest probability to give the final classification.

Now, let's see exactly what the softmax layer does—given a set of a collection of N real
numbers $(c_0, ..., c_{N-1})$, we first compute the sum of the exponential function on each number
$(S = e^{c_0} + ... + e^{c_{N-1}})$, and then calculate the exponential of each number divided by this
sum to yield the softmax:

$$(e^{c_0}/S, ..., e^{c_{N-1}}/S)$$

Let's start with our implementation. We will start by writing two very short CUDA kernels:
one that takes the exponential of each input, and another that takes the mean over all of the
points:

```
SoftmaxExpCode='''
__global__ void softmax_exp( int num, float *x, float *y, int batch_size)
{
 int i = blockIdx.x * blockDim.x + threadIdx.x;

 if (i < num)
 {
  for (int k=0; k < batch_size; k++)
  {
   y[num*k + i] = expf(x[num*k+i]);
  }
 }
}
'''
```

```
exp_mod = SourceModule(SoftmaxExpCode)
exp_ker = exp_mod.get_function('softmax_exp')

SoftmaxMeanCode='''
__global__ void softmax_mean( int num, float *x, float *y, int batch_size)
{
 int i = blockDim.x*blockIdx.x + threadIdx.x;

 if (i < batch_size)
 {
  float temp = 0.0f;

  for(int k=0; k < num; k++)
   temp += x[i*num + k];


  for(int k=0; k < num; k++)
   y[i*num+k] = x[i*num+k] / temp;
 }

 return;
}'''

mean_mod = SourceModule(SoftmaxMeanCode)
mean_ker = mean_mod.get_function('softmax_mean')
```

Now, let's write a Python wrapper class, like we did previously. First, we will start with the constructor, and we will indicate the number of both inputs and outputs with num. We can also specify a default stream, if we wish:

```
class SoftmaxLayer:
    def __init__(self, num=None, stream=None):
      self.num = np.int32(num)
      self.stream = stream
```

Now, let's write eval_ function in a way that is similar to the dense layer:

```
def eval_(self, x, y=None, batch_size=None, stream=None):
 if stream is None:
 stream = self.stream

 if type(x) != pycuda.gpuarray.GPUArray:
  temp = np.array(x,dtype=np.float32)
  x = gpuarray.to_gpu_async( temp , stream=stream)

 if batch_size==None:
  if len(x.shape) == 2:
   batch_size = np.int32(x.shape[0])
```

```
    else:
     batch_size = np.int32(1)
   else:
     batch_size = np.int32(batch_size)

   if y is None:
     if batch_size == 1:
       y = gpuarray.empty((self.num,), dtype=np.float32)
   else:
     y = gpuarray.empty((batch_size, self.num), dtype=np.float32)

   exp_ker(self.num, x, y, batch_size, block=(32,1,1), grid=(int( np.ceil(
   self.num / 32) ), 1, 1), stream=stream)

   mean_ker(self.num, y, y, batch_size, block=(32,1,1), grid=(int( np.ceil(
   batch_size / 32)), 1,1), stream=stream)

   return y
```

Implementation of Cross-Entropy loss

Now, let's implement what is known as the **cross-entropy loss** function. This is used to measure how accurate an NN is on a small subset of data points during the training process; the bigger the value that is output by our loss function, the more inaccurate our NN is at properly classifying the given data. We do this by calculating a standard mean log-entropy difference between the expected output and the actual output of the NN. For numerical stability, we will limit the value of the output to 1:

```
MAX_ENTROPY = 1

def cross_entropy(predictions=None, ground_truth=None):

 if predictions is None or ground_truth is None:
   raise Exception("Error! Both predictions and ground truth must be float32
arrays")

 p = np.array(predictions).copy()
 y = np.array(ground_truth).copy()

 if p.shape != y.shape:
   raise Exception("Error! Both predictions and ground_truth must have same
shape.")

 if len(p.shape) != 2:
   raise Exception("Error! Both predictions and ground_truth must be 2D
```

```
arrays.")

total_entropy = 0

for i in range(p.shape[0]):
 for j in range(p.shape[1]):
  if y[i,j] == 1:
    total_entropy += min( np.abs( np.nan_to_num( np.log( p[i,j] ) ) ) ),
MAX_ENTROPY)
   else:
    total_entropy += min( np.abs( np.nan_to_num( np.log( 1 - p[i,j] ) ) ) ),
MAX_ENTROPY)

 return total_entropy / p.size
```

Implementation of a sequential network

Now, let's implement one final class that will combine multiple dense layer and softmax layer objects into a single coherent feed-forward sequential neural network. This will be implemented as another class, which will subsume the other classes. Let's first start by writing the constructor—we will be able to set the max batch size here, which will affect how much memory is allocated for the use of this network – we'll store some allocated memory used for weights and input/output for each layer in the list variable, network_mem. We will also store the DenseLayer and SoftmaxLayer objects in the list network, and information about each layer in the NN in network_summary. Notice how we can also set up some training parameters here, including the delta, how many streams to use for gradient descent (we'll see this later), as well as the number of training epochs.

We can also see one other input at the beginning called layers. Here, we can indicate the construction of the NN by describing each layer, which the constructor will create by iterating through each element of layers and calling the add_layer method, which we will implement next:

```
class SequentialNetwork:
 def __init__(self, layers=None, delta=None, stream = None,
max_batch_size=32, max_streams=10, epochs = 10):

 self.network = []
 self.network_summary = []
 self.network_mem = []

 if stream is not None:
  self.stream = stream
 else:
```

```
  self.stream = drv.Stream()

  if delta is None:
    delta = 0.0001

  self.delta = delta
  self.max_batch_size=max_batch_size
  self.max_streams = max_streams
  self.epochs = epochs

  if layers is not None:
    for layer in layers:
      add_layer(self, layer)
```

Now, let's implement the `add_layer` method. We will use a dictionary data type to pass all of the relevant information about the layer to the sequential network—including the type of layer (dense, softmax, and so on), the number of inputs/outputs, weights, and biases. This will append the appropriate object and information to the object's network and `network_summary` list variables, as well as appropriately allocate `gpuarray` objects to the `network_mem` list:

```
def add_layer(self, layer):
  if layer['type'] == 'dense':
    if len(self.network) == 0:
      num_inputs = layer['num_inputs']
    else:
      num_inputs = self.network_summary[-1][2]

    num_outputs = layer['num_outputs']
    sigmoid = layer['sigmoid']
    relu = layer['relu']
    weights = layer['weights']
    b = layer['bias']

    self.network.append(DenseLayer(num_inputs=num_inputs,
num_outputs=num_outputs, sigmoid=sigmoid, relu=relu, weights=weights, b=b))
    self.network_summary.append( ('dense', num_inputs, num_outputs))

    if self.max_batch_size > 1:
      if len(self.network_mem) == 0:
self.network_mem.append(gpuarray.empty((self.max_batch_size,
self.network_summary[-1][1]), dtype=np.float32))
      self.network_mem.append(gpuarray.empty((self.max_batch_size,
self.network_summary[-1][2] ), dtype=np.float32 ) )
    else:
      if len(self.network_mem) == 0:
      self.network_mem.append( gpuarray.empty( (self.network_summary[-1][1], ),
```

```
dtype=np.float32 ) )
  self.network_mem.append( gpuarray.empty((self.network_summary[-1][2], ),
dtype=np.float32 ) )

 elif layer['type'] == 'softmax':

  if len(self.network) == 0:
   raise Exception("Error! Softmax layer can't be first!")

  if self.network_summary[-1][0] != 'dense':
   raise Exception("Error! Need a dense layer before a softmax layer!")


  num = self.network_summary[-1][2]
  self.network.append(SoftmaxLayer(num=num))
  self.network_summary.append(('softmax', num, num))

  if self.max_batch_size > 1:
   self.network_mem.append(gpuarray.empty((self.max_batch_size,
self.network_summary[-1][2] ), dtype=np.float32))
  else:
   self.network_mem.append( gpuarray.empty((self.network_summary[-1][2], ),
dtype=np.float32))
```

Implementation of inference methods

We will now add two methods for inference to our `SequentialNetwork` class—that is, for predicting an output given for a particular input. The first method we will just call `predict`, which will be used by the end user. In the course of the training process, we will have to make predictions based on a partial result from only some of the layers, and we will make another method to this end called `partial_predict`.

Let's start by implementing *predict*. This will take two inputs—a collection of samples in the form of a one- or two-dimensional NumPy array, and possibly a user-defined CUDA stream. We will start by doing some type-checks and formatting on the samples (here, called x), remembering that the samples will be stored row-wise:

```
def predict(self, x, stream=None):

 if stream is None:
  stream = self.stream

 if type(x) != np.ndarray:
  temp = np.array(x, dtype = np.float32)
  x = temp
```

```
if(x.size == self.network_mem[0].size):
  self.network_mem[0].set_async(x, stream=stream)
else:

  if x.size > self.network_mem[0].size:
   raise Exception("Error: batch size too large for input.")

  x0 = np.zeros((self.network_mem[0].size,), dtype=np.float32)
  x0[0:x.size] = x.ravel()
  self.network_mem[0].set_async(x0.reshape( self.network_mem[0].shape),
stream=stream)

if(len(x.shape) == 2):
  batch_size = x.shape[0]
else:
  batch_size = 1
```

Now, let's perform the actual inference step. We just have to iterate through our entire neural network, performing an `eval_` on each layer:

```
for i in xrange(len(self.network)):
  self.network[i].eval_(x=self.network_mem[i], y= self.network_mem[i+1],
batch_size=batch_size, stream=stream)
```

We will now pull the final output of the NN, the GPU, and return it to the user. If the number of samples in x is actually smaller than the maximum batch size, we will slice the output array appropriately before it is returned:

```
y = self.network_mem[-1].get_async(stream=stream)

if len(y.shape) == 2:
  y = y[0:batch_size, :]

return y
```

Now, with that done, let's implement `partial_predict`. Let's briefly discuss the idea behind this. When we are in the training process, we will evaluate a collection of samples, and then look at how a subtle change of adding *delta* to each weight and bias individually will affect the outputs. To save time, we can calculate the outputs of each layer and store them for a given collection of samples, and then only recompute the output for the layer where we change the weight, as well as for all subsequent layers. We'll see the idea behind this in a little more depth soon, but for now, we can implement this like so:

```
def partial_predict(self, layer_index=None, w_t=None, b_t=None,
partial_mem=None, stream=None, batch_size=None, delta=None):

  self.network[layer_index].eval_(x=self.network_mem[layer_index], y =
```

```
partial_mem[layer_index+1], batch_size=batch_size, stream = stream,
w_t=w_t, b_t=b_t, delta=delta)

 for i in xrange(layer_index+1, len(self.network)):
   self.network[i].eval_(x=partial_mem[i], y =partial_mem[i+1],
batch_size=batch_size, stream = stream)
```

Gradient descent

We will now make a full implementation of the training method for our NN in the form of **batch-stochastic gradient descent (BSGD)**. Let's think about what this means, word by word. **Batch** means that this training algorithm will operate on a collection of training samples at once, rather than all of the samples simultaneously, while **stochastic** indicates that each batch is chosen randomly. **Gradient** means that we will be using a gradient from calculus—which, here, is the collection of derivatives for each weight and bias on the loss function. Finally, **descent** means that we are trying to reduce the loss function—we do this by iteratively making subtle changes on the weights and biases by *subtracting* the Gradient.

Remember from calculus that the gradient of a point always points in the direction of the greatest *increase*, with its opposite direction being that of the greatest *decrease*. Since we want a *decrease*, we subtract the gradient.

We will now implement BSGD as the `bsgd` method in our `SequentialNetwork` class. Let's go over the input parameters of `bsgd`, one by one:

- `training` will be a two-dimensional NumPy array of training samples
- `labels` will be the desired output of the final layer of the NN corresponding to each training sample
- `delta` will indicate how much we should increase a weight for the calculation of derivatives by
- `max_streams` will indicate the maximum number of concurrent CUDA streams that BSGD will perform calculations over
- `batch_size` will indicate how large we want the batches that we will calculate the loss function on for each update of the weights
- `epochs` will indicate how many times we shuffle the order of the current set of samples, break into a collection of batches, and then perform BSGD on
- `training_rate` will indicate the rate at which we will update our weights and biases with our gradient calculations

We'll start out this method as usual and perform some checks and typecasting, set up the collection of CUDA stream objects into a Python list, and allocate some additional needed GPU memory in another list:

```
def bsgd(self, training=None, labels=None, delta=None, max_streams = None,
batch_size = None, epochs = 1, training_rate=0.01):

 training_rate = np.float32(training_rate)

 training = np.float32(training)
 labels = np.float32(labels)

 if( training.shape[0] != labels.shape[0] ):
  raise Exception("Number of training data points should be same as
labels!")

 if max_streams is None:
  max_streams = self.max_streams

 if epochs is None:
 epochs = self.epochs

 if delta is None:
 delta = self.delta

 streams = []
 bgd_mem = []

 # create the streams needed for training
 for _ in xrange(max_streams):
  streams.append(drv.Stream())
  bgd_mem.append([])


 # allocate memory for each stream
 for i in xrange(len(bgd_mem)):
  for mem_bank in self.network_mem:
   bgd_mem[i].append( gpuarray.empty_like(mem_bank) )
```

Now, we can begin training. We will start by doing an iteration of the entire BSGD for each epoch, performing a random shuffle of the entire dataset for each epoch. We'll print some information to the terminal as well so that the user will have some status updates in the training process:

```
num_points = training.shape[0]

 if batch_size is None:
```

```
    batch_size = self.max_batch_size

    index = range(training.shape[0])

    for k in xrange(epochs):

        print '-----------------------------------------------------------'
        print 'Starting training epoch: %s' % k
        print 'Batch size: %s , Total number of training samples: %s' %
        (batch_size, num_points)
        print '-----------------------------------------------------------'

        all_grad = []

        np.random.shuffle(index)
```

Now, we will make a loop that iterates over each batch in the shuffled dataset. We start by calculating the entropy from the current batch, and we will print this as well. If the user sees decreases in entropy, then they will know that gradient descent is working here:

```
    for r in xrange(int(np.floor(training.shape[0]/batch_size))):

        batch_index = index[r*batch_size:(r+1)*batch_size]

        batch_training = training[batch_index, :]
        batch_labels = labels[batch_index, :]

        batch_predictions = self.predict(batch_training)

        cur_entropy = cross_entropy(predictions=batch_predictions,
        ground_truth=batch_labels)

        print 'entropy: %s' % cur_entropy
```

We will now iterate through each dense layer of our NN, calculating the gradient for the entire set of weights and biases. We will store these derivatives for the weights and biases in *flattened* (one-dimensional) arrays, which will correspond to the `w_t` and `b_t` indices in our CUDA kernels, which are also flattened. Since we will have multiple streams process different outputs for different weights, we will use a Python Queue container to store the set of weights and biases that are yet to be processed for this batch: we can then just pop values off the top of this container to the next available stream (we'll store these as tuples, with the first element indicating whether this is a weight or bias, in particular):

```
    for i in xrange(len(self.network)):

        if self.network_summary[i][0] != 'dense':
            continue
```

```
all_weights = Queue()

grad_w = np.zeros((self.network[i].weights.size,), dtype=np.float32)
grad_b = np.zeros((self.network[i].b.size,), dtype=np.float32)

for w in xrange( self.network[i].weights.size ):
 all_weights.put( ('w', np.int32(w) ) )

for b in xrange( self.network[i].b.size ):
 all_weights.put(('b', np.int32(b) ) )
```

Now, we need to iterate over each and every weight and bias, which we can do with a `while` loop that checks if the `queue` object we just set up is empty. We will set up another queue, `stream_weights`, that will help us organize which weights and biases each stream has processed. After setting up the weight and bias inputs appropriately, we can now use `partial_predict` by using the current stream and corresponding GPU memory arrays:

 Notice that we already performed a `predict` for this batch of samples to calculate the entropy, so we are now able to perform `partial_predict` on this batch, provided we are careful about which memory and layers we use.

```
while not all_weights.empty():

 stream_weights = Queue()

 for j in xrange(max_streams):

  if all_weights.empty():
    break

  wb = all_weights.get()

  if wb[0] == 'w':
   w_t = wb[1]
   b_t = None
  elif wb[0] == 'b':
   b_t = wb[1]
   w_t = None

  stream_weights.put( wb )

  self.partial_predict(layer_index=i, w_t=w_t, b_t=b_t,
partial_mem=bgd_mem[j], stream=streams[j], batch_size=batch_size,
delta=delta)
```

We have only computed the prediction of the output for alterations of a small set of weights and biases. We will have to compute the entropy for each, and then store the value of the derivative in the flattened arrays:

```
for j in xrange(max_streams):

 if stream_weights.empty():
  break

 wb = stream_weights.get()

 w_predictions = bgd_mem[j][-1].get_async(stream=streams[j])

 w_entropy = cross_entropy(predictions=w_predictions[ :batch_size,:],
ground_truth=batch_labels)



 if wb[0] == 'w':
  w_t = wb[1]
  grad_w[w_t] = -(w_entropy - cur_entropy) / delta

 elif wb[0] == 'b':
  b_t = wb[1]
  grad_b[b_t] = -(w_entropy - cur_entropy) / delta
```

We have now finished the `while` loop. Once we reach the outside of this, we will know that we've calculated the derivatives for all weights and biases for this particular layer. Before we iterate to the next layer, we will append the calculated values for the gradient of the current set of weights and biases into the `all_grad` list. We will also reshape the flattened list of weights back into the original shape while we're at it:

```
all_grad.append([np.reshape(grad_w,self.network[i].weights.shape) ,
grad_b])
```

After we are done iterating over every layer, we can perform the optimization of the weights and biases of our NN on this batch. Notice how if the `training_rate` variable is far less than 1, this will reduce how fast the weights are updated:

```
for i in xrange(len(self.network)):
 if self.network_summary[i][0] == 'dense':
  new_weights = self.network[i].weights.get()
  new_weights += training_rate*all_grad[i][0]
  new_bias = self.network[i].b.get()
  new_bias += training_rate*all_grad[i][1]
  self.network[i].weights.set(new_weights)
  self.network[i].b.set(new_bias)
```

We have fully implemented a (very simple) GPU-based DNN!

Conditioning and normalizing data

Before we move on to training and testing our brand-new NN, we need to step back for a moment and talk about **conditioning** and **normalizing** data. NNs are highly susceptible to numerical error, especially when inputs have a large variance in scale. This can be mitigated by properly **conditioning** our training data; this means that for each point in an input sample, we will calculate the mean and variance of each point over all samples, and then subtract the mean and divide by the standard deviation for each point in each sample before it is input into the NN for either training or inference (prediction). This method is known as **normalization**. Let's put together a small Python function that can do this for us:

```python
def condition_data(data, means=None, stds=None):

  if means is None:
   means = np.mean(data, axis=0)

  if stds is None:
   stds = np.std(data, axis = 0)

  conditioned_data = data.copy()
  conditioned_data -= means
  conditioned_data /= stds

  return (conditioned_data, means, stds)
```

The Iris dataset

We will now construct our very own DNN for a real-life problem: classification of flower types based on the measurements of petals. We will be working with the well-known *Iris dataset* for this. This dataset is stored as a comma-separated value (CSV) text file, with each line containing four different numerical values (petal measurements), followed by the flower type (here, there are three classes—*Iris setosa*, *Iris versicolor*, and *Iris virginica*). We will now design a small DNN that will classify the type of iris, based on this set.

Before we continue, please download the Iris dataset and put it into your working directory. This is available from the UC Irvine Machine Learning repository, which can be found here: https://archive.ics.uci.edu/ml/machine-learning-databases/iris/iris.data.

We will start by processing this file into appropriate data arrays that we can use for training and validating our DNN. Let's start by opening up our main function; we will need to translate the names of the flowers into actual classes that a DNN can output, so let's make a small dictionary that will give us a corresponding label for each class. We will also set up some empty lists to store our training data and labels:

```
if __name__ == '__main__':
 to_class = { 'Iris-setosa' : [1,0,0] , 'Iris-versicolor' : [0,1,0], 'Iris-
virginica' : [0,0,1]}

 iris_data = []
 iris_labels = []
```

Now, let's read from the CSV file. We will use the `reader` function from Python's `csv` module, which we imported earlier:

```
with open('C:/Users/btuom/examples/9/iris.data', 'rb') as csvfile:
 csvreader = csv.reader(csvfile, delimiter=',')
 for row in csvreader:
  newrow = []
  if len(row) != 5:
   break
  for i in range(4):
   newrow.append(row[i])
  iris_data.append(newrow)
  iris_labels.append(to_class[row[4]])
```

We will now randomly shuffle the data and use two-third of these samples as training data. The remaining one-third will be used for test (validation) data:

```
iris_len = len(iris_data)
shuffled_index = list(range(iris_len))
np.random.shuffle(shuffled_index)
iris_data = np.float32(iris_data)
iris_labels = np.float32(iris_labels)
iris_data = iris_data[shuffled_index, :]
iris_labels = iris_labels[shuffled_index,:]

t_len = (2*iris_len) // 3

iris_train = iris_data[:t_len, :]
label_train = iris_labels[:t_len, :]

iris_test = iris_data[t_len:,:]
label_test = iris_labels[t_len:, :]
```

Now, finally, we can begin building our DNN! First, let's create a `SequentialNetwork` object. We'll set the `max_batch_size` to 32:

```
sn = SequentialNetwork( max_batch_size=32 )
```

Now, let's create our NN. This will consist of four dense layers (two hidden) and a softmax layer. We will increment the number of neurons in each layer until the final layer, which will only have three outputs (one for each class). This increasing amount of neurons per layer allows us to capture some of the subtleties of the data:

```
sn.add_layer({'type' : 'dense', 'num_inputs' : 4, 'num_outputs' : 10,
'relu': True, 'sigmoid': False, 'weights' : None, 'bias' : None} )
sn.add_layer({'type' : 'dense', 'num_inputs' : 10, 'num_outputs' : 15,
'relu': True, 'sigmoid': False, 'weights': None, 'bias' : None} )
sn.add_layer({'type' : 'dense', 'num_inputs' : 15, 'num_outputs' : 20,
'relu': True, 'sigmoid': False, 'weights': None, 'bias' : None} )
sn.add_layer({'type' : 'dense', 'num_inputs' : 20, 'num_outputs' : 3,
'relu': True, 'sigmoid': False, 'weights': None , 'bias': None } )
sn.add_layer({'type' : 'softmax'})
```

We will now condition our training data and begin the training with our BSGD method that we just implemented. We will train with `batch_size` set to 16, `max_streams` set to 10, the number of `epochs` set to 100, the `delta` set to 0.0001, and the `training_rate` set to 1—these will be admissible parameters for virtually any modern GPU. We will also time the training procedure while we're at it, which can be rather time-consuming:

```
ctrain, means, stds = condition_data(iris_train)

t1 = time()
sn.bsgd(training=ctrain, labels=label_train, batch_size=16, max_streams=20,
epochs=100 , delta=0.0001, training_rate=1)
training_time = time() - t1
```

Now, our DNN is fully trained. We are ready to begin the validation process! Let's set up a Python variable called `hits` to count the total number of correct classifications. We will also need to condition the validation/testing data too. One more thing—we determine the class by the index corresponding to the largest value of the softmax layer of our DNN. We can check whether this gives us the correct classification by using NumPy's `argmax` function, like so:

```
hits = 0
ctest, _, _ = condition_data(iris_test, means=means, stds=stds)
for i in range(ctest.shape[0]):
  if np.argmax(sn.predict(ctest[i,:])) == np.argmax( label_test[i,:]):
    hits += 1
```

Now, we are ready to check how well our DNN actually works. Let's output the accuracy as well as the total training time:

```
print 'Percentage Correct Classifications: %s' % (float(hits ) /
ctest.shape[0])
print 'Total Training Time: %s' % training_time
```

Now, we are done. We can now fully implement a DNN with Python and CUDA! Generally speaking, you can expect an accuracy ranging from 80%-97% for this particular problem, with a training time of 10-20 minutes on any Pascal-level GPU.

 The code for this chapter is available in the `deep_neural_network.py` file, under the appropriate directory in this book's GitHub repository.

Summary

In this chapter, we started by giving the definition of an artificial neural network, and showed you how individual ANs can be combined into dense layers, which combine together into a full-on deep neural network. We then implemented a dense layer in CUDA-C and made an appropriate corresponding Python wrapper class. We also included functionality to add ReLU and sigmoid layers on the outputs of a dense layer. We saw the definition and motivation of using a softmax layer, which is used for classification problems, and then implemented this in CUDA-C and Python. Finally, we implemented a Python class so that we could build a sequential feed-forward DNN from the prior classes; we implemented a cross-entropy loss function, and then used this in our loss function in our implementation of gradient descent to train the weights and biases in our DNN. Finally, we used our implementation to construct, train, and test a DNN on a real-life dataset.

We now have a great deal of self-confidence in our CUDA programming abilities, since we can write our own GPU-based DNN! We will now move on to some very advanced material in the next two chapters, where we will look at how we can write our own interfaces to compiled CUDA code, as well as some of the very technical ins and outs of NVIDIA GPUs.

Questions

1. Suppose you construct a DNN and after training it, it yields only garbage. After inspection, you find that all of the weights and biases are either huge numbers or NaNs. What might the problem be?
2. Name one possible problem with a small `training_rate` value.
3. Name one possible problem with a large `training_rate` value.
4. Suppose we want to train a DNN that will assign multiple labels to an image of an animal ("slimey", "furry", "red", "brown", and so on). Should we use a sigmoid or softmax layer at the end of the DNN?
5. Suppose we want to classify an image of a single animal as either a cat or dog. Do we use sigmoid or softmax?
6. If we decrease the batch size, will there be more or less updates to the weights and biases during gradient descent training?

Working with Compiled GPU Code

10

Throughout the course of this book, we have generally been reliant on the PyCUDA library to interface our inline CUDA-C code for us automatically, using just-in-time compilation and linking with our Python code. We might recall, however, that sometimes the compilation process can take a while. In Chapter 3, *Getting Started With PyCUDA*, we even saw in detail how the compilation process can contribute to slowdown, and how it can even be somewhat arbitrary as to when inline code will be compiled and retained. In some cases, this may be inconvenient and cumbersome given the application, or even unacceptable in the case of a real-time system.

To this end, we will finally see how to use pre-compiled GPU code from Python. In particular, we will look at three distinct ways to do this. First, we will look at how we can do this by writing a host-side CUDA-C function that can indirectly launch a CUDA kernel. This method will involve invoking the host-side function with the standard Python Ctypes library. Second, we will compile our kernel into what is known as a PTX module, which is effectively a DLL file containing compiled binary GPU. We can then load this file with PyCUDA and launch our kernel directly. Finally, we will end this chapter by looking at how to write our own full-on Ctypes interface to the CUDA Driver API. We can then use the appropriate functions from the Driver API to load our PTX file and launch a kernel.

The learning outcomes for this chapter are as follows:

- Launching compiled (host-side) code with the Ctypes module
- Using host-side CUDA C wrappers with Ctypes to launch a kernel from Python
- How to compile a CUDA C module into a PTX file
- How to load a PTX module into PyCUDA to launch pre-compiled kernels
- How to write your own custom Python interface to the CUDA Driver API

Launching compiled code with Ctypes

We will now give a brief overview of the Ctypes module from the Python Standard Library. Ctypes is used for calling functions from the Linux `.so` (shared object) or Windows. DLL (Dynamically Linked Library) pre-compiled binaries. This will allow us to break out of the world of pure Python and interface with libraries and code that have been written in compiled languages, notably C and C++—it just so happens that Nvidia only provides such pre-compiled binaries for interfacing with our CUDA device, so if we want to sidestep PyCUDA, we will have to use Ctypes.

Let's start with a very basic example: we will show you how to call `printf` directly from Ctypes. Open up an instance of IPython and type `import ctypes`. We are now going to look at how to call the standard `printf` function from Ctypes. First, we will have to import the appropriate library: in Linux, load the LibC library by typing `libc = ctypes.CDLL('libc.so.6')` (in Windows, replace `'libc.so.6'` with `'msvcrt.dll'`). We can now directly call `printf` from the IPython prompt by typing `libc.printf("Hello from ctypes!\n")`. Try it for yourself!

Now let's try something else: type `libc.printf("Pi is approximately %f.\n", 3.14)` from IPython; you should get an error. This is because the `3.14` was not appropriately typecast from a Python float variable to a C double variable—we can do this with Ctypes like so:

```
libc.printf("Pi is approximately %f.\n", ctypes.c_double(3.14))
```

The output should be as expected. As in the case of launching a CUDA kernel from PyCUDA, we have to be equally careful to typecast inputs into functions with Ctypes.

Always be sure to appropriately typecast inputs into any function that you call with Ctypes from Python to the appropriate C datatypes (in Ctypes, these are preceded by c_: `c_float`, `c_double`, `c_char`, `c_int`, and so on).

The Mandelbrot set revisited (again)

Let's revisit the Mandelbrot set that we looked at in Chapter 1, *Why GPU Programming?*, and Chapter 3, *Getting Started with PyCUDA*. First, we will write a full-on CUDA kernel that will compute the Mandelbrot set, given a particular set of parameters, along with an appropriate host-side wrapper function that we may interface to from Ctypes later. We will first be writing these functions into a single CUDA-C .cu source file and then compile this into a DLL or .so binary with the NVCC compiler. Finally, we will write some Python code so that we can run our binary code and display the Mandelbrot set.

We will now apply our knowledge of Ctypes to launch a pre-compiled CUDA kernel from Python without any assistance from PyCUDA. This will require us to write a host-side *kernel launcher* wrapper function in CUDA-C that we may call directly, which itself has been compiled into a dynamic library binary with any necessary GPU code—that is, a Dynamically Linked Library (DLL) binary on Windows, or a shared-object (so) binary on Linux.

We will start, of course, by writing our CUDA-C code, so open up your favorite text editor and follow along. We will begin with the standard include statements:

```
#include <cuda_runtime.h>
#include <stdio.h>
#include <stdlib.h>
#include <math.h>
```

We'll now jump directly into writing our kernel. Notice extern "C" in the code, which will allow us to link to this function externally:

```
extern "C" __global__ void mandelbrot_ker(float * lattice, float *
mandelbrot_graph, int max_iters, float upper_bound_squared, int
lattice_size)
{
```

Let's think for a minute about how this will work: we will use a single one-dimensional array for both the real and imaginary components called lattice, which is of length lattice_size. We will use this to compute a two-dimensional Mandelbrot graph of the shape (lattice_size, lattice_size) into the pre-allocated array, mandelbrot_graph. We will specify the number of iterations to check for divergence at each point with max_iters, specifying the maximum upper bound as before by providing its squared value with upper_bound_squared. (We'll look at the motivation for using the square in a second.)

We will launch this kernel over a one-dimensional grid/block structure, with each thread corresponding to a single point in the graph image of the Mandelbrot set. We can then determine the real/imaginary lattice values for the corresponding point, like so:

```
int tid = blockIdx.x * blockDim.x + threadIdx.x;
if ( tid < lattice_size*lattice_size )
{
    int i = tid % lattice_size;
    int j = lattice_size - 1 - (tid / lattice_size);
    float c_re = lattice[i];
    float c_im = lattice[j];
```

Let's talk about this for a minute. First, remember that we may have to use slightly more threads than necessary, so it's important that we check that the thread ID will correspond to some point in the output image with the `if` statement. Let's also remember that the output array, `mandelbrot_graph`, will be stored as a one-dimensional array that represents a two-dimensional image stored in a row-wise format, and that we will be using `tid` as the index to write in this array. We will use i and j, as well as the x and y coordinates of the graph on the complex plane. Since lattice is a series of real values sorted from small to large, we will have to reverse their order to get the appropriate imaginary values. Also, notice that we will be using plain floats here, rather than some structure or object to represent a complex value. Since there are real and imaginary components in every complex number, we will have to use two floats here to store the complex number corresponding to this thread's lattice point (`c_re` and `c_im`).

We will set up two more variables to handle the divergence check, `z_re` and `z_im`, and set the initial value of this thread's point on the graph to 1 before we check for divergence:

```
float z_re = 0.0f;
float z_im = 0.0f;
mandelbrot_graph[tid] = 1;
```

Now we will do our check for divergence; if it does diverge after `max_iters` iterations, we set the point to 0. Otherwise, it is left at 1:

```
for (int k = 0; k < max_iters; k++)
{
    float temp;
    temp = z_re*z_re - z_im*z_im + c_re;
    z_im = 2*z_re*z_im + c_im;
    z_re = temp;
    if ( (z_re*z_re + z_im*z_im) > upper_bound_squared )
    {
        mandelbrot_graph[tid] = 0;
        break;
```

```
        }
    }
```

Let's talk about this chunk of code for a minute before we continue. Let's remember that each iteration of a Mandelbrot set is computed with complex multiplication and addition for example, `z_new = z*z + c`. Since we are not working with a class that will handle complex values for us, the preceding operation is exactly what we need to do to compute the new real and imaginary values of `z`. We also need to compute the absolute value and see if it exceeds a particular value—remember that the absolute value of a complex number, $c = x + iy$, is computed with $\sqrt{(x^2+y^2)}$. It will actually save us some time here to compute the square of the upper bound and then plug that into the kernel, since it will save us the time of computing the square root of `z_re*z_re + z_im*z_im` for each iteration here.

We're now pretty much done with this kernel—we just need to close off the `if` statement and return from the kernel, and we're done:

```
        }
    return;
}
```

However, we are not completely finished just yet. We need to write a host-side wrapper function with only `extern "C"` in the case of Linux, and `extern "C"` `__declspec(dllexport)` in the case of Windows. (In contrast to a compiled CUDA kernel, this extra word is necessary if we want to be able to access a host-side function from Ctypes in Windows.) The parameters that we put into this function will correspond directly to those that go into the kernel, except these will be stored on the host:

```
extern "C" __declspec(dllexport) void launch_mandelbrot(float * lattice,
float * mandelbrot_graph, int max_iters, float upper_bound, int
lattice_size)
{
```

Now, the first task we will have to do is allocate sufficient memory to store the lattice and output on the GPU with `cudaMalloc`, and then copy the lattice to the GPU with `cudaMemcpy`:

```
    int num_bytes_lattice = sizeof(float) * lattice_size;
    int num_bytes_graph = sizeof(float)* lattice_size*lattice_size;
    float * d_lattice;
    float * d_mandelbrot_graph;
    cudaMalloc((float **) &d_lattice, num_bytes_lattice);
    cudaMalloc((float **) &d_mandelbrot_graph, num_bytes_graph);
    cudaMemcpy(d_lattice, lattice, num_bytes_lattice,
cudaMemcpyHostToDevice);
```

Like many of our other kernels, we will launch this over one-dimensional blocks of size 32 over a one-dimensional grid. We will take the ceiling value of the number of output points to compute, divided by 32, to determine the grid size, like so:

```
int grid_size = (int)  ceil(  ( (double) lattice_size*lattice_size ) /
( (double) 32 ) );
```

Now we are ready to launch our kernel by using the traditional CUDA-C triple-triangle brackets to specify grid and block size. Notice how we square the upper bound beforehand here:

```
mandelbrot_ker <<< grid_size, 32 >>> (d_lattice,  d_mandelbrot_graph,
max_iters, upper_bound*upper_bound, lattice_size);
```

Now we just need to copy the output to the host after this is done, and then call `cudaFree` on the appropriate arrays. Then we can return from this function:

```
cudaMemcpy(mandelbrot_graph, d_mandelbrot_graph, num_bytes_graph,
cudaMemcpyDeviceToHost);
cudaFree(d_lattice);
cudaFree(d_mandelbrot_graph);
}
```

And with that, we are done with all of the CUDA-C code that we will need. Save this to a file named `mandelbrot.cu`, and let's continue to the next step.

 You can also download this file from `https://github.com/btuomanen/` `handsongpuprogramming/blob/master/10/mandelbrot.cu`.

Compiling the code and interfacing with Ctypes

Now let's compile the code we just wrote into a DLL or `.so` binary. This is actually fairly painless: if you are a Linux user, type the following into the command line to compile this file into `mandelbrot.so`:

```
nvcc -Xcompiler -fPIC -shared -o mandelbrot.so mandelbrot.cu
```

If you are a Windows user, type the following into the command line to compile the file into `mandelbrot.dll`:

```
nvcc -shared -o mandelbrot.dll mandelbrot.cu
```

Now we can write our Python interface. We will start with the appropriate import statements, excluding PyCUDA completely and using just Ctypes. For ease of use, we'll just import all of the classes and functions from Ctypes directly into the default Python namespace, like so:

```
from __future__ import division
from time import time
import matplotlib
from matplotlib import pyplot as plt
import numpy as np
from ctypes import *
```

Let's set up an interface for the `launch_mandelbrot` host-side function using Ctypes. First, we will have to load our compiled DLL or `.so` file as such (Linux users will, of course, have to change the file name to `mandelbrot.so`):

```
mandel_dll = CDLL('./mandelbrot.dll')
```

Now we can get a reference to `launch_mandelbrot` from the library, like so; we'll call it `mandel_c` for short:

```
mandel_c = mandel_dll.launch_mandelbrot
```

Now before we call a function with Ctypes, we will have to make Ctypes aware of what the input types are. Let's remember that for `launch_mandelbrot`, the inputs were `float-pointer`, `float-pointer`, `integer`, `float`, and `integer`. We set this up with the `argtypes` parameter, using the appropriate Ctypes datatypes (`c_float`, `c_int`), as well as the Ctypes `POINTER` class:

```
mandel_c.argtypes = [POINTER(c_float), POINTER(c_float), c_int, c_float,
c_int]
```

Now let's write a Python function that will run this for us. We will specify the width and height of the square output image with `breadth`, and the minimum and maximum values in the complex lattice for both the real and imaginary components. We will also specify the maximum number of iterations, as well as the upper bound:

```
def mandelbrot(breadth, low, high, max_iters, upper_bound):
```

Now, we will create our lattice array with NumPy's `linspace` function, like so:

```
lattice = np.linspace(low, high, breadth, dtype=np.float32)
```

Let's remember that we will have to pass a pre-allocated float array to `launch_mandelbrot` to get the output in the form of an output graph. We can do this by calling NumPy's `empty` command to set up an array of the appropriate shape and size, which will act as a C `malloc` call here:

```
out = np.empty(shape=(lattice.size,lattice.size), dtype=np.float32)
```

Now, we are ready to compute the Mandelbrot graph. Notice that we can pass the NumPy arrays to C by using their `ctypes.data_as` method with the appropriate corresponding types. After we have done this, we can return the output; that is, the Mandelbrot graph in the form of a two-dimensional NumPy array:

```
mandel_c(lattice.ctypes.data_as(POINTER(c_float)),
out.ctypes.data_as(POINTER(c_float)), c_int(max_iters),
c_float(upper_bound), c_int(lattice.size) )
 return out
```

Now, let's write our main function to compute, time, and view the Mandelbrot graph with Matplotlib:

```
if __name__ == '__main__':
    t1 = time()
    mandel = mandelbrot(512,-2,2,256, 2)
    t2 = time()
    mandel_time = t2 - t1
    print 'It took %s seconds to calculate the Mandelbrot graph.' %
mandel_time
    plt.figure(1)
    plt.imshow(mandel, extent=(-2, 2, -2, 2))
    plt.show()
```

We will now try running this. You should get an output that looks exactly like the Mandelbrot graph from Chapter 1, *Why GPU Programming?* and Chapter 3, *Getting Started with PyCUDA*:

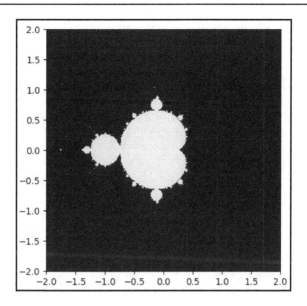

The code for this Python example is also available as the file
`mandelbrot_ctypes.py` in the GitHub repository.

Compiling and launching pure PTX code

We have just seen how to call a pure-C function from Ctypes. In some ways, this may seem
a little inelegant, as our binary file must contain both host code as well as the compiled
GPU code, which may seem cumbersome. Can we just use pure, compiled GPU code and
then launch it appropriately onto the GPU without writing a C wrapper each and every
time? Fortunately, we can.

The NVCC compiler compiles CUDA-C into **PTX (Parallel Thread Execution)**, which is an
interpreted pseudo-assembly language that is compatible across NVIDIA 's various GPU
architectures. Whenever you compile a program that uses a CUDA kernel with NVCC into
an executable EXE, DLL, `.so`, or ELF file, there will be PTX code for that kernel contained
within the file. We can also directly compile a file with the extension PTX, which will
contain only the compiled GPU kernels from a compiled CUDA .cu file. Luckily for us,
PyCUDA includes an interface to load a CUDA kernel directly from a PTX, freeing us from
the shackles of just-in-time compilation while still allowing us to use all of the other nice
features from PyCUDA.

Now let's compile the Mandelbrot code we just wrote into a PTX file; we don't need to make any changes to it. Just type the following into the command line in either Linux or Windows:

```
nvcc -ptx -o mandelbrot.ptx mandelbrot.cu
```

Now let's modify the Python program from the last section to use PTX code instead. We will remove ctypes from the imports and add the appropriate PyCUDA imports:

```
from __future__ import division
from time import time
import matplotlib
from matplotlib import pyplot as plt
import numpy as np
import pycuda
from pycuda import gpuarray
import pycuda.autoinit
```

Now let's load the PTX file using PyCUDA's module_from_file function, like so:

```
mandel_mod = pycuda.driver.module_from_file('./mandelbrot.ptx')
```

Now we can get a reference to our kernel with get_function, just like did with PyCUDA's SourceModule:

```
mandel_ker = mandel_mod.get_function('mandelbrot_ker')
```

We can now rewrite the Mandelbrot function to handle using this kernel with the appropriate gpuarray objects and typecast inputs. (We won't go over this one line-by-line since its functionality should be obvious at this point.):

```
def mandelbrot(breadth, low, high, max_iters, upper_bound):
    lattice = gpuarray.to_gpu(np.linspace(low, high, breadth, dtype=np.
    out_gpu = gpuarray.empty(shape=(lattice.size,lattice.size),
dtype=np.float32)
    gridsize = int(np.ceil(lattice.size**2 / 32))
    mandel_ker(lattice, out_gpu, np.int32(256), np.float32(upper_bound**2),
np.int32(lattice.size), grid=(gridsize, 1, 1), block=(32,1,1))
    out = out_gpu.get()

    return out
```

The main function will be exactly the same as in the last section:

```
if __name__ == '__main__':
    t1 = time()
    mandel = mandelbrot(512,-2,2,256,2)
```

```
    t2 = time()
    mandel_time = t2 - t1
    print 'It took %s seconds to calculate the Mandelbrot graph.' %
mandel_time
    plt.figure(1)
    plt.imshow(mandel, extent=(-2, 2, -2, 2))
    plt.show()
```

Now, try running this to ensure that the output is correct. You may also notice some speed improvements over the Ctypes version.

 This code is also available in the `mandelbrot_ptx.py` file under the "10" directory in this book's GitHub repository.

Writing wrappers for the CUDA Driver API

We will now look at how we can write our very own wrappers for some pre-packaged binary CUDA library functions using Ctypes. In particular, we will be writing wrappers for the CUDA Driver API, which will allow us to perform all of the necessary operations needed for basic GPU usage—including GPU initialization, memory allocation/transfers/deallocation, kernel launching, and context creation/synchronization/destruction. This is a very powerful piece of knowledge; it will allow us to use our GPU without going through PyCUDA, and also without writing any cumbersome host-side C-function wrappers.

We will now write a small module that will act as a wrapper library for the **CUDA Driver API**. Let's talk about what this means for a minute. The Driver API is slightly different and a little more technical than the **CUDA Runtime API**, the latter being what we have been working within this text from CUDA-C. The Driver API is designed to be used with a regular C/C++ compiler rather than with NVCC, with some different conventions like using the `cuLaunchKernel` function to launch a kernel rather than using the `<<< gridsize, blocksize >>>` bracket notation. This will allow us to directly access the necessary functions that we need to launch a kernel from a PTX file with Ctypes.

Let's start writing this module by importing all of the Ctypes into the module's namespace, and then importing the sys module. We will make our module usable from both Windows and Linux by loading the proper library file (either `nvcuda.dll` or `libcuda.so`) by checking the system's OS with `sys.platform`, like so:

```
from ctypes import *
import sys
if 'linux' in sys.platform:
 cuda = CDLL('libcuda.so')
elif 'win' in sys.platform:
 cuda = CDLL('nvcuda.dll')
```

We have successfully loaded the CUDA Driver API, and we can now begin writing wrappers for the necessary functions for basic GPU usage. We will look at the prototypes of each Driver API function as we go along, which is generally necessary to do when you are writing Ctypes wrappers.

The reader is encouraged to look up all of the functions we will be using in this section in the official Nvidia CUDA Driver API Documentation, which is available here: `https://docs.nvidia.com/cuda/cuda-driver-api/`.

Let's start with the most fundamental function from the Driver API, `cuInit`, which will initialize the Driver API. This takes an unsigned integer used for flags as an input parameter and returns a value of type CUresult, which is actually just an integer value. We can write our wrapper like so:

```
cuInit = cuda.cuInit
cuInit.argtypes = [c_uint]
cuInit.restype = int
```

Now let's start on the next function, `cuDeviceCount`, which will tell us how many NVIDIA GPUs we have installed on our computer. This takes in an integer pointer as its single input, which is actually a single integer output value that is returned by reference. The return value is another CUresult integer—all of the functions will use CUresult, which is a standardization of the error values for all of the Driver API functions. For instance, if any function we see returns a 0, this means the result is CUDA_SUCCESS, while non-zero results will always mean an error or warning:

```
cuDeviceGetCount = cuda.cuDeviceGetCount
cuDeviceGetCount.argtypes = [POINTER(c_int)]
cuDeviceGetCount.restype = int
```

Now let's write a wrapper for `cuDeviceGet`, which will return a device handle by reference in the first input. This will correspond to the ordinal GPU given in the second input. The first parameter is of the type `CUdevice *`, which is actually just an integer pointer:

```
cuDeviceGet = cuda.cuDeviceGet
cuDeviceGet.argtypes = [POINTER(c_int), c_int]
cuDeviceGet.restype = int
```

Let's remember that every CUDA session will require at least one CUDA Context, which can be thought of as analogous to a process running on the CPU. Since this is handled automatically with the Runtime API, here we will have to create a context manually on a device (using a device handle) before we can use it, and we will have to destroy this context when our CUDA session is over.

We can create a CUDA context with the `cuCtxCreate` function, which will, of course, create a context. Let's look at the prototype listed in the documentation:

```
CUresult cuCtxCreate ( CUcontext* pctx, unsigned int flags, CUdevice dev )
```

Of course, the return value is `CUresult`. The first input is a pointer to a type called `CUcontext`, which is actually itself a pointer to a particular C structure used internally by CUDA. Since our only interaction with `CUcontext` from Python will be to hold onto its value to pass between other functions, we can just store `CUcontext` as a C `void *` type, which is used to store a generic pointer address for any type. Since this is actually a pointer to a CU context (again, which is itself a pointer to an internal data structure—this is another pass-by-reference return value), we can set the type to be just a plain `void *`, which is a `c_void_p` type in Ctypes. The second value is an unsigned integer, while the final value is the device handle on which to create the new context—let's remember that this is itself just an integer. We are now prepared to create our wrapper for `cuCtxCreate`:

```
cuCtxCreate = cuda.cuCtxCreate
cuCtxCreate.argtypes = [c_void_p, c_uint, c_int]
cuCtxCreate.restype = int
```

You can always use the `void *` type in C/C++ (`c_void_p` in Ctypes) to point to any arbitrary data or variable—even structures and objects whose definition may not be available.

The next function is `cuModuleLoad`, which will load a PTX module file for us. The first argument is a CUmodule by reference (again, we can just use a `c_void_p` here), and the second is the file name, which will be a typical null-terminated C-string—this is a `char *`, or `c_char_p` in Ctypes:

```
cuModuleLoad = cuda.cuModuleLoad
cuModuleLoad.argtypes = [c_void_p, c_char_p]
cuModuleLoad.restype = int
```

The next function is for synchronizing all launched operations over the current CUDA context, and is called `cuCtxSynchronize` (this takes no arguments):

```
cuCtxSynchronize = cuda.cuCtxSynchronize
cuCtxSynchronize.argtypes = []
cuCtxSynchronize.restype = int
```

The next function is used for retrieving a kernel function handle from a loaded module so that we may launch it onto the GPU, which corresponds exactly to PyCUDA's `get_function` method, which we've seen many times at this point. The documentation tells us that the prototype is `CUresult cuModuleGetFunction ( CUfunction* hfunc, CUmodule hmod, const char* name )`. We can now write the wrapper:

```
cuModuleGetFunction = cuda.cuModuleGetFunction
  cuModuleGetFunction.argtypes = [c_void_p, c_void_p, c_char_p ]
  cuModuleGetFunction.restype = int
```

Now let's write the wrappers for the standard dynamic memory operations; these will be necessary since we won't have the vanity of using PyCUDA gpuarray objects. These are practically the same as the CUDA runtime operations that we have worked with before; that is, `cudaMalloc`, `cudaMemcpy`, and `cudaFree`:

```
cuMemAlloc = cuda.cuMemAlloc
cuMemAlloc.argtypes = [c_void_p, c_size_t]
cuMemAlloc.restype = int

cuMemcpyHtoD = cuda.cuMemcpyHtoD
cuMemcpyHtoD.argtypes = [c_void_p, c_void_p, c_size_t]
cuMemAlloc.restype = int

cuMemcpyDtoH = cuda.cuMemcpyDtoH
cuMemcpyDtoH.argtypes = [c_void_p, c_void_p, c_size_t]
cuMemcpyDtoH.restype = int

cuMemFree = cuda.cuMemFree
cuMemFree.argtypes = [c_void_p]
cuMemFree.restype = int
```

Now, we will write a wrapper for the `cuLaunchKernel` function. Of course, this is what we will use to launch a CUDA kernel onto the GPU, provided that we have already initialized the CUDA Driver API, set up a context, loaded a module, allocated memory and configured inputs, and have extracted the kernel function handle from the loaded module. This one is a little more complex than the other functions, so we will look at the prototype:

```
CUresult cuLaunchKernel ( CUfunction f, unsigned int gridDimX, unsigned int
    gridDimY, unsigned int gridDimZ, unsigned int blockDimX, unsigned int
    blockDimY, unsigned int blockDimZ, unsigned int sharedMemBytes, CUstream
    hStream, void** kernelParams, void** extra )
```

The first parameter is a handle to the kernel function we want to launch, which we can represent as `c_void_p`. The six `gridDim` and `blockDim` parameters are used to indicate the grid and block dimensions. The unsigned integer, `sharedMemBytes`, is used to indicate how many bytes of shared memory will be allocated for each block upon kernel launch. `CUstream hStream` is an optional parameter that we can use to set up a custom stream, or set to NULL (0) if we wish to use the default stream, which we can represent as `c_void_p` in Ctypes. Finally, the `kernelParams` and `extra` parameters are used to set the inputs to a kernel; these are a little involved, so for now just know that we can also represent these as `c_void_p`:

```
cuLaunchKernel = cuda.cuLaunchKernel
cuLaunchKernel.argtypes = [c_void_p, c_uint, c_uint, c_uint, c_uint,
c_uint, c_uint, c_uint, c_void_p, c_void_p, c_void_p]
cuLaunchKernel.restype = int
```

Now we have one last function to write a wrapper for, `cuCtxDestroy`. We use this at the end of a CUDA session to destroy a context on the GPU. The only input is a `CUcontext` object, which is represented by `c_void_p`:

```
cuCtxDestroy = cuda.cuCtxDestroy
cuCtxDestroy.argtypes = [c_void_p]
cuCtxDestroy.restype = int
```

Let's save this into the `cuda_driver.py` file. We have now completed our Driver API wrapper module! Next, we will look at how to load a PTX module and launch a kernel using only our module and our Mandelbrot PTX.

 This example is also available as the `cuda_driver.py` file in this book's GitHub repository.

Using the CUDA Driver API

We will now translate our little Mandelbrot generation program so that we can use our wrapper library. Let's start with the appropriate import statements; notice how we load all of our wrappers into the current namespace:

```
from __future__ import division
from time import time
import matplotlib
from matplotlib import pyplot as plt
import numpy as np
from cuda_driver import *
```

Let's put all of our GPU code into the `mandelbrot` function, as we did previously. We will start by initializing the CUDA Driver API with `cuInit` and then checking if there is at least one GPU installed on the system, raising an exception otherwise:

```
def mandelbrot(breadth, low, high, max_iters, upper_bound):
 cuInit(0)
 cnt = c_int(0)
 cuDeviceGetCount(byref(cnt))
 if cnt.value == 0:
  raise Exception('No GPU device found!')
```

Notice the `byref` here: this is the Ctypes equivalent of the reference operator (`&`) from C programming. We'll now apply this idea again, remembering that the device handle and CUDA context can be represented as `c_int` and `c_void_p` with Ctypes:

```
cuDevice = c_int(0)
cuDeviceGet(byref(cuDevice), 0)
cuContext = c_void_p()
cuCtxCreate(byref(cuContext), 0, cuDevice)
```

We will now load our PTX module, remembering to typecast the filename to a C string with `c_char_p`:

```
cuModule = c_void_p()
cuModuleLoad(byref(cuModule), c_char_p('./mandelbrot.ptx'))
```

Now we will set up the lattice on the host side, as well as a NumPy array of zeros called `graph` that will be used to store the output on the host side. We will also allocate memory on the GPU for both the lattice and the graph output, and then copy the lattice to the GPU with `cuMemcpyHtoD`:

```
lattice = np.linspace(low, high, breadth, dtype=np.float32)
lattice_c = lattice.ctypes.data_as(POINTER(c_float))
```

```
lattice_gpu = c_void_p(0)
graph = np.zeros(shape=(lattice.size, lattice.size), dtype=np.float32)
cuMemAlloc(byref(lattice_gpu), c_size_t(lattice.size*sizeof(c_float)))
graph_gpu = c_void_p(0)
cuMemAlloc(byref(graph_gpu), c_size_t(lattice.size**2 * sizeof(c_float)))
cuMemcpyHtoD(lattice_gpu, lattice_c,
c_size_t(lattice.size*sizeof(c_float)))
```

Now we will get a handle to the Mandelbrot kernel with `cuModuleGetFunction` and set up some of the inputs:

```
mandel_ker = c_void_p(0)
cuModuleGetFunction(byref(mandel_ker), cuModule,
c_char_p('mandelbrot_ker'))
max_iters = c_int(max_iters)
upper_bound_squared = c_float(upper_bound**2)
lattice_size = c_int(lattice.size)
```

The next step is a little complex to understand. Before we continue, we have to understand how the parameters are passed into a CUDA kernel with `cuLaunchKernel`. Let's see how this works in CUDA-C first.

We express the input parameters in `kernelParams` as an array of `void *` values, which are, themselves, pointers to the inputs we desire to plug into our kernel. In the case of our Mandelbrot kernel, it would look like this:

```
void * mandel_params [] = {&lattice_gpu, &graph_gpu, &max_iters,
&upper_bound_squared, &lattice_size};
```

Now let's see how we can express this in Ctypes, which isn't immediately obvious. First, let's put all of our inputs into a Python list, in the proper order:

```
mandel_args0 = [lattice_gpu, graph_gpu, max_iters, upper_bound_squared,
lattice_size ]
```

Now we need pointers to each of these values, typecast to the `void *` type. Let's use the Ctypes function `addressof` to get the address of each Ctypes variable here (which is similar to `byref`, only not bound to a particular type), and then typecast it to `c_void_p`. We'll store these values in another list:

```
mandel_args = [c_void_p(addressof(x)) for x in mandel_args0]
```

Now let's use Ctypes to convert this Python list to an array of `void *` pointers, like so:

```
mandel_params = (c_void_p * len(mandel_args))(*mandel_args)
```

We can now set up our grid's size, as we did previously, and launch our kernel with this set of parameters using `cuLaunchKernel`. We then synchronize the context afterward:

```
gridsize = int(np.ceil(lattice.size**2 / 32))
cuLaunchKernel(mandel_ker, gridsize, 1, 1, 32, 1, 1, 10000, None,
mandel_params, None)
cuCtxSynchronize()
```

We will now copy the data from the GPU into our NumPy array using `cuMemcpyDtoH` with the NumPy `array.ctypes.data` member, which is a C pointer that will allow us to directly access the array from C as a chunk of heap memory. We will typecast this to `c_void_p` using the Ctypes typecast function `cast`:

```
cuMemcpyDtoH( cast(graph.ctypes.data, c_void_p), graph_gpu,
c_size_t(lattice.size**2 *sizeof(c_float)))
```

We are now done! Let's free the arrays we allocated on the GPU and end our GPU session by destroying the current context. We will then return the graph NumPy array to the calling function:

```
cuMemFree(lattice_gpu)
cuMemFree(graph_gpu)
cuCtxDestroy(cuContext)
return graph
```

Now we can set up our `main` function exactly as before:

```
if __name__ == '__main__':
t1 = time()
mandel = mandelbrot(512,-2,2,256, 2)
t2 = time()
mandel_time = t2 - t1
print 'It took %s seconds to calculate the Mandelbrot graph.' %
mandel_time

fig = plt.figure(1)
plt.imshow(mandel, extent=(-2, 2, -2, 2))
plt.show()
```

Now try running this function to ensure that it yields the same output as the other Mandelbrot programs we just wrote.

Congratulations—you've just written a direct interface to the low-level CUDA Driver API and successfully launched a kernel with it!

 This program is also available as the `mandelbrot_driver.py` file under the directory in this book's GitHub repository.

Summary

We started this chapter with a brief overview of the Python Ctypes library, which is used to interface directly with compiled binary code, and particularly dynamic libraries written in C/C++. We then looked at how to write a C-based wrapper with CUDA-C that launches a CUDA kernel, and then used this to indirectly launch our CUDA kernel from Python by writing an interface to this function with Ctypes. We then learned how to compile a CUDA kernel into a PTX module binary, which can be thought of as a DLL but with CUDA kernel functions, and saw how to load a PTX file and launch pre-compiled kernels with PyCUDA. Finally, we wrote a collection of Ctypes wrappers for the CUDA Driver API and saw how we can use these to perform basic GPU operations, including launching a pre-compiled kernel from a PTX file onto the GPU.

We will now proceed to what will arguably be the most technical chapter of this book: Chapter 11, *Performance Optimization in CUDA*. In this chapter, we will learn about some of the technical ins and outs of NVIDIA GPUs that will assist us in increasing performance levels in our applications.

Questions

1. Suppose that you use `nvcc` to compile a single `.cu` file containing both host and kernel code into an EXE file, and also into a PTX file. Which file will contain the host functions, and which file will contain the GPU code?

2. Why do we have to destroy a context if we are using the CUDA Driver API?

3. At the beginning of this chapter when we first saw how to use Ctypes, notice that we had to typecast the floating point value 3.14 to a Ctypes `c_double` object in a call to `printf` before it would work. Yet we can see many working cases of not typecasting to Ctypes in this chapter. Why do you think `printf` is an exception here?

4. Suppose you want to add functionality to our Python CUDA Driver interface module to support CUDA streams. How would you represent a single stream object in Ctypes?

5. Why do we use `extern "C"` for functions in `mandelbrot.cu`?

6. Look at `mandelbrot_driver.py` again. Why do we *not* use the `cuCtxSynchronize` function after GPU memory allocations and host/GPU memory transfers, and only after the single kernel invocation?

11
Performance Optimization in CUDA

In this penultimate chapter, we will cover some fairly advanced CUDA features that we can use for low-level performance optimizations. We will start by learning about dynamic parallelism, which allows kernels to launch and manage other kernels on the GPU, and see how we can use this to implement quicksort directly on the GPU. We will learn about vectorized memory access, which can be used to increase memory access speedups when reading from the GPU's global memory. We will then look at how we can use CUDA atomic operations, which are thread-safe functions that can operate on shared data without thread synchronization or *mutex* locks. We will learn about Warps, which are fundamental blocks of 32 or fewer threads, in which threads can read or write to each other's variables directly, and then make a brief foray into the world of PTX Assembly. We'll do this by directly writing some basic PTX Assembly inline within our CUDA-C code, which itself will be inline in our Python code! Finally, we will bring all of these little low-level tweaks together into one final example, where we will apply them to make a blazingly fast summation kernel, and compare this to PyCUDA's sum.

The learning outcomes for this chapter are as follows:

- Dynamic parallelism in CUDA
- Implementing quicksort on the GPU with dynamic parallelism
- Using vectorized types to speed up device memory accesses
- Using thread-safe CUDA atomic operations
- Basic PTX Assembly
- Applying all of these concepts to write a performance-optimized summation kernel

Dynamic parallelism

First, we will take a look at **dynamic parallelism**, a feature in CUDA that allows a kernel to launch and manage other kernels without any interaction or input on behalf of the host. This also makes many of the host-side CUDA-C features that are normally available also available on the GPU, such as device memory allocation/deallocation, device-to-device memory copies, context-wide synchronizations, and streams.

Let's start with a very simple example. We will create a small kernel over N threads that will print a short message to the terminal from each thread, which will then recursively launch another kernel over $N - 1$ threads. This process will continue until N reaches 1. (Of course, beyond illustrating how dynamic parallelism works, this example would be pretty pointless.)

Let's start with the `import` statements in Python:

```
from __future__ import division
import numpy as np
from pycuda.compiler import DynamicSourceModule
import pycuda.autoinit
```

Notice that we have to import `DynamicSourceModule` rather than the usual `SourceModule`! This is due to the fact that the dynamic parallelism feature requires particular configuration details to be set by the compiler. Otherwise, this will look and act like a usual `SourceModule` operation. Now we can continue writing the kernel:

```
DynamicParallelismCode='''
__global__ void dynamic_hello_ker(int depth)
{
 printf("Hello from thread %d, recursion depth %d!\\n", threadIdx.x,
depth);
 if (threadIdx.x == 0 && blockIdx.x == 0 && blockDim.x > 1)
 {
  printf("Launching a new kernel from depth %d .\\n", depth);
  printf("-------------------------------------------\\n");
  dynamic_hello_ker<<< 1, blockDim.x - 1 >>>(depth + 1);
 }
}'''
```

The most important thing here to note is this: we must be careful that we have only a single thread launch the next iteration of kernels with a single thread with a well-placed `if` statement that checks the `threadIdx` and `blockIdx` values. If we don't do this, then each thread will launch far more kernel instances than necessary at every depth iteration. Also, notice how we could just launch the kernel in a normal way with the usual CUDA-C triple-bracket notation—we don't have to use any obscure or low-level commands to make use of dynamic parallelism.

> When using the CUDA dynamic parallelism feature, always be careful to avoid unnecessary kernel launches. This can be done by having a designated thread launch the next iteration of kernels.

Now let's finish this up:

```
dp_mod = DynamicSourceModule(DynamicParallelismCode)
hello_ker = dp_mod.get_function('dynamic_hello_ker')
hello_ker(np.int32(0), grid=(1,1,1), block=(4,1,1))
```

Now we can run the preceding code, which will give us the following output:

```
PS C:\Users\btuom\examples\11> python .\dynamic_hello.py
Hello from thread 0, recursion depth 0!
Hello from thread 1, recursion depth 0!
Hello from thread 2, recursion depth 0!
Hello from thread 3, recursion depth 0!
Launching a new kernel from depth 0 .
-------------------------------------------
Hello from thread 0, recursion depth 1!
Hello from thread 1, recursion depth 1!
Hello from thread 2, recursion depth 1!
Launching a new kernel from depth 1 .
-------------------------------------------
Hello from thread 0, recursion depth 2!
Hello from thread 1, recursion depth 2!
Launching a new kernel from depth 2 .
-------------------------------------------
Hello from thread 0, recursion depth 3!
PS C:\Users\btuom\examples\11>
```

> This example can also be found in the `dynamic_hello.py` file under the directory in this book's GitHub repository.

Quicksort with dynamic parallelism

Now let's look at a slightly more interesting and utilitarian application of dynamic parallelism—the **Quicksort Algorithm**. This is actually a well-suited algorithm for parallelization, as we will see.

Let's start with a brief review. Quicksort is a recursive and in-place sorting algorithm that has an average and best case performance of *O(N log N)*, and worst-case performance of *O(N²)*. Quicksort is performed by choosing an arbitrary point called a *pivot* in an unsorted array, and then partitioning the array into a left array (which contains all points less than the pivot), a right array (which contains all points equal to or greater than the pivot), with the pivot in-between the two arrays. If one or both of the arrays now has a length greater than 1, then we recursively call quicksort again on one or both of the sub-arrays, with the pivot point now in its final position.

 Quicksort can be implemented in a single line in pure Python using functional programming:
```
qsort = lambda xs : [] if xs == [] else
qsort(filter(lambda x: x < xs[-1] , xs[0:-1])) + [xs[-1]]
+ qsort(filter(lambda x: x >= xs[-1] , xs[0:-1]))
```

We can see where parallelism will come into play by the fact that quicksort is recursively called on both the right and left arrays—we can see how this will start with one thread operating on an initial large array, but by the time the arrays get very small, there should be many threads working on them. Here, we will actually accomplish this by launching all of the kernels over one *single thread each*!

Let's get going, and start with the import statements. (We will ensure that we import the `shuffle` function from the standard random module for the example that we will go over later.):

```
from __future__ import division
import numpy as np
from pycuda.compiler import DynamicSourceModule
import pycuda.autoinit
from pycuda import gpuarray
from random import shuffle
```

Now we'll write our quicksort kernel. We'll write a `device` function for the partitioning step, which will take an integer pointer, the lowest point of the subarray to partition, and the highest point of the subarray. This function will also use the highest point of this subarray as the pivot. Ultimately, after this function is done, it will return the final resting place of the pivot:

```
DynamicQuicksortCode='''
__device__ int partition(int * a, int lo, int hi)
{
 int i = lo;
 int pivot = a[hi];
 int temp;

 for (int k=lo; k<hi; k++)
 {
  if (a[k] < pivot)
  {
   temp = a[k];
   a[k] = a[i];
   a[i] = temp;
   i++;
  }
 }

 a[hi] = a[i];
 a[i] = pivot;
 return i;
}
```

Now we can write the kernel that implements this partition function into a parallel quicksort. We'll have to use the CUDA-C conventions for streams, which we haven't seen so far: to launch a kernel *k* in a stream *s* in CUDA-C, we use k<<<grid, block, sharedMemBytesPerBlock, s>>>(...). By using two streams here, we can be sure that they are launched in parallel. (Considering that we won't be using shared memory, we'll set the third launch parameter to "0".) The creation and destruction of the stream objects should be self-explanatory:

```
__global__ void quicksort_ker(int *a, int lo, int hi)
{

 cudaStream_t s_left, s_right;
 cudaStreamCreateWithFlags(&s_left, cudaStreamNonBlocking);
 cudaStreamCreateWithFlags(&s_right, cudaStreamNonBlocking);

 int mid = partition(a, lo, hi);
 if(mid - 1 - lo > 0)
```

```
    quicksort_ker<<< 1, 1, 0, s_left >>>(a, lo, mid - 1);
  if(hi - (mid + 1) > 0)
    quicksort_ker<<< 1, 1, 0, s_right >>>(a, mid + 1, hi);
  cudaStreamDestroy(s_left);
  cudaStreamDestroy(s_right);


}
'''
```

Now let's randomly shuffle a list of 100 integers and have our kernel sort this for us. Notice how we launch the kernel over a single thread:

```
qsort_mod = DynamicSourceModule(DynamicQuicksortCode)

qsort_ker = qsort_mod.get_function('quicksort_ker')

if __name__ == '__main__':
    a = range(100)
    shuffle(a)
    a = np.int32(a)
    d_a = gpuarray.to_gpu(a)
    print 'Unsorted array: %s' % a
    qsort_ker(d_a, np.int32(0), np.int32(a.size - 1), grid=(1,1,1),
block=(1,1,1))
    a_sorted = list(d_a.get())
    print 'Sorted array: %s' % a_sorted
```

 This program is also available in the `dynamic_quicksort.py` file in this book's GitHub repository.

Vectorized data types and memory access

We will now look at CUDA's Vectorized Data Types. These are *vectorized* versions of the standard datatypes, such as int or double, in that they can store multiple values. There are *vectorized* versions of the 32-bit types of up to size 4 (for example, `int2`, `int3`, `int4`, and `float4`), while 64-bit variables can only be vectorized to be twice their original size (for example, `double2` and `long2`). For a size 4 vectorized variable, we access each individual element using the C "struct" notation for the members x, y, z, and w, while we use x,y, and z for a 3-member variable and just x and y for a 2-member variable.

These may seem pointless right now, but these datatypes can be used to improve the performance of loading arrays from the global memory. Now, let's do a small test to see how we can load some int4 variables from an array of integers, and double2s from an array of doubles—we will have to use the CUDA `reinterpret_cast` operator to do this:

```
from __future__ import division
import numpy as np
from pycuda.compiler import SourceModule
import pycuda.autoinit
from pycuda import gpuarray

VecCode='''
__global__ void vec_ker(int *ints, double *doubles) {

 int4 f1, f2;

 f1 = *reinterpret_cast<int4*>(ints);
 f2 = *reinterpret_cast<int4*>(&ints[4]);

 printf("First int4: %d, %d, %d, %d\\n", f1.x, f1.y, f1.z, f1.w);
 printf("Second int4: %d, %d, %d, %d\\n", f2.x, f2.y, f2.z, f2.w);

 double2 d1, d2;

 d1 = *reinterpret_cast<double2*>(doubles);
 d2 = *reinterpret_cast<double2*>(&doubles[2]);

 printf("First double2: %f, %f\\n", d1.x, d1.y);
 printf("Second double2: %f, %f\\n", d2.x, d2.y);

}'''
```

Notice how we have to use the `dereference` operator `*` to set the vectorized variables, and how we have to jump to the next address by reference (`&ints[4]`, `&doubles[2]`) to load the second `int4` and `double2` by using the reference operator `&` on the array:

```
PS C:\Users\btuom\examples\11> python .\vectorized_memory.py
Vectorized Memory Test:
First int4: 1, 2, 3, 4
Second int4: 5, 6, 7, 8
First double2: 1.110000, 2.220000
Second double2: 3.330000, 4.440000
```

This example is also available in the `vectorized_memory.py` file in this book's GitHub repository.

Thread-safe atomic operations

We will now learn about **atomic operations** in CUDA. Atomic operations are very simple, thread-safe operations that output to a single global array element or shared memory variable, which would normally lead to race conditions otherwise.

Let's think of one example. Suppose that we have a kernel, and we set a local variable called x across all threads at some point. We then want to find the maximum value over all xs, and then set this value to the shared variable we declare with `__shared__ int x_largest`. We can do this by just calling `atomicMax(&x_largest, x)` over every thread.

Let's look at a brief example of atomic operations. We will write a small program for two experiments:

- Setting a variable to 0 and then adding 1 to this for each thread
- Finding the maximum thread ID value across all threads

Let's start out by setting the `tid` integer to the global thread ID as usual, and then set the global `add_out` variable to 0. In the past, we would do this by having a single thread alter the variable using an `if` statement, but now we can use `atomicExch(add_out, 0)` across all threads. Let's do the imports and write our kernel up to this point:

```
from __future__ import division
import numpy as np
from pycuda.compiler import SourceModule
import pycuda.autoinit
from pycuda import gpuarray
import pycuda.driver as drv

AtomicCode='''
__global__ void atomic_ker(int *add_out, int *max_out)
{

  int tid = blockIdx.x*blockDim.x + threadIdx.x;

  atomicExch(add_out, 0);
```

It should be noted that while Atomics are indeed thread-safe, they by no means guarantee that all threads will access them at the same time, and they may be executed at different times by different threads. This can be problematic here, since we will be modifying `add_out` in the next step. This might lead to `add_out` being reset after it's already been partially modified by some of the threads. Let's do a block-synchronization to guard against this:

```
__syncthreads();
```

We can now use `atomicAdd` to add 1 to `add_out` for each thread, which will give us the total number of threads:

```
atomicAdd(add_out, 1);
```

Now let's check what the maximum value of `tid` is for all threads by using `atomicMax`. We can then close off our CUDA kernel:

```
atomicMax(max_out, tid);

}
'''
```

We will now add the test code; let's try launching this over 1 block of 100 threads. We only need two variables here, so we will have to allocate some `gpuarray` objects of only size 1. We will then print the output:

```
atomic_mod = SourceModule(AtomicCode)
atomic_ker = atomic_mod.get_function('atomic_ker')

add_out = gpuarray.empty((1,), dtype=np.int32)
max_out = gpuarray.empty((1,), dtype=np.int32)

atomic_ker(add_out, max_out, grid=(1,1,1), block=(100,1,1))

print 'Atomic operations test:'
print 'add_out: %s' % add_out.get()[0]
print 'max_out: %s' % max_out.get()[0]
```

Now we are prepared to run this:

```
PS C:\Users\btuom\examples\11> python .\atomic.py
Atomic operations test:
add_out: 64
max_out: 127
```

 This example is also available as the `atomic.py` file in this book's GitHub repository.

Warp shuffling

We will now look at what is known as **warp shuffling**. This is a feature in CUDA that allows threads that exist within the same CUDA Warp concurrently to communicate by directly reading and writing to each other's registers (that is, their local stack-space variables), without the use of *shared* variables or global device memory. Warp shuffling is actually much faster and easier to use than the other two options. This almost sounds too good to be true, so there must be a *catch*—indeed, the *catch* is that this only works between threads that exist on the same CUDA Warp, which limits shuffling operations to groups of threads of size 32 or less. Another catch is that we can only use datatypes that are 32 bits or less. This means that we can't shuffle 64-bit *long long* integers or *double* floating point values across a Warp.

 Only 32-bit (or smaller) datatypes can be used with CUDA Warp shuffling! This means that while we can use integers, floats, and chars, we cannot use doubles or *long long* integers!

Let's briefly review CUDA Warps before we move on to any coding. (You might wish to review the section entitled *The warp lockstep property* in `Chapter 6`, *Debugging and Profiling Your CUDA Code*, before we continue.) A CUDA **Warp** is the minimal execution unit in CUDA that consists of 32 threads or less, that runs on exactly 32 GPU cores. Just as a Grid consists of blocks, blocks similarly consist of one or more Warps, depending on the number of threads the Block uses – if a Block consists of 32 threads, then it will use one Warp, and if it uses 96 threads, it will consist of three Warps. Even if a Warp is of a size less than 32, it is also considered a full Warp: this means that a Block with only one single thread will use 32 cores. This also implies that a block of 33 threads will consist of two Warps and 31 cores.

To remember what we looked at in Chapter 6, *Debugging and Profiling Your CUDA Code*, a Warp has what is known as the **Lockstep Property**. This means that every thread in a warp will iterate through every instruction, perfectly in parallel with every other thread in the Warp. That is to say, every thread in a single Warp will step through the same exact instructions simultaneously, *ignoring* any instructions that are not applicable to a particular thread – this is why any divergence among threads within a single Warp is to be avoided as much as possible. NVIDIA calls this execution model **Single Instruction Multiple Thread**, or **SIMT**. By now, you should understand why we have tried to always use Blocks of 32 threads consistently throughout the text!

We need to learn one more term before we get going—a **lane** in a Warp is a unique identifier for a particular thread within the warp, which will be between 0 and 31. Sometimes, this is also called the **Lane ID**.

Let's start with a simple example: we will use the __shfl_xor command to swap the values of a particular variable between all even and odd numbered Lanes (threads) within our warp. This is actually very quick and easy to do, so let's write our kernel and take a look:

```
from __future__ import division
import numpy as np
from pycuda.compiler import SourceModule
import pycuda.autoinit
from pycuda import gpuarray


ShflCode='''
__global__ void shfl_xor_ker(int *input, int * output) {

int temp = input[threadIdx.x];

temp = __shfl_xor (temp, 1, blockDim.x);

output[threadIdx.x] = temp;

}'''
```

Everything here is familiar to us except `__shfl_xor` . This is how an individual CUDA thread sees this: this function takes the value of `temp` as an input from the current thread. It performs an XOR operation on the binary Lane ID of the current thread with 1, which will be either its left neighbor (if the least significant digit of this thread's Lane is "1" in binary), or its right neighbor (if the least significant digit is "0" in binary). It then sends the current thread's `temp` value to its neighbor, while retrieving the neighbor's temp value, which is `__shfl_xor`. This will be returned as output right back into `temp`. We then set the value in the output array, which will swap our input array values.

Now let's write the rest of the test code and then check the output:

```
shfl_mod = SourceModule(ShflCode)
shfl_ker = shfl_mod.get_function('shfl_xor_ker')

dinput = gpuarray.to_gpu(np.int32(range(32)))
doutout = gpuarray.empty_like(dinput)

shfl_ker(dinput, doutout, grid=(1,1,1), block=(32,1,1))

print 'input array: %s' % dinput.get()
print 'array after __shfl_xor: %s' % doutout.get()
```

The output for the preceding code is as follows:

```
PS C:\Users\btuom\examples\11> python .\shfl_xor.py
input array: [ 0  1  2  3  4  5  6  7  8  9 10 11 12 13 14 15 16 17 18 19 20 21 22 23 24
 25 26 27 28 29 30 31]
array after __shfl_xor: [ 1  0  3  2  5  4  7  6  9  8 11 10 13 12 15 14 17 16 19 18 21 20 23 22 25
 24 27 26 29 28 31 30]
```

Let's do one more warp-shuffling example before we move on—we will implement an operation to sum a single local variable over all of the threads in a Warp. Let's recall the Naive Parallel Sum algorithm from Chapter 4, *Kernels, Threads, Blocks, and Grids*, which is very fast but makes the *naive* assumption that we have as many processors as we do pieces of data—this is one of the few cases in life where we actually will, assuming that we're working with an array of size 32 or less. We will use the `__shfl_down` function to implement this in a single warp. `__shfl_down` takes the thread variable in the first parameter and works by *shifting* a variable between threads by the certain number of steps indicated in the second parameter, while the third parameter will indicate the total size of the Warp.

Let's implement this right now. Again, if you aren't familiar with the Naive Parallel Sum or don't remember why this should work, please review Chapter 4, *Kernels, Threads, Blocks, and Grids*. We will implement a straight-up sum with __shfl_down, and then run this on an array that includes the integers 0 through 31. We will then compare this against NumPy's own sum function to ensure correctness:

```
from __future__ import division
import numpy as np
from pycuda.compiler import SourceModule
import pycuda.autoinit
from pycuda import gpuarray


ShflSumCode='''
__global__ void shfl_sum_ker(int *input, int *out) {

 int temp = input[threadIdx.x];

 for (int i=1; i < 32; i *= 2)
     temp += __shfl_down (temp, i, 32);

 if (threadIdx.x == 0)
     *out = temp;

}'''

shfl_mod = SourceModule(ShflSumCode)
shfl_sum_ker = shfl_mod.get_function('shfl_sum_ker')

array_in = gpuarray.to_gpu(np.int32(range(32)))
out = gpuarray.empty((1,), dtype=np.int32)

shfl_sum_ker(array_in, out, grid=(1,1,1), block=(32,1,1))

print 'Input array: %s' % array_in.get()
print 'Summed value: %s' % out.get()[0]
print 'Does this match with Python''s sum? : %s' % (out.get()[0] ==
sum(array_in.get()) )
```

This will give us the following output:

```
PS C:\Users\btuom\examples\11> python .\shfl_sum.py
Input array: [ 0  1  2  3  4  5  6  7  8  9 10 11 12 13 14 15 16 17 18 19 20 21 22 23 24
 25 26 27 28 29 30 31]
Summed value: 496
Does this match with Pythons sum? : True
```

 The examples in this section are also available as the `shfl_sum.py` and `shfl_xor.py` files under the `Chapter11` directory in this book's GitHub repository.

Inline PTX assembly

We will now scratch the surface of writing PTX (Parallel Thread eXecution) Assembly language, which is a kind of a pseudo-assembly language that works across all Nvidia GPUs, which is, in turn, compiled by a Just-In-Time (JIT) compiler to the specific GPU's actual machine code. While this obviously isn't intended for day-to-day usage, it will let us work at an even a lower level than C if necessary. One particular use case is that you can easily disassemble a CUDA binary file (a host-side executable/library or a CUDA .cubin binary) and inspect its PTX code if no source code is otherwise available. This can be done with the `cuobjdump.exe -ptx  cuda_binary` command in both Windows and Linux.

As stated previously, we will only cover some of the basic usages of PTX from within CUDA-C, which has a particular syntax and usage which is similar to that of using the inline host-side assembly language in GCC. Let's get going with our code—we will do the imports and start writing our GPU code:

```
from __future__ import division
import numpy as np
from pycuda.compiler import SourceModule
import pycuda.autoinit
from pycuda import gpuarray

PtxCode='''
```

We will do several mini-experiments here by writing the code into separate device functions. Let's start with a simple function that sets an input variable to zero. (We can use the C++ pass-by-reference operator & in CUDA, which we will use in the device function.):

```
__device__ void set_to_zero(int &x)
{
  asm("mov.s32 %0, 0;" : "=r"(x));
}
```

Let's break this down before we move on. asm, of course, will indicate to the nvcc compiler that we are going to be using assembly, so we will have to put that code into quotes so that it can be handled properly. The mov instruction just copies a constant or other value, and inputs this into a **register**. (A register is the most fundamental type of on-chip storage unit that a GPU or CPU uses to store or manipulate values; this is how most *local* variables are used in CUDA.) The .s32 part of mov.s32 indicates that we are working with a signed, 32-bit integer variable—PTX Assembly doesn't have *types* for data in the sense of C, so we have to be careful to use the correct particular operations. %0 tells nvcc to use the register corresponding to the 0th argument of the string here, and we separate this from the next *input* to mov with a comma, which is the constant 0. We then end the line of assembly with a semicolon, like we would in C, and close off this string of assembly code with a quote. We'll have to then use a colon (not a comma!) to indicate the variables we want to use in our code. The "=r" means two things: the = will indicate to nvcc that the register will be written to as an output, while the r indicates that this should be handled as a 32-bit integer datatype. We then put the variable we want to be handled by the assembler in parentheses, and then close off the asm, just like we would with any C function.

All of that exposition to set the value of a single variable to 0! Now, let's make a small device function that will add two floating-point numbers for us:

```
__device__ void add_floats(float &out, float in1, float in2)
{
  asm("add.f32 %0, %1, %2 ;" : "=f"(out) : "f"(in1) , "f"(in2));
}
```

Let's stop and notice a few things. First, of course, we are using add.f32 to indicate that we want to add two 32-bit floating point values together. We also use "=f" to indicate that we will be writing to a register, and f to indicate that we will be only reading from it. Also, notice how we use a colon to separate the write registers from the only read registers for nvcc.

Let's look at one more simple example before we continue, that is, a function akin to the ++ operator in C that increments an integer by 1:

```
__device__ void plusplus(int &x)
{
  asm("add.s32 %0, %0, 1;" : "+r"(x));
}
```

First, notice that we use the "0th" parameter as both the output and the first input. Next, notice that we are using +r rather than =r—the + tells nvcc that this register will be read from *and* written to in this instruction.

Now, we won't be getting any fancier than this, as even writing a simple if statement in assembly language is fairly involved. However, let's look at some more examples that will come in useful when using CUDA Warps. Let's start with a small function that will give us the lane ID of the current thread; this is particularly useful, and actually far more straightforward than doing this with CUDA-C, since the lane ID is actually stored in a special register called %laneid that we can't access in pure C. (Notice how we use two % symbols in the code, which will indicate to nvcc to directly use the % in the assembly code for the %laneid reference rather than interpret this as an argument to the asm command.):

```
__device__ int laneid()
{
  int id;
  asm("mov.u32 %0, %%laneid; " : "=r"(id));
  return id;
}
```

Now let's write two more functions that will be useful for dealing with CUDA Warps. Remember, you can only pass a 32-bit variable across a Warp using a shuffle command. This means that to pass a 64-bit variable over a warp, we have to split this into two 32-bit variables, shuffle both of those to another thread individually, and then re-combine these 32-bit values back into the original 64-bit variable. We can use the mov.b64 command for the case of splitting a 64-bit double into two 32-bit integers—notice how we have to use d to indicate a 64-bit floating-point double:

Notice our use of volatile in the following code, which will ensure that these commands are executed exactly as written after they are compiled. We do this because sometimes a compiler will make its own optimizations to or around inline assembly code, but for particularly delicate operations such as this, we want this done exactly as written.

```
__device__ void split64(double val, int & lo, int & hi)
{
 asm volatile("mov.b64 {%0, %1}, %2; ":"=r"(lo),"=r"(hi):"d"(val));
}

__device__ void combine64(double &val, int lo, int hi)
{
 asm volatile("mov.b64 %0, {%1, %2}; ":"=d"(val):"r"(lo),"r"(hi));
}
```

Now let's write a simple kernel that will test all of the PTX assembly device functions we wrote. We will then launch it over one single thread so that we can check everything:

```
__global__ void ptx_test_ker() {

int x=123;

printf("x is %d \\n", x);

set_to_zero(x);

printf("x is now %d \\n", x);

plusplus(x);

printf("x is now %d \\n", x);

float f;

add_floats(f, 1.11, 2.22 );

printf("f is now %f \\n", f);

printf("lane ID: %d \\n", laneid() );

double orig = 3.1415;

int t1, t2;

split64(orig, t1, t2);

double recon;

combine64(recon, t1, t2);

printf("Do split64 / combine64 work? : %s \\n", (orig == recon) ? "true" :
"false");
```

```
}'''

ptx_mod = SourceModule(PtxCode)
ptx_test_ker = ptx_mod.get_function('ptx_test_ker')
ptx_test_ker(grid=(1,1,1), block=(1,1,1))
```

We will now run the preceding code:

```
PS C:\Users\btuom\examples\11> python .\ptx_assembly.py
x is 123
x is now 0
x is now 1
f is now 3.330000
lane ID: 0
Do split64 / combine64 work? : true
```

 This example is also available as the `ptx_assembly.py` file under the `Chapter11` directory in this book's GitHub repository.

Performance-optimized array sum

For the final example of this book, we will now make a standard array summation kernel for a given array of doubles, except this time we will use every trick that we've learned in this chapter to make it as fast as possible. We will check the output of our summing kernel against NumPy's `sum` function, and then we will run some tests with the standard Python `timeit` function to compare how our function compares to PyCUDA's own `sum` function for `gpuarray` objects.

Let's get started by importing all of the necessary libraries, and then start with a `laneid` function, similar to the one we used in the previous section:

```
from __future__ import division
import numpy as np
from pycuda.compiler import SourceModule
import pycuda.autoinit
from pycuda import gpuarray
import pycuda.driver as drv
from timeit import timeit

SumCode='''
__device__ void __inline__ laneid(int & id)
{
```

```
asm("mov.u32 %0, %%laneid; " : "=r"(id));
}
```

Let's note a few things—notice that we put a new inline statement in the declaration of our device function. This will effectively make our function into a macro, which will shave off a little time from calling and branching to a device function when we call this from the kernel. Also, notice that we set the `id` variable by reference instead of returning a value—in this case, there may actually be two integer registers that should be used, and there should be an additional copy command. This guarantees that this won't happen.

Let's write the other device functions in a similar fashion. We will need to have two more device functions so that we can split and combine a 64-bit double into two 32-bit variables:

```
__device__ void __inline__ split64(double val, int & lo, int & hi)
{
  asm volatile("mov.b64 {%0, %1}, %2; ":"=r"(lo),"=r"(hi):"d"(val));
}

__device__ void __inline__ combine64(double &val, int lo, int hi)
{
  asm volatile("mov.b64 %0, {%1, %2}; ":"=d"(val):"r"(lo),"r"(hi));
}
```

Let's start writing the kernel. We will take in an array of doubles called input, and then output the entire sum to `out`, which should be initialized to 0. We will start by getting the lane ID for the current thread and loading two values from global memory into the current thread with vectorized memory loading:

```
__global__ void sum_ker(double *input, double *out)
{

  int id;
  laneid(id);

  double2 vals = *reinterpret_cast<double2*> ( &input[(blockDim.x*blockIdx.x
+ threadIdx.x) * 2] );
```

Now let's sum these values from the double2 `vals` variable into a new double variable, `sum_val`, which will keep track of all the summations across this thread. We will create two 32-bit integers, `s1` and `s2`, that we will use for splitting this value and sharing it with Warp Shuffling, and then create a `temp` variable for reconstructed values we receive from other threads in this Warp:

```
double sum_val = vals.x + vals.y;

double temp;

int s1, s2;
```

Now let's use a Naive Parallel sum again across the warp, which will be the same as summing 32-bit integers across a Warp, except we will be using our `split64` and `combine64` PTX functions on `sum_val` and `temp` for each iteration:

```
for (int i=1; i < 32; i *= 2)
{

    // use PTX assembly to split
    split64(sum_val, s1, s2);

    // shuffle to transfer data
    s1 = __shfl_down (s1, i, 32);
    s2 = __shfl_down (s2, i, 32);
    // PTX assembly to combine
    combine64(temp, s1, s2);
    sum_val += temp;
}
```

Now that we are done, let's have the `0th` thread of every single warp add their end value to `out` using the thread-safe `atomicAdd`:

```
if (id == 0)
    atomicAdd(out, sum_val);
}'''
```

We will now write our test code with `timeit` operations to measure the average time of our kernel and PyCUDA's sum over 20 iterations of both on an array of 10000*2*32 doubles:

```
sum_mod = SourceModule(SumCode)
sum_ker = sum_mod.get_function('sum_ker')

a = np.float64(np.random.randn(10000*2*32))
a_gpu = gpuarray.to_gpu(a)
out = gpuarray.zeros((1,), dtype=np.float64)
```

```
sum_ker(a_gpu, out, grid=(int(np.ceil(a.size/64)),1,1), block=(32,1,1))
drv.Context.synchronize()

print 'Does sum_ker produces the same value as NumPy\'s sum (according
allclose)? : %s' % np.allclose(np.sum(a) , out.get()[0])

print 'Performing sum_ker / PyCUDA sum timing tests (20 each)...'

sum_ker_time = timeit('''from __main__ import sum_ker, a_gpu, out, np, drv
\nsum_ker(a_gpu, out, grid=(int(np.ceil(a_gpu.size/64)),1,1),
block=(32,1,1)) \ndrv.Context.synchronize()''', number=20)
pycuda_sum_time = timeit('''from __main__ import gpuarray, a_gpu, drv
\ngpuarray.sum(a_gpu) \ndrv.Context.synchronize()''', number=20)

print 'sum_ker average time duration: %s, PyCUDA\'s gpuarray.sum average
time duration: %s' % (sum_ker_time, pycuda_sum_time)
print '(Performance improvement of sum_ker over gpuarray.sum: %s )' %
(pycuda_sum_time / sum_ker_time)
```

Let's run this from IPython. Make sure that you have run both gpuarray.sum and sum_ker beforehand to ensure that we aren't timing any compilation by nvcc as well:

```
In [14]: run sum_ker.py
Does sum_ker produces the same value as NumPy's sum (according allclose)? : True
Performing sum_ker / PyCUDA sum timing tests (20 each)...
sum_ker average time duration: 0.00553162831763, PyCUDA's gpuarray.sum average time duration: 0.0278831109579
(Performance improvement of sum_ker over gpuarray.sum: 5.04066964677 )
```

So, while summing is normally pretty boring, we can be excited by the fact that our clever use of hardware tricks can speed up such a bland and trivial algorithm quite a bit.

This example is available as the performance_sum_ker.py file under the Chapter11 directory in this book's GitHub repository.

Summary

We started this chapter by learning about dynamic parallelism, which is a paradigm that allows us to launch and manage kernels directly on the GPU from other kernels. We saw how we can use this to implement a quicksort algorithm on the GPU directly. We then learned about vectorized datatypes in CUDA, and saw how we can use these to speed up memory reads from global device memory. We then learned about CUDA Warps, which are small units of 32 threads or less on the GPU, and we saw how threads within a single Warp can directly read and write to each other's registers using Warp Shuffling. We then looked at how we can write a few basic operations in PTX assembly, including import operations such as determining the lane ID and splitting a 64-bit variable into two 32-bit variables. Finally, we ended this chapter by writing a new performance-optimized summation kernel that is used for arrays of doubles, applying almost most of the tricks we've learned in this chapter. We saw that this is actually faster than the standard PyCUDA sum on double arrays with a length of an order of 500,000.

We have gotten through all of the technical chapters of this book! You should be proud of yourself, since you are now surely a skilled GPU programmer with many tricks up your sleeve. We will now embark upon the final chapter, where we will take a brief tour of a few of the different paths you can take to apply and extend your GPU programming knowledge from here.

Questions

1. In the atomic operations example, try changing the grid size from 1 to 2 before the kernel is launched while leaving the total block size at 100. If this gives you the wrong output for add_out (anything other than 200), then why is it wrong, considering that atomicExch is thread-safe?

2. In the atomic operations example, try removing __syncthreads, and then run the kernel over the original parameters of grid size 1 and block size 100. If this gives you the wrong output for add_out (anything other than 100), then why is it wrong, considering that atomicExch is thread-safe?

3. Why do we not have to use __syncthreads to synchronize over a block of size 32 or less?

4. We saw that `sum_ker` is around five times faster than PyCUDA's sum operation for random-valued arrays of length 640,000 (`10000*2*32`). If you try adding a zero to the end of this number (that is, multiply it by 10), you'll notice that the performance drops to the point where `sum_ker` is only about 1.5 times as fast as PyCUDA's sum. If you add another zero to the end of that number, you'll notice that `sum_ker` is only 75% as fast as PyCUDA's sum. Why do you think this is the case? How can we improve `sum_ker` to be faster on larger arrays?

5. Which algorithm performs more addition operations (counting both calls to the C + operator and atomicSum as a single operation): `sum_ker` or PyCUDA's `sum`?

12
Where to Go from Here

This book has been a journey, much like a daring mountain hike... but now, at last, we have arrived at the end of our trek. We now stand upon the summit of mount introductory-GPU-programming, and we stand proud as we gaze back upon our native village of serial-programming-ville and smile as we think about the quaint naivity of our old one-dimensional programming traditions, where we considered *forking* a process in Unix to be our entire understanding of the notion of *parallel programming*. We have braved many pitfalls and dangers to arrive at this point, and we may have even made such mishaps as installing a broken NVIDIA driver module in Linux, or maybe downloading the wrong Visual Studio version over a slow 100k connection while visiting our parents for vacation. But these setbacks were only temporary, leaving wounds that developed into calluses that made us even stronger against the forces of (GPU) nature.

But, in the corner of our eye, we can see two wooden signs a few meters away from where we are standing; we avert our gaze from the little village of our past and now take a look at them. The first has an arrow pointing in the direction from which we are currently faced, with only one word on it—PAST. The other is pointing in the opposite direction, also with only one word—FUTURE. We turn around in the direction pointing to FUTURE, and we see a large glimmering metropolis strewn out before us to the horizon, beckoning us. Now that we have finally caught our breath, we can start walking into the future...

In this chapter, we will go over some of the options that you now have so that you can continue your education and career in fields related to GPU programming. Whether you are trying to build a career, a hobbyist doing this for fun, an engineering student studying GPUs for a class, a programmer or engineer trying to enhance your technical background, or an academic scientist trying to apply GPUs to a research project, there are many, many options that you now have at this point. Much like our metaphorical metropolis, it is easy to get lost, and it is difficult to determine where we should go. We hope to provide something akin to a brief tour guide in this final chapter, providing you with some of the options for where you can go next.

We will now take a look at the following paths in this chapter:

- Advanced CUDA and GPGPU programming
- Graphics
- Machine learning and computer vision
- Blockchain technology

Furthering your knowledge of CUDA and GPGPU programming

The first option you have is, of course, to learn more about CUDA and **General-Purpose GPU** (**GPGPU**) programming in particular. In this case, you have probably already found a good application of this and want to write even more advanced or optimized CUDA code. You may find it interesting for its own sake, or perhaps you want to get a job as a CUDA/GPU programmer. With a strong GPU programming foundation in place (which was provided by this book), we will now look at some of the advanced topics in this field that we are now prepared to learn about.

Multi-GPU systems

The first major topic that comes to mind would be to learn how to program systems with more than one GPU installed. Many professional workstations and servers contain several GPUs that have been installed with the intention of processing far more data that requires not one, but several top-of-the-line GPUs. To this end, there exists a subfield called Multi-GPU programming. Much of the work is focused on load balancing, which is the art of using each GPU at its peak capacity, ensuring that no GPU gets saturated with too much work while the other goes without being fully utilized. Another topic here is Inter-GPU Communication, which is generally concerned about the issue of one GPU directly copying memory arrays to or from another using CUDA's GPUDirect **peer-to-peer** (**P2P**) memory access.

 NVIDIA provides a brief introduction to Multi-GPU programming here: https://www.nvidia.com/docs/IO/116711/sc11-multi-gpu.pdf.

Cluster computing and MPI

Another topic is cluster computing, that is, writing programs that make collective use of a multitude of servers containing GPUs. These are the *server farms* that populate the data-processing facilities of well-known internet companies such as Facebook and Google, as well as the scientific supercomputing facilities used by governments and militaries. Clusters are generally programmed with a programming paradigm called **message-passing interface** (**MPI**), which is an interface used with languages such as C++ or Fortran that allows you to program many computers that are connected to the same network.

 More information about using CUDA with MPI is available here: `https:/ /devblogs.nvidia.com/introduction-cuda-aware-mpi/`.

OpenCL and PyOpenCL

CUDA isn't the only language that can be used to program a GPU. CUDA's most major competitor is called Open Computing Language, or OpenCL. Where CUDA is a closed and proprietary system that will work exclusively on only NVIDIA hardware, OpenCL is an open standard that's developed and supported by the nonprofit Khronos Group. OpenCL can be used to program not only an NVIDIA GPU, but also AMD Radeon GPUs and even Intel HD GPUs—most major technology companies have committed to supporting OpenCL in their products. Additionally, the author of PyCUDA, Professor Andreas Kloeckner of UIUC, has written another excellent (and free) Python library called PyOpenCL, which provides an equally user-friendly interface to OpenCL, with nearly the same syntax and notions as PyCUDA.

 Information on OpenCL is provided by NVIDIA here: `https://developer.nvidia.com/opencl`.

Information on the free PyOpenCL library is available from Andreas Kloeckner's website here:

`https://mathema.tician.de/software/pyopencl/`.

Graphics

Obviously, the **G** in GPU stands for **graphics**, which we really haven't seen much of in this book. Even though machine learning applications are now NVIDIA's bread and butter, it all started with rendering nice-looking graphics. We will provide some resources to get you started here, whether you want to develop video game engines, render CGI movies, or develop CAD software. CUDA can actually be used hand in hand with graphics applications, and is actually used in professional software such as Adobe's Photoshop and After Effects, as well as in many recent video games such as the *Mafia* and *Just Cause* series. We will briefly cover some of the major APIs you might consider starting with here.

OpenGL

The Open Graphics Language, or OpenGL, is an industry open standard that has existed since the early 90's. While in some ways it is showing its age, it is a stable API that enjoys widespread support, and if you write a program that makes use of this, it is pretty much guaranteed to work on any relatively modern GPU in existence. The CUDA samples folder actually contains many examples of how OpenGL can interface with CUDA (particularly in the `2_Graphics` subdirectory), so interested readers may consider going over these examples. (The default location is `C:\ProgramData\NVIDIA Corporation\CUDA Samples` in Windows, and `/usr/local/cuda/samples` in Linux.)

Information about OpenGL is available directly from NVIDIA here: `https://developer.nvidia.com/opengl`.

PyCUDA also provides an interface for the NVIDIA OpenGL driver. Information is available here: `https://documen.tician.de/pycuda/gl.html`.

DirectX 12

DirectX 12 is the latest iteration of Microsoft's well-known and well-supported graphics API. While this is proprietary for Windows PCs and Microsoft Xbox game consoles, these systems obviously have a wide install base of hundreds of millions of users. Furthermore, a variety of GPUs are supported on Windows PCs besides NVIDIA cards, and the Visual Studio IDE provides a great ease of use. DirectX 12 actually supports low-level GPGPU programming-type concepts and can utilize multiple GPUs.

Microsoft's DirectX 12 Programming Guide is available here: `https://docs.microsoft.com/en-us/windows/desktop/direct3d12/directx-12-programming-guide`.

Vulkan

Vulkan can be thought of as the open equivalent of DirectX 12, which was developed by the Khronos Group as the *next-gen* successor of OpenGL. Along with Windows, Vulkan is also supported on macOS and Linux, as well as on the Sony PlayStation 4, Nintendo Switch, and Xbox One consoles. Vulkan has many of the same features as DirectX 12, such as quasi-GPGPU programming. Vulkan is providing some serious competition to DirectX 12, with video games such as the 2016 *DOOM* remake.

The *Beginner's Guide to Vulkan* is available from the Khronos Group here: `https://www.khronos.org/blog/beginners-guide-to-vulkan`.

Machine learning and computer vision

Of course, the elephant in the room of this chapter is machine learning and its fraternal twin computer vision. It goes without saying that machine learning (particularly the subfields of deep neural networks and convolutional neural networks) is what is keeping a roof over NVIDIA CEO Jensen Huang's head these days. (Okay, we admit that was the understatement of the decade...) If you need a reminder as to why GPUs are so applicable and useful in this field, please take another look at Chapter 9, *Implementation of a Deep Neural Network*. A large number of parallel computations and mathematical operations, as well as the user-friendly mathematical libraries, have made NVIDIA GPUs the hardware backbone of the machine learning industry.

The basics

While you now know many of the intricacies of low-level GPU programming, you won't be able to apply this knowledge to machine learning immediately. If you don't have the basic skills in this field, like how to do a basic statistical analysis of a dataset, you really should stop and familiarize yourself with them. Stanford Professor Andrew Ng, the founder of Google Brain, provides many materials that are available for free on the web and on YouTube. Professor Ng's work is generally considered to be the gold standard of educational material on machine learning.

 Professor Ng provides a free introductory machine learning class on the web here: http://www.ml-class.org.

cuDNN

NVIDIA provides an optimized GPU library for deep neural network primitives called cuDNN. These primitives include operations such as forward propagation, convolutions, back propagation, activation functions (such as sigmoid, ReLU, and tanh), and gradient descent. cuDNN is what most of the mainstream deep neural network frameworks such as Tensorflow use as a backend for NVIDIA GPUs. This is provided for free by NVIDIA , but has to be downloaded separately from the CUDA Toolkit.

 More information on cuDNN is available here: https://developer. nvidia.com/cudnn.

Tensorflow and Keras

Tensorflow is, of course, Google's well-known neural network framework. This is a free and open source framework that is usable with Python and C++, and has been available to the general public since 2015.

 Tutorials on Tensorflow are available from Google here: https://www. tensorflow.org/tutorials/.

Keras is a higher level library that provides a more *user-friendly* interface to Tensorflow, which was originally written by Google Brain's Francois Chollet. Readers may actually consider starting with Keras before moving on to Tensorflow.

 Information on Keras is available here: `https://keras.io/`.

Chainer

Chainer is another neural network API that was developed by Seiya Tokui, who is currently a PhD student at the University of Tokyo in Japan. While it is less mainstream than Tensorflow, it is very well-respected due to its incredible speed and efficiency. Moreover, readers may find Chainer of particular interest, since this was originally developed using PyCUDA. (This was later switched to CuPy, which is a PyCUDA branch that was developed to provide an interface that is more similar to NumPy.)

 Information on Chainer is available here: `https://chainer.org/`.

OpenCV

The Open Source computer vision Library (OpenCV) has been around since 2001. This library provides many of the tools from classical computer vision and image processing, which are still extremely useful in this age of the deep neural network. Most of the algorithms in OpenCV have been ported to CUDA in recent years, and it interfaces very easily with PyCUDA.

 Information on OpenCV is here: `https://opencv.org/`.

Blockchain technology

Last, but certainly not least, is **blockchain technology**. This is the underlying cryptographic technology that powers cryptocurrencies such as Bitcoin and Ethereum. This is, of course, a very new field, which was first described by Bitcoin's mysterious creator, Satoshi Nakamoto, in a white paper published in 2008. GPUs were applied to this field almost immediately after its invention—generating a unit of currency comes down to brute-force cracking a cryptographic puzzle, and a GPU can attempt to brute-force crack more combinations in parallel than any other piece of hardware available to the general public today. This process is known as **mining**.

Those who are interested in blockchain technology are suggested to read Satoshi Nakamoto's original white paper on Bitcoin, which is available here: `https://bitcoin.org/bitcoin.pdf`.

GUIMiner, an open source, CUDA-based Bitcoin miner, is available here: `https://guiminer.org/`.

Summary

In this chapter, we went over some of the options and paths for those that are interested in furthering their background in GPU programming, which is beyond the scope of this book. The first path we covered was expanding your background in pure CUDA and GPGPU programming—some of the things you can learn about that weren't covered in this book include programming systems with multiple GPUs and networked clusters. We also looked at some of the parallel programming languages/APIs besides CUDA, such as MPI and OpenCL. Next, we discussed some of the well-known APIs available to those who are interested in applying GPUs to rendering graphics, such as Vulkan and DirectX 12. We then looked at machine learning and went into some of the basic backgrounds that you should have as well as some of the major frameworks available for developing deep neural networks. Finally, we ended by taking a brief look at blockchain technology and GPU-based cryptocurrency mining.

As the author, I would like to say *thank you* to everyone who has pushed through this book and made it here, to the end. GPU programming is one of the trickiest subfields of programming that I have encountered, and I hope my text has helped you come to grips with the essentials. As the reader, you should now feel free to indulge in a slice of the richest, most calorie-laden slice of chocolate cake you can find—just know that you've *earned* it. (But only one slice!)

Questions

1. Use Google or some other search engine to find at least one application of GPU programming that is not featured in this chapter.
2. Try to find at least one programming language or API that can be used to program a GPU that is not featured in this chapter.
3. Look up Google's new Tensor Processing Unit (TPU) chips. How do these differ from GPUs?
4. Do you think it is a better idea to connect computers together into a cluster using Wi-Fi or wired Ethernet cables?

Assessment

Chapter 1, Why GPU Programming?

1. The first two `for` loops iterate over every pixel, whose outputs are invariant to each other; we can thus parallelize over these two `for` loops. The third `for` loop calculates the final value of a particular pixel, which is intrinsically recursive.

2. Amdahl's Law doesn't account for the time it takes to transfer memory between the GPU and the host.

3. 512 x 512 amounts to 262,144 pixels. This means that the first GPU can only calculate the outputs of half of the pixels at once, while the second GPU can calculate all of the pixels at once; this means the second GPU will be about twice as fast as the first here. The third GPU has more than sufficient cores to calculate all pixels at once, but as we saw in problem 1, the extra cores will be of no use to us here. So the second and third GPUs will be equally fast for this problem.

4. One issue with generically designating a certain segment of code as parallelizable with regards to Amdahl's Law is that this makes the assumption that the computation time for this piece of code will be close to 0 if the number of processors, N, is very large. As we can see from the last problem, this is not the case.

5. First, using *time* consistently can be cumbersome, and it might not zero in on the bottlenecks of your program. Second, a profiler can tell you the exact computation time of all of your code from the perspective of Python, so you can tell whether some library function or background activity of your operating system is at fault rather than your code.

Chapter 2, Setting Up Your GPU Programming Environment

1. No, CUDA only supports Nvidia GPUs, not Intel HD or AMD Radeon
2. This book only uses Python 2.7 examples
3. Device Manager
4. `lspci`
5. `free`
6. `.run`

Chapter 3, Getting Started with PyCUDA

1. Yes.
2. Memory transfers between host/device, and compilation time.
3. You can, but this will vary depending on your GPU and CPU setup.
4. Do this using the C ? operator for both the point-wise and reduce operations.
5. If a `gpuarray` object goes out of scope its destructor is called, which will deallocate (free) the memory it represents on the GPU automatically.
6. `ReductionKernel` may perform superfluous operations, which may be necessary depending on how the underlying GPU code is structured. A *neutral element* will ensure that no values are altered as a result of these superfluous operations.
7. We should set `neutral` to the smallest possible value of a signed 32-bit integer.

Chapter 4, Kernels, Threads, Blocks, and Grids

1. Try it.
2. All of the threads don't operate on the GPU simultaneously. Much like a CPU switching between tasks in an OS, the individual cores of the GPU switch between the different threads for a kernel.
3. O(n/640 log n), that is, O(n log n).
4. Try it.

5. There is actually no internal grid-level synchronization in CUDA—only block-level (with `__syncthreads`). We have to synchronize anything above a single block with the host.

6. Naive: 129 addition operations. Work-efficient: 62 addition operations.

7. Again, we can't use `__syncthreads` if we need to synchronize over a large grid of blocks. We can also launch over fewer threads on each iteration if we synchronize on the host, freeing up more resources for other operations.

8. In the case of a naive parallel sum, we will likely be working with only a small number of data points that should be equal to or less than the total number of GPU cores, which can likely fit in the maximum size of a block (1032); since a single block can be synchronized internally, we should do so. We should use the work-efficient algorithm only if the number of data points are far greater than the number of available cores on the GPU.

Chapter 5, Streams, Events, Contexts, and Concurrency

1. The performance improves for both; as we increase the number of threads, the GPU reaches peak utilization in both cases, reducing the gains made through using streams.

2. Yes, you can launch an arbitrary number of kernels asynchronously and synchronize them to with `cudaDeviceSynchronize`.

3. Open up your text editor and try it!

4. High standard deviation would mean that the GPU is being used unevenly, overwhelming the GPU at some points and under-utilizing it at others. A low standard deviation would mean that all launched operations are running generally smoothly.

5. i. The host can generally handle far fewer concurrent threads than a GPU. ii. Each thread requires its own CUDA context. The GPU can become overwhelmed with excessive contexts, since each has its own memory space and has to handle its own loaded executable code.

Chapter 6, Debugging and Profiling Your CUDA Code

1. Memory allocations are automatically synchronized in CUDA.
2. The `lockstep` property only holds in single blocks of size 32 or less. Here, the two blocks would properly diverge without any `lockstep`.
3. The same thing would happen here. This 64-thread block would actually be split into two 32-thread warps.
4. Nvprof can time individual kernel launches, GPU utilization, and stream usage; any host-side profiler would only see CUDA host functions being launched.
5. Printf is generally easier to use for small-scale projects with relatively short, inline kernels. If you write a very involved CUDA kernel with thousands of lines, then probably you would want to use the IDE to step through and debug your kernel line by line.
6. This tells CUDA which GPU we want to use.
7. `cudaDeviceSynchronize` will ensure that interdependent kernel launches and mem copies are indeed synchronized, and that they won't launch before all necessary operations have finished.

Chapter 7, Using the CUDA Libraries with Scikit-CUDA

1. SBLAH starts with an S, so this function uses 32-bit real floats. ZBLEH starts with a Z, which means it works with 128-bit complex floats.
2. Hint: set `trans = cublas._CUBLAS_OP['T']`
3. Hint: use the Scikit-CUDA wrapper to the dot product, `skcuda.cublas.cublasSdot`
4. Hint: build upon the answer to the last problem.
5. You can put the cuBLAS operations in a CUDA stream and use event objects with this stream to precisely measure the computation times on the GPU.
6. Since the input appears as being complex to cuFFT, it will calculate all of the values as NumPy.
7. The dark edge is due to the zero-buffering around the image. This can be mitigated by *mirroring* the image on its edges rather than by using a zero-buffer.

Chapter 8, The CUDA Device Function Libraries and Thrust

1. Try it. (It's actually more accurate than you'd think.)
2. One application: a Gaussian distribution can be used to add `white noise` to samples to augment a dataset in machine learning.
3. No, since they are from different seeds, these lists may have a strong correlation if we concatenate them together. We should use subsequences of the same seed if we plan to concatenate them together.
4. Try it.
5. Hint: remember that matrix multiplication can be thought of as a series of matrix-vector multiplications, while matrix-vector multiplication can be thought of as a series of dot products.
6. `Operator()` is used to define the actual function.

Chapter 9, Implementation of a Deep Neural Network

1. One problem could be that we haven't normalized our training inputs. Another could be that the training rate was too large.
2. With a small training rate a set of weights might converge very slowly, or not at all.
3. A large training rate can lead to a set of weights being over-fit to particular batch values or this training set. Also, it can lead to numerical overflows/underflows as in the first problem.
4. Sigmoid.
5. Softmax.
6. More updates.

Chapter 10, Working with Compiled GPU Code

1. Only the EXE file will have the host functions, but both the PTX and EXE will contain the GPU code.
2. `cuCtxDestory`.
3. `printf` with arbitrary input parameters. (Try looking up the `printf` prototype.)
4. With a Ctypes `c_void_p` object.
5. This will allow us to link to the function with its original name from Ctypes.
6. Device memory allocations and memcopies between device/host are automatically synchronized by CUDA.

Chapter 11, Performance Optimization in CUDA

1. The fact that `atomicExch` is thread-safe doesn't guarantee that all threads will execute this function at the same time (which is not the case since different blocks in a grid can be executed at different times).
2. A block of size 100 will be executed over multiple warps, which will not be synchronized within the block unless we use __syncthreads. Thus, `atomicExch` may be called at multiple times.
3. Since a warp executes in lockstep by default, and blocks of size 32 or less are executed with a single warp, __syncthreads would be unnecessary.
4. We use a naïve parallel sum within the warp, but otherwise, we are doing as many sums with`atomicAdd` as we would do with a serial sum. While CUDA automatically parallelizes many of these `atomicAdd` invocations, we could reduce the total number of required `atomicAdd` invocations by implementing a work-efficient parallel sum.
5. Definitely `sum_ker`. It's clear that PyCUDA's sum doesn't use the same hardware tricks as we do since ours performs better on smaller arrays, but by scaling the size to be much larger, the only explanation as to why PyCUDA's version is better is that it performs fewer addition operations.

Chapter 12, Where to Go from Here

1. Two examples: DNA analysis and physics simulations.
2. Two examples: OpenACC, Numba.
3. TPUs are only used for machine learning operations and lack the components required to render graphics.
4. Ethernet.

Other Books You May Enjoy

If you enjoyed this book, you may be interested in these other books by Packt:

Hands-On GPU-Accelerated Computer Vision with OpenCV and CUDA
Bhaumik Vaidya

ISBN: 9781789348293

- Understand how to access GPU device properties and capabilities from CUDA programs
- Learn how to accelerate searching and sorting algorithms
- Detect shapes such as lines and circles in images
- Explore object tracking and detection with algorithms
- Process videos using different video analysis techniques in Jetson TX1
- Access GPU device properties from the PyCUDA program
- Understand how kernel execution works

OpenCV 3 Computer Vision with Python Cookbook
Alexey Spizhevoy, Aleksandr Rybnikov

ISBN: 9781788474443

- Get familiar with low-level image processing methods
- See the common linear algebra tools needed in computer vision
- Work with different camera models and epipolar geometry
- Find out how to detect interesting points in images and compare them
- Binarize images and mask out regions of interest
- Detect objects and track them in videos

Leave a review - let other readers know what you think

Please share your thoughts on this book with others by leaving a review on the site that you bought it from. If you purchased the book from Amazon, please leave us an honest review on this book's Amazon page. This is vital so that other potential readers can see and use your unbiased opinion to make purchasing decisions, we can understand what our customers think about our products, and our authors can see your feedback on the title that they have worked with Packt to create. It will only take a few minutes of your time, but is valuable to other potential customers, our authors, and Packt. Thank you!

Index